Praise f

The book is a wonderful guide for gleaning the contribution of Caribbean Lutheranism—and beyond it, of mainline Latin American Protestantism—to decolonial possibilities for living out the Christian faith. Of particular interest is the careful attention to the contribution of women: from teachers, missionaries, and lay leaders to bishops. Without glossing over its complexities and ambiguities, Rodríguez shows how Lutheranism in the Caribbean has contributed to the gospel "giving more of itself" as good news.

—Dr. Nancy Elizabeth Bedford, Georgia Harkness Professor of Theology, Garrett-Evangelical Theological Seminary, and coauthor (with Guillermo Hansen) of *Nuestra fe: Una introducción a la teología cristiana*

José D. Rodríguez offers a sharp historiography channeling the faith of the Lutheran church in Puerto Rico from a Caribbean standpoint. Flowing in sacred spaces like that of a Lutheran tailor, Mr. John Christopher Owen Browne, *Caribbean Lutherans* deepens in accounts of pastors, lay leaders, Indigenous peoples, and women whose legacy affirms agency and the active role of people's transformational involvement in the mission. This unique book is a doorway for further research contributing to academia on matters of history, mission, and Lutheran identity.

—The Rev. Dr. Patricia Cuyatti Chavez, former regional secretary for Latin America, the Caribbean, and North America in the Lutheran World Federation; pastor in the Metropolitan Chicago Synod of the Evangelical Lutheran Church in America; author of *Hanging On and Rising Up: Renewing, Re-envisioning, and Rebuilding the Cross from the "Marginalized"*

This groundbreaking study of the mission of the Lutheran Church in Puerto Rico makes two significant contributions, relevant also to the study of the mission work of other Christian denominations on the island. First, it combines traditional historiographical methods with postcolonial and postmodern methods, and exhaustively examines documents and other authoritative classical sources as well as stories, music, poetry, and other art forms that depict the struggle of

resistance against prejudice and cultural assimilation. In so doing, it uplifts the significant contributions that marginal populations have made to the mission of the church. The second is the theological grounding of this historical analysis: Mission work has its beginning and end in God. It is a theology of radical inclusion that brings all of us to forward justice, peace, and love. This theocentric perspective makes it clear that the purpose of mission is not church growth nor the well-being of the denomination. We are all subjects and objects of that mission whose purpose ultimately is to announce and to be a sign of the Kingdom that calls us to overcome all obstacles that impede the formation of beloved communities.
—Dr. Ismael Garcia, emeritus professor of Christian ethics, Austin Presbyterian Theological Seminary

This is the first comprehensive history of the Caribbean Synod as part of the history of the Evangelical Lutheran Church in America and its predecessors. In his narrative—which includes important contextual and historical connections, inspiring stories, and detailed statistics—Dr. Rodríguez turns our invisibility in our Lutheran history books and denominational life into a text that documents important dimensions of the Lutheran traditional missionary ethos and its relationship with communities at the margins. Many of the dilemmas and issues presented by Rodríguez are *vivitos y coleando* (alive and kicking) in our days. As we launch efforts to renew and reform our denomination, this book is a must-read to help us be *a church of the cross.*
—The Rev. Dr. Francisco Javier Goitía-Padilla, director for Formation for Leadership, Church Community and Leadership, ELCA

Many readers will be surprised to learn that the presence of Lutherans in the Caribbean much predates the existence of Lutheranism in the continental US. Rodríguez's book concentrates on the history of the Lutheran church in Puerto Rico and has the merit of exploring the historical periods before the arrival of US missionaries in the wake of the Spanish-American war. The stories of fleeing slaves from the Danish West Indies, of freedom fighters against Spanish colonialism, of women leaders, and of people of color who identified with the Lutheran church are intertwined with the reports and letters of the first US missionaries and their ambiguous mix of American idealism, dubious colonialist assumptions, and honest zeal in spreading the gospel and serving the people of Puerto Rico. The result is a very illuminating, well-balanced, and judicious exposition of a denominational history set amid the larger political, economic, and cultural forces that have traversed Puerto Rico since Spanish colonization.

—Dr. Guillermo Hansen, professor of theology and global Christianity, Luther Seminary, Saint Paul, Minnesota

It is very comfortable to talk about voiceless people and cultures but, providentially, Rodríguez is not deaf. Only a sympathetic historian, systematician, and pastor such as he could have done justice to our—in this order—Taino, Jamaican, Virgin Islands, and Scandinavian Lutheran and Moravian DNA. This comprehensive essay decolonizes North Atlantic white supremacy. By doing that, José David makes the Greater Caribbean political-religious narratives part of church history, and no longer a mere footnote of "missions."

—The Rev. Dr. Eliseo Pérez-Álvarez, professor of systematic theology, Seminario Evangélico de Puerto Rico, and author of *The Vexing Gadfly: The Late Kierkegaard on Economic Matters*

This long-awaited book is a treasure trove of information about the origins of the Lutheran witness to the gospel in the Caribbean. But for many of us, it is much more than that. It is our family history: the good, the bad, the ugly, and the beautiful. With decolonial sensitivity, Prof. Rodríguez has collected and curated for us the "little stories" of how we, Caribbean Puerto Rican Lutherans, came to be. It is a fascinating narrative that interweaves great sacrifices from early missionaries, chaplains, and deaconesses; Bibles being smuggled by Lutheran pirates and corsairs; courageous leadership from wise local lay leaders, especially the women; and all happening against the backdrop of two world wars, increasing racial tensions, and

imperial-colonial intrigues. Yet somehow, it all worked, and the Caribbean Puerto Rican Lutheran presence continues to be strong, now sending pastors to the mission field in the mainland US and leadership to the ELCA Churchwide organization! Gracias, José, por rescatar nuestra historia.
—The Rev. Dr. Carmelo Santos, director for Theological Diversity and Engagement Office of the Presiding Bishop, ELCA

José David Rodríguez's book is the first academic history by a Puerto Rican about the Lutheran church, which arrived with the rest of the Protestant churches after the Hispanic American War. The book has an excellent introduction on Lutheran Protestantism in the Caribbean starting in the seventeenth century, when Dutch, German, and Danish missionaries first arrived on the islands. Dr. José David Rodríguez was the program director of the Hispanic Ministries program and director of the PhD program at the Lutheran School of Theology at Chicago in the US, as well as rector (president) at the Institute of Theological Education (ISEDET) in Buenos Aires, Argentina. He is a fitting researcher to write this history, as he was raised in the Lutheran tradition and his father was a professor of theology at ISEDET in Argentina and at the Evangelical Seminary of Puerto Rico, where students from all Protestant denominations on the island attend. The book contains a rich chapter on the development of the leadership role of women in the Lutheran church, which gives us a more contemporary vision of the history of his denomination.

Few studies on denominational history in Puerto Rico have been made with equal academic rigor, even among those of the Baptist, Methodist, Presbyterian, Episcopal, and United Evangelical churches, as well as the other Protestant denominations that arrived alongside the Lutherans after 1898. *Caribbean Lutherans* is therefore not only a contribution to the history of the church, but no doubt also a valuable contribution to the history of Puerto Rico as a whole.
—Dr. Samuel Silva Gotay, distinguished professor, retired, University of Puerto Rico

CARIBBEAN LUTHERANS

CARIBBEAN LUTHERANS

The History of the Church in Puerto Rico

José David Rodríguez

Foreword by Idalia Negrón

Afterword by Luis N. Rivera-Pagán

FORTRESS PRESS
MINNEAPOLIS

CARIBBEAN LUTHERANS
The History of the Church in Puerto Rico

Copyright © 2024 Fortress Press, an imprint of 1517 Media. All rights reserved. Except for brief quotations in critical articles and reviews, no part of this book may be reproduced in any manner without prior written permission from the publisher. Email copyright@1517.media or write to Permissions, Fortress Press, PO Box 1209, Minneapolis, MN 55440-1209.

All Scripture quotations, unless otherwise indicated, are from the New Revised Standard Version Bible, copyright © 1989 National Council of the Churches of Christ in the United States of America. Used by permission. All rights reserved worldwide.

Library of Congress Cataloging-in-Publication Data

Names: Rodríguez, José David, author.
Title: Caribbean Lutherans : the history of the church in Puerto Rico / José David Rodríguez.
Description: Minneapolis : Fortress Press, 2024. | Includes bibliographical references and index.
Identifiers: LCCN 2023029113 (print) | LCCN 2023029114 (ebook) | ISBN 9781506496184 (paperback) | ISBN 9781506496191 (ebook)
Subjects: LCSH: Lutheran Church--Puerto Rico--History. | Lutheran Church--Missions--Caribbean Area. | Puerto Rico--Religion.
Classification: LCC BX8063.P9 R63 2024 (print) | LCC BX8063.P9 (ebook) | DDC 284.1/7295--dc23/eng/20231017
LC record available at https://lccn.loc.gov/2023029113
LC ebook record available at https://lccn.loc.gov/2023029114

Cover design: Kristin Miller
Cover art: Vintage engraving from 1878 showing a Map of Central America and West India Islands, from duncan1890/Getty Images

Print ISBN: 978-1-5064-9618-4
eBook ISBN: 978-1-5064-9619-1

I dedicate this book to my four grandchildren, Víctor, Felipe, Jonathan, and Luca. Also, to all the pastors and lay leaders that have participated in the Lutheran mission in Puerto Rico in the past and continue their labor in the present.

Contents

*Foreword by Bishop Idalia Negrón,
Caribbean Synod* — ix

Introduction — 1

1. Lutheran Mission in the Caribbean — 11
2. Setting the Stage for an Emerging Protestantism — 35
3. Lutherans Begin Their Mission in Puerto Rico — 69
4. The Mission and Its Trailblazers — 89
5. A Mission Coming of Age — 123
6. The Leadership of Women in the Mission — 159
7. Findings — 175

Conclusion — 193

*Afterword by Dr. Luis N. Rivera-Pagán,
Princeton Theological Seminary* — 203

Bibliography — 205

Index — 223

Foreword

Dear friend of my youth, I must write to you what the singer Pedro Vargas said: very grateful, very grateful, very grateful to be applauded. Today I say "thank you" for writing the history of the Evangelical Lutheran Church in Puerto Rico. I remember that, about eleven years ago, we went to the Historical Archive of Puerto Rico to look for information on how the Lutheran mission began and we left very frustrated because there was no information. Today I thank God, because you were persistent and later you informed me very humbly, "I am studying history to know more where to look and prepare the history of our beloved church."

The great advantage of this publication is that you extended your investigation to the Caribbean; that is why the first chapters you present to us begin in 1666, and address how the faith was spread by laypeople who taught the foundations of how the Christian and Lutheran faith reached the islands.

As I continue reading the next chapters, I find that you intertwine the growth of the Lutheran faith on the island with the situation of being a colony of Spain, and subsequently a colony of the United States. In addition, you give us the good news of the church's growth and you point out the importance of the brave laypeople who oversaw bringing the good news and establishing the kingdom of God and his justice in Puerto Rico. You also give a special thanks to the deaconesses and the wives of the pastors who, using their talents, promoted the knowledge of the Word and social work in the congregations.

In telling this story you confront us with the poverty in Puerto Rico, the political situation, and how the Lutherans did not comment,

FOREWORD

in their newspaper dedicated to the fiftieth anniversary, on what happened in the Nationalist Revolt of 1950. You recount the famous story of Santa Claus coming to the "Cuchilla" and you present this as a clear attempt to indoctrinate us through the imposition of the English language; however, our people continue to use their vernacular language, which is Spanish.

You also examine the history of the Lutheran Churches in the Virgin Islands and how the Caribbean Synod was founded. Despite the differences in language, we are united by the Lutheran faith base and the common denominator of being colonies of the United States.

Rev. Idalia Negrón
Bishop, Caribbean Synod
Evangelical Lutheran Church in America
March 8, 2023

Introduction

During my early years as a member of the faculty at the Lutheran School of Theology at Chicago (LSTC), I participated in a gathering of Lutheran theologians sponsored by the Evangelical Lutheran Church in America (ELCA). At that time, the topic explored was "our Lutheran legacy." Those making presentations referred to studies written by scholars from their various ethnic backgrounds on this topic. I was quite embarrassed because I could only speak from my personal experience, since there have not been any scholarly publications focusing on the Lutheran experience in Puerto Rico. Even today, some Lutheran historians provide just a brief note in their scholarly works on the story of Lutheranism in the Caribbean archipelago.[1]

One of the goals of this book is to provide such a history. Its content is the product of a dissertation I presented on this subject at the University of the West Indies (UWI) in Jamaica in 2023, for my PhD degree in history. The title of the dissertation was "The Lutheran Mission in Puerto Rico: Challenge and Promise."[2]

Before I engage in reporting this story, I need to clarify that, while there have been a variety of meanings of the term "mission" throughout history,[3] in this study I will use the term as the Puerto Rican scholar Carlos F. Cardoza-Orlandi suggests:

> Mission is a spiritual discipline, informed by prayer, devotion, communal worship, biblical study, and critical theological

reflection. *Mission is the participation of the people of God in God's action in the world.* The theological and critical reflection about mission is called missiology.[4]

Another important consideration I want to make at the beginning of this narrative relates to the specific approach I will be using in addressing the topic of missions. My reflections on the subject will be from the perspective of a Lutheran Puerto Rican, born and raised in Puerto Rico, yet living in the diaspora of Chicago for the last forty-plus years. This means, among other things, that my understanding of the Lutheran mission in Puerto Rico will be from the experience of being missionized. This indicates, as Cardoza Orlandi suggests, that "I become aware of my dual identity" of being both "the object and subject of mission."

In other words, I find myself in an exciting paradox, between *discontinuity and continuity*, as I seek for tools that will help Christian communities be in mission without losing the awareness that we are both *objects and subjects of mission.*[5]

During my previous advanced studies in history at the Interamerican University in Puerto Rico,[6] I learned that, although written communication has been a valuable instrument to transmit our knowledge of the past, it is a relatively recent development.[7] It is generally acknowledged that, before writing was invented, people used spoken language, sometimes in the form of poetry and song, to communicate. One example is the emergence of Greek historical communication laid in epic poetry such as Homer's *Iliad* and *Odyssey*, later written by the Greek prose historians.[8] Another important instance is the pre-Columbian peoples of the Americas who used *quipus*, along with oral recital, or painting, to preserve and recall the past.[9]

At the same time, I also became aware that the writing of history can have an important strategic value. In my course on the history of the Americas, we studied the life and writings of Gómez Suárez de

Figueroa, better known as Garcilaso de la Vega, El Inca (1539–1616), the great chronicler of the Incas. He was the mestizo son of the Spanish conquistador and *encomendero* Sebastián Garcilaso de la Vega and the Inca noblewoman Isabel Chimpo Ocllo.[10] Two of his works were *The Florida of the Inca* (1605)[11] and the *Royal Commentaries of the Incas: And General History of Perú* (1609),[12] the latter considered his best-known work. With these two early chronicles, Garcilaso El Inca achieved a feat that still stands as encouragement for us today. While he never lost his esteem for his Spanish heritage, his works were a witness to his devotion for his Inca birth right and empathy for his mother's people. By writing the story of the ancient Incas, he dignified their past, and in time they had some impact in the struggle of Latin Americans for their independence from Spain. For this and other reasons, my hope is that the present work may stimulate a stronger interest in Caribbean Lutheranism, as well as in the experience of Lutheranism in my country of origin, Puerto Rico.

Another important goal of this book is to read this story from a Caribbeanist perspective. Gustav Warneck, considered the founder of the science of mission studies,[13] and most investigations of the Lutheran mission around the world since the late nineteenth century, including in the Caribbean, have commonly used what B. W. Higman calls a historiographical written approach, "physically located in, and ideologically oriented to, the metropolitan centers of imperial control"[14] to provide an account of their inquiries. For most historians this approach, which has traditionally dominated the professionalization of this area of studies since the nineteenth century, has been described as Eurocentrism; yet for Daniel Woolf, a more crucial problem in this Western historiography lies in its tendency to deny the very existence of other suitable alternatives.[15]

In this book, my intention is to employ a different historiography, which scholars such as Peter Burke have described as "new perspectives on historical writing."[16] One of my key concerns is to follow the lead in approaching Caribbean history from such influential works as that of Elsa V. Goveia,[17] which has been described as Caribbean historiography.[18] This type of historiography can be traced back to an increasing number of Caribbean professional historians at Caribbean academies since the 1950s. It also follows broader trends in historical practice associated with movements toward independence after 1945 and the Cuban revolution in 1959, when anticolonial and nationalist ideologies became important topics to explore. While following the classical approach of privileging data preserved in writing, this approach is progressively exploring alternative sources and analysis of evidence recognized and identified as suitable for the study of the past, such as the oral tradition, historical archaeology, social history, history from below, women's history, environmental history, gay and lesbian history, and the history of science.[19]

I will enrich this Caribbean historiography, employing a postcolonial or decolonial perspective.[20] Along with the use of postcolonial hermeneutics, I will employ some elements proposed by the distinguished sociopolitical scholar James C. Scott in exploring subaltern movements of resistance in his analysis of Asian societies.[21] My specific interest in the works of James C. Scott is in understanding topics such as "public" and "hidden" transcripts, along with what he called the "weapons of the weak" in his analysis of domination and the arts of resistance.

The content of this book is organized in seven chapters and a short conclusion. Chapter 1 offers a brief yet substantial description of Lutheran identity. While not a book on Lutheranism per se (since the focus of my research is the Lutheran mission in Puerto Rico), in this chapter I provide a specific framework of the type of Lutheran distinctiveness that impacted the missionary enterprise in the island. This endeavor, rather than providing a generic typology of Lutheran missions, aims to advance a more specific understanding of Lutheran missions characteristic of the Caribbean and, in particular, of the island of Puerto Rico.

In chapters 2 through 6, I explore the foundations for the Lutheran Mission on the island of Puerto Rico, along with its development up to the time when the Caribbean Evangelical Lutheran Synod of the United Lutheran Church in America was initiated in 1952. For this task, I drew on articles published in the mission's own journal, *El*

INTRODUCTION

Testigo, other Protestant studies in journals,[22] newspaper commentaries published on this topic,[23] church bulletins,[24] bibliographical resources available at the libraries of the Seminario Evangélico de Puerto Rico, the University of Puerto Rico, the Interamerican University, and government archives located in the island of Puerto Rico. I also examined the reports of the Puerto Rico Mission Board to the General Council of the Evangelical Lutheran Church in North America, those of the Board of the West Indies Mission of the United Lutheran Church in America, and other valuable first and secondary sources, such as the *Lutheran* magazine published in the United States, that shed light on this development.[25]

The final chapter, chapter 7, focuses on the promise and challenge of the dynamics of a Lutheran identity developed by the Caribbean Synod and its contribution to the Lutheran legacy in the United States and worldwide. This review of important stages and components in the emergence of the Caribbean Synod aims at facilitating a better understanding of further developments in its historical expansion. It also aims to provide a more informed understanding of its contribution to other Lutheran global expressions.

The book ends with a short conclusion, providing a summary of my findings and a brief depiction of recent developments in the Caribbean Synod that shows the continuing relevance of its mission and ministry for the Evangelical Lutheran Church in America and its predecessor bodies.

The origin of this book can be traced back to the time when I was a pastor in the Caribbean Synod. However, my interest in pursuing a PhD degree in history and writing a dissertation on this topic developed from a conversation I had with my sister, Rev. Dr. Raquel E. Rodríguez, while she served as director for Mexico, the Caribbean, and Latin America at the Global Mission Unit of the Evangelical Lutheran Church in America (ELCA). She informed me about the continuing support provided by ELCA to the United Theological College of the West Indies (UTCWI) in Jamaica, and its connection to the University of the West Indies (UWI). Her supervisor, Rev. Dr. Rafael Malpica-Padilla, executive director for the Global Mission

Unit of the ELCA, provided assistance, encouragement, and financial support for my venture in pursuing my interest in this project. On various occasions I served as a visiting scholar at UTCWI, which gave me the opportunity to register at the university for a PhD in the Department of History. I want to thank my colleagues, Dr. Justo L. González, Dr. Luis N. Rivera Pagán, Dr. Ismael García, Dr. Agustina Luvis, and Dr. Eliseo Pérez, who were willing to support me in this venture and write letters of recommendation on my behalf for my entrance to the program. I also want to express my appreciation to Dr. David Cook and his wife Mary, who not only supported my interest in the advanced program in history at the university but provided valuable time and efforts to encourage my interest and facilitate my conversations with colleagues at UTCWI and the university.

I first began my part-time studies at UWI in 2006, but had to withdraw due to my many commitments. At that time Dr. Waibinte Wariboco was the head of the Department of History and was very helpful in providing guidance and encouragement while I was a student in the program. Later on, after a short tenure as rector (president) of the University Institute ISEDET in Buenos Aires, Argentina, I registered once more as a candidate for the PhD in history at UWI. At that time, Dr. Enrique Okenve was the head of the Department of History and facilitated my joining the program once more. Thanks to Dr. Okenve and my academic advisor, Dr. James Robertson, I've been able to complete the requirements established by the officers for advanced studies at the university. To Dr. Robertson I owe a great debt for the suggestions of important bibliographical resources for my research, as well as for his assistance in framing its content in a scholarly manner. I also want to express my gratitude to Barry Hopkins, interim director of the JKM Library at the Lutheran School of Theology at Chicago, Milka T. Vigo Verestín, director of the library at the Seminario Evangélico de Puerto Rico, Joel Thorensen, a member of the staff at the archives of the Evangelical Lutheran Church in America, along with Mr. Cody Swisher and the staff at the Krauth Memorial Branch Library of the United Lutheran Seminary Philadelphia Campus, whose patient and extraordinary support allowed me to find valuable bibliographical documents for my research.

I also want to express my gratitude to Dr. Laura Gifford, Lisa Eaton, Louise Spencely, and other staff at Fortress Press, whose ability to transform my scholarly writing style to make it available to a wider audience made this project possible; and to Fortress Press, the publisher willing to take the risk of supporting my contribution to highlight the impact of the Caribbean Synod of the ELCA in broadening the Lutheran legacy among us.

Last, but not least, I want to thank my wife Kathryn L. Baker, my daughter Taina, and other members of my family whose diligence gave me the support I needed to complete my program of studies at UWI. To these, and to all the other colleagues who have accompanied me on this journey, I want to express my sincere thanks and appreciation.

NOTES

1 See Mark Granquist, *Lutherans in America: A New History* (Minneapolis: Fortress Press, 2015), 353. Also, E. Theodore Bachmann and Mercia Brenne Bachmann, *Lutheran Churches in the World: A Handbook* (Minneapolis: Augsburg, 1989), 483–86. The most recent reference to Lutheranism in Puerto Rico comes from Martin J. Lohrmann, *Stories from Global Lutheranism: A Historical Timeline* (Minneapolis: Fortress Press, 2021), 187.
2 José David Rodríguez, "The Lutheran Mission in Puerto Rico: Challenge and Promise" (a dissertation submitted to the Faculty of the University of the West Indies, Department of History, in partial fulfillment of the requirements for the degree of Doctor in Philosophy, 2023).
3 Gustav Warneck, the father of the theory of mission, described Protestant missions in his book, *Abriß einer Geschichte der protestantische Missionen von der Reformation bis auf die Gegenwart: Mit einem unhang über die Catholischen Missionen* (Berlin: Verlag von Martin Barned, 1905), available in an English-language translation, *Outline of a History of Protestant Missions from the Reformation to the Present Time* (New York, Chicago, and Toronto: Fleming H. Revell Company, 1901), as the church's task of witnessing to God's gracious work of salvation for human beings in all parts of the world: "So haben wir in der Lehre von der Rechtfertigung durch der

Glauben ein univerßales heilsbedürß, eine univerßales heilsgnade und eine univerßales heildbedingung. Mit logischer wir mit dogmatißer und ethicher Notwendigkeit folgt daraus auch eine univerßale heilsambiengtung, i.e. die Gendungsveranßtaltung durch die ganze Welt (Röm. 10, 4–17)," 3. "We have therefore in the doctrine of justification by faith a universal need of salvation, a universal grace of salvation, and a universal condition of salvation. From this there follows also, of logical as well as of dogmatic and ethical necessity, a universal offer of salvation, i.e., the institution of missions throughout the whole world (Rom. x. 4–17)," Warneck, Outline of a History of Protestant Missions from the Reformation, to the Present Time: With an Appendix Concerning Roman Catholic Missions, Third English Edition Being Authorized Translation from the Eighth German Ed., ed. George Robson DD (Edinburgh and London: Oliphant Anderson & Ferrier, 1906), 5. You can also find this edition online at https://missiology.org.uk/pdf/e-books/warneck_gustav/history-of-protestant-missions_warneck.pdf (accessed July 12, 2023). In chapter 1 of this study, I will provide a brief but more thorough understanding of the notion of mission from a Lutheran perspective, emerging in the sixteenth century up to the end of the nineteenth century. For a brief but valuable biography of Warneck, see https://www.bu.edu/missiology/missionary-biography/w-x-y-z/warneck-gustav-1834-1910/ (accessed May 20, 2020).
4 Carlos F. Cardoza Orlandi, *Mission: An Essential Guide* (Nashville: Abingdon Press, 2002), 14–15, original emphasis.
5 Cardoza Orlandi, *Mission*, 12, original emphasis.
6 From January to May 2011, I took two advanced courses in the Department of History at the Metropolitan site of the Interamerican University of Puerto Rico: Historia de las Américas and Historia de Puerto Rico. I appreciate the support I received from my colleague and friend Dr. Angel Vélez to engage in these advanced studies.
7 Daniel Woolf argues that it dates back "at most five millennia to the earliest cuneiform tablets in Mesopotamia, to hieroglyphics in Egypt, and to bone inscriptions in China." He also claims that, even in the modern era, writing as such does not constitute the essential means of historical communication. Daniel Woolf, *A Global History of History* (Cambridge: Cambridge University Press, 2011), 2.
8 "Greek contact with the Phoenicians, who in turn had had dealings with Mesopotamia and Egypt, probably resulted in the acquisition of alphabetic writing, and the Homeric epics, previously transmitted orally, were finally written down several centuries after they first were performed." Woolf, *A Global History of History*, 34. In his book *The Singer of Tales*, Albert Bates Lord offers a fascinating alternative to the centuries-old mystery of the Homeric texts of the *Iliad* and the *Odyssey*. In his analysis of Homer and the modern Balkan Singer of Tales, Avdo Mededovic of Bijelo Polje

from Yugoslavia, Lord also provides a well-informed process detailing the various ways the oral narrative poetry may have been consigned in writing (chapter 8). See Albert B. Lord, *The Singer of Tales* (Cambridge, MA: Harvard University Press, 1964), 124–38.

9 Lord, *The Singer of Tales*, 6–7. *Quipus* (kee-poo): the word *quipu* comes from the Quechua word for "knot." A *quipu* usually consisted of colored, spun, and plied thread or strings from llama hair. Historic documents indicate that *quipus* were used for record keeping and sending messages by runner throughout the empire. Most of the existing *quipus* are from the Inka period, approximately 1400–1532 CE. Information from the Smithsonian Institution, https://www.si.edu/newsdesk/snapshot/quipu (accessed June 19, 2023).

10 For a biography of this Peruvian figure, see John Grier Varner, *El Inca: The Life and Times of Garcilaso de la Vega* (Austin and London: University of Texas Press, 1968).

11 An account of Hernando de Soto's voyage and journey in Florida.

12 It was written in two sections and volumes. The first was mostly about Inca life, the second about the Spanish conquest of Perú.

13 See Warneck biography: https://www.bu.edu/missiology/missionary-biography/w-x-y-z/warneck-gustav-1834-1910/ (accessed June 19, 2023).

14 B. W. Higman, "The Development of Historical Disciplines in the Caribbean," in *General History of the Caribbean*, vol. VI: *Methodology and Historiography of the Caribbean*, ed. B. W. Higman (London and Oxford: UNESCO Publishing/Macmillan Education, 1999), 3.

15 Woolf, *A Global History of History*, 15.

16 Peter Burke, *New Perspectives on Historical Writing*, 2nd ed. (University Park: The Pennsylvania State University Press, 2001), 1–24.

17 Elsa V. Goveia, *A Study on the Historiography of the British West Indies to the End of the Nineteenth Century* (Mexico: Instituto Panamericano de Geografía e Historia, 1956). While in her work Goveia's research shows her knowledge and use of sources available in what we have earlier called "metropolitan centers of imperial control," her most important contributions lie, according to Mary Chamberlain, in her innovative historical approach endorsing the philosophy and goals of the New World Group of which she had been an early and active member. "New World is a movement which aims to transform the mode of living and thinking in the region. The movement rejects uncritical acceptance of dogmas and ideologies imported from outside and bases its ideas for the future of the area on an unfettered analysis of the experience and existing conditions of the region." Mary Chamberlain, "Elsa Goveia: History and Nation," *History Workshop Journal* 58 (November 3, 2015): 167–68.

18 Higman, *General History of the Caribbean*, 6–9. See also D. A. G. Waddell, "The British West Indies," in *The Historiography of the British*

Empire-Commonwealth: Trends, Interpretations, and Resources, ed. Robin W. Winks (Durham, NC: Duke University Press, 1966), 344–56; and my analysis influenced by discussions in HIST6712: Theory and Method of History (2016).

19 For a more precise description of these and other tendencies in historiography see Burke, *New Perspectives on Historical Writing*, 25–297, and Higman, *General History of the Caribbean*, 19–307.

20 See Robert J. C. Young, *Postcolonialism: A Very Short Introduction* (Oxford: Oxford University Press, 2003), and Dane Kennedy, *Decolonization: A Very Short Introduction* (Oxford: Oxford University Press, 2016). In some parts of my investigation, I use one or the other to bring more clarity to my analysis of the subject. Here I must clarify a close similarity between postcolonial and decolonial hermeneutics. While there are differences between the two as methodological tools, a common assumption and goal is to explore and analyze the factors that led to the collapse of European imperial regimes after World War II (1939–45), as well as the fact that, instead of disappearing from the scene, these empires reconstituted themselves in new forms.

21 Two of this author's most valuable books for my research have been *Weapons of the Weak: Everyday Forms of Peasant Resistance* (New Haven, CT, and London: Yale University Press, 1985), and *Domination and the Arts of Resistance: Hidden Transcripts* (New Haven, CT, and London: Yale University Press, 1990).

22 Such as the *Puerto Rico Evangélico, El Misionero*, and the Roman Catholic journal *El Ideal Católico*.

23 For this research I reviewed articles related to the Lutheran mission since 1898 in Puerto Rican newspapers such as *La Correspondencia* (1903–23), *El Boletín Mercantil* (1903–9), *La Democracia* (from 1906 to 1923), *El Imparcial* (1922–23), *El Mundo* (1919–1952), and *El Nuevo Día* (1909–).

24 Such as the *Bulletin for the Fiftieth Anniversary of the Ministry of Rev. Eduardo Roig Vélez Iglesia Luterana El Buen Pastor*, and the *Bulletin for the Celebration of the 69th Anniversary of the Lutheran Church Divino Salvador*.

25 These bibliographical resources are at the Archives of the Evangelical Lutheran Church in America, located at 321 Bonnie Lane, Elk Grove Village, IL 60007, USA.

CHAPTER 1

Lutheran Mission in the Caribbean

When I came to Chicago to begin my advanced studies back in the early 1970s, I shockingly learned that one of the biggest challenges for people from Spanish or Latin American backgrounds in the United States is that of identity.[1] While the US government uses the term "Hispanics," other terms used to identify people like me coming from Puerto Rico are "Latino," "Puertorriqueños," Boricuas, and recently the word "Latinx," which has appeared as a gender- and LGBTQ-inclusive term.[2] The fact is that the ways people in the United States from Spanish or Latin American backgrounds describe their identity differs across immigrant generations. Something similar seems to happen in trying to define with precision the distinct character of Lutheranism.

Lutheran identity has usually been associated with Martin Luther, and the Reformation movement in Germany during the sixteenth century of which he was a major leader. Even Karl Marx, in his introduction to the *Critique of Hegel's Philosophy of Right*, argues that Germany's past revolutionary experience was the sixteenth-century European Reformation. This revolutionary experience began in the mind of the Augustinian monk Martin Luther. Unfortunately, for Marx this revolutionary past of Germany was limited to a theoretical revolution, whereas Germany's radical revolution needed to be a practical and real one.

> Even from the historical point of view, theoretical emancipation has a specific practical importance for Germany. Germany's revolutionary past is precisely theoretical: it is the Reformation. As at that time it was a monk, so now it is the philosopher in whose brain the revolution begins.
>
> Luther, to be sure, overcame servitude based on devotion, but by replacing it with servitude based on conviction. He shattered faith in authority by restoring the authority of faith. He transformed priests into laymen by changing the laymen into priests. He liberated man from external religiosity by making religiosity that which is innermost to man. He freed the body of chains by putting the heart in chains.
>
> But if Protestantism was not the real solution it at least posed the problem correctly. . . . A radical revolution can only be a revolution of radical needs, whose preconditions and birthplaces appear to be lacking.[3]

However, even today there are debates about the precise distinctiveness of this religious movement.[4] Probably one of the reasons for this continuous debate emerged from Luther himself. At a time when some of his followers intended to recognize Luther as the mastermind of the sixteenth-century Reformation movement in Europe, he rebuked them with the following argument:

> In the first place, I ask that men make no reference to my name; let them call themselves Christians, not Lutherans. What is Luther? After all, the teaching is not mine (John 7:16). Neither was I crucified for anyone (1Cor. 1:13). Saint Paul, in I Corinthians 3, would not allow the Christians to call themselves Pauline or Petrine, but Christians. How then should I – poor stinking maggot-fodder that I am – come to have men call the children of Christ by my wretched name? Not so, my dear friends; let

us abolish all party names and call ourselves Christians, after him whose teachings we hold. The papists deservedly have a party name, because they are not content with the teachings and name of Christ, but want to be papists as well. Let them be papists then, since the pope is their master. I neither am nor want to be anyone's master. I hold, together with the universal church, the one universal teaching of Christ, who is our only master (Matt. 23:8).[5]

In any case, it is commonly acknowledged that Lutheranism emerged as a Reformation movement seeking to correct existing errors, eradicate conflicts and misinterpretations about the faith within Western Roman Catholic Christendom, instead of initiating a new form of Christianity. In spite of this fact, and unforeseen by Luther and his followers, historical incidents contributed to the development of autonomous Lutheran churches with their own confessional witness to the gospel.[6] The Lutheran historian Eric W. Gritsch argues that the name "Lutheran" was used by Roman Catholic adversaries, particularly the Dominican theologian John Eck (1486–1543), to demean its followers, for sixteenth-century Lutheran theologians usually spoke of the movement as of an evangelical-Catholic church (*ecclesia catholica evangelica*). Whatever the case may be, the notion of "Lutheran churches" started to emerge in the seventeenth century.[7]

LUTHERAN MISSIONS IN HISTORICAL PERSPECTIVE

Regarding the contribution of Lutheranism in the area of mission, James A. Scherer argues that Lutheran missionary endeavors have a history of about 450 years; yet this historical legacy has been riddled with many controversies since its beginning. During the nineteenth century Gustav Warneck, the "father of mission science," upheld the view that Luther was not truly aware of the need for the missionary endeavor of the church.[8] Scherer says,

Warneck was critical of Luther chiefly because the reformer had not issued a call in support of "a regular sending of messengers of the Gospel to non-Christian nations, with the view of Christianizing them."⁹

Ensuing studies by Luther scholars have shown that the claim of Warneck and his contemporaries disregarded Luther's deeper missionary insights; and powerful renewal movements within Lutheranism in succeeding generations recovered and deepened the work of the Reformation in the areas of mission, evangelism, church renewal, and Christian unity.¹⁰

One such early study, which was unfortunately overlooked by many scholars at the time, was the one produced by Gustav Leopold Plitt (1836–80).¹¹ For this early Lutheran mission scholar, as for others that succeeded him, Warneck's oversight was that Luther's contribution was more radical than the one proposed by nineteenth-century missionary movements.

> For Luther, said Plitt, mission was the essential task of the church in every age, but only a church itself grounded in the gospel can do mission. This interpretation which credits Luther with being the father of genuine church-centered evangelical mission work based on the gospel, is true as far as it goes, but it misses the radicality of Luther's missionary thinking.¹²

As Scherer and other contemporary Lutheran missiologists contend, while nineteenth-century missiology tended to ascribe the church as the starting point of missionary work (a view that would mesh with state-sponsored missions to imperial territories), for Luther mission is always primarily the work of the Triune God—*missio Dei*—and its goal and outcome are the coming of God's reign:¹³ "It is always God's own mission that dominates Luther's thought, and the coming kingdom of God represents its final culmination."¹⁴ In this way, Luther foresaw the present-day missionary perspective which makes God's initiative the starting point of mission and the kingdom of God, instead of the church, its vital concept.[15]

During the seventeenth century, a period characterized by scholastic orthodoxy, Lutheranism was led to "dogmatic hairsplitting and ecclesiastical retrenchment."[16] Given the concession granted to territorial rulers by the proviso of *cuius regio, eius religio*, they were given the right to establish the religious adherence of their subjects.[17] However, for Lutherans a monarch's missionary duty was not expected to go beyond the territories ruled, particularly if these territories were governed by a Christian prince at home or abroad. Furthermore, in defense against their Roman Catholic opponents, and based on exegetical and dogmatic ground, Lutheran scholars, guided by the notable theologian of Lutheran orthodoxy Johann Gerhard, claimed the termination of the evangelistic instruction of the great commission.

> The gifts and powers of the apostolate, said Gerhard, now devolved corporately upon the church and were mediated through regular ecclesiastical calls to settle parochial ministries. No theological basis existed for a call to preach the gospel to distant heathen.[18]

An interesting exception to this position was proposed by the Lutheran layman Justinian Weltz, who called on his fellow Christians to send student volunteer evangelists to preach the gospel to the heathen, but he was found a heretic by leading theologians at the Imperial Diet meeting of 1664.[19]

With the emergence of Philip Jacob Spener (1635-1705), the "father of Pietism," the ground was prepared to set the stage for the breakdown of the intransigent denial and unbending controls of orthodoxy by Lutheran pietists, to recover some of Luther's important contributions for Christian missions.[20] These pietist incentives were further developed by August Hermann Francke at the University of Halle (1695-1727), which led to the initiation of an evangelical mission in South India[21] and a ministry in Pennsylvania (USA) by Henry Melchior Muhlenberg (1711–87).[22]

During the nineteenth century, while Lutherans began to establish relationships with ecumenical partners on a regional basis to renew their commitment for mission work overseas,[23] a resurgence of faithfulness to the confessional benchmarks of the Reformation led to separating themselves from other evangelical Christians in order to establish churches with a "pure" Lutheran identity abroad.

Believing that their own confessional teachings were closer to biblical truth than those of other churches, and that they were somehow the "purest" of visible churches, many Lutherans began to break off ecumenical ties formed under the influence of the Awakening.[24]

The beginning of the Lutheran recovery of faithfulness to its confessional benchmarks of the sixteenth-century Reformation began in Europe during the middle third of the nineteenth century, particularly after the year 1836. For the first time, mission work was embarked upon in the name of the Evangelical Lutheran Church. Lutherans broke away from ecumenical relationships established under the auspices of the Evangelical Awakening, withdrawing from union evangelical societies to form unambiguously Lutheran societies based on the teachings of the Lutheran confessions.[25]

Nevertheless, in spite of the mission field opened by the Lutheran Missouri Synod in India in 1894,[26] for the Lutheran historian and missiologist James Scherer, Lutheranism made no uniform response in the nineteenth century to the challenges of mission and unity; and Lutheran attitudes during the twentieth century became the continuation of nineteenth-century developments.[27] To be sure, the early Lutheran missionaries in Puerto Rico that I will mention in a later section of this study were not affected by the confessional trend followed by the Lutheran Church-Missouri Synod, because they came from a different Lutheran group, the one related to the United Lutheran Church in America.

In the twentieth century, the Lutheran response to world developments such as the end of colonialism, the collapse of Christendom, and the growth of a Christian world community in the six continents, along with the accessibility of common instruments for ecumenical consultation (The Lutheran World Federation, 1947) and missionary cooperation (The World Council of Churches, 1948), allowed for overcoming "their 19th century confessional exclusivism and placing them in the mainstream of the new missionary and ecumenical movements."[28]

LUTHERAN MISSIONS IN THE CARIBBEAN

The Lutheran missionary venture to the Caribbean and Latin America can be traced back, as mentioned earlier in this chapter,[29] to the seventeenth century. Alicia Mayer, a Mexican historian who has endeavored to pursue this issue in her scholarly research, claims that Lutheranism stood as an ideological pernicious image projected against other expressions of the Protestant reformed movement as a strategic resource developed by the Roman Catholic historiography to legitimate the conquest of these lands.[30]

> The metropolis and its colonies participated in the assimilation or transmission of a legacy carrying an ideological message.... Catholic historiography created a very negative stereotype of the Wittenberg theologian. In part, this was due to the intellectual climate of the epoch in which the antihispanic "black legend" prevailed, in other words, the attack against the opponent nations of Spanish conquest and civilizing labor in the Americas... Luther's stereotype released by the Hispanic world could have been seen as a reaction or counterpoint to the "black legend...." The formulation of Luther as an antihero, as a metaphor of evil could be used to legitimate the conquest, above all in the missionary work of the Spanish Crown against its rival powers, most of all those of different confessions.[31]

In spite of this claim, the Lutheran Reformation movement had a presence in this area earlier in the sixteenth century.³² In his book *Teología y Misión en América Latina* (Theology and mission in Latin America), the Lutheran missiologist Rodolfo Blank argues that, to achieve an adequate understanding of the sixteenth-century conquest in what today we call Latin America, we need to look at the great European conquistadores, not just as grand navigators and soldiers, but also as theologians and missionaries.³³ The Paraguayan historian Pablo Alberto Deiros argues that during the sixteenth century this interpretation was also introduced by immigrants and missionaries authorized by European hegemonic powers like Germany, Holland, Sweden, Denmark, Great Britain, and their commercial companies.³⁴ Pirates and corsairs of these nations increasingly began to sail the Latin American continent bringing Bibles and books written by European reformers, and threatening to establish colonies. While at first the Spanish religious leaders seemed in favor of the circulation of the Bible in Spanish (probably the one produced by Casiodoro de Reina in 1569), as the reading and diffusion of the Bible became increasingly identified with the emergence of Protestantism, the Inquisition began to prohibit this diffusion, especially of those in the vernacular.³⁵

In a 1961 study commemorating the fourth centenary of Bartolomé Welser's death, Juan Friede provides one of the most comprehensive examinations of Welser's conquest of Venezuela from 1528 to 1551.³⁶ This study, using the best research available at the time, describes the reality of the first face of what historians call the conquest, pacification, and colonization of the Americas, challenging some of the worst accusations by the early Spanish colonial chroniclers and even some modern historians of this German venture.³⁷

The Welsers were a commercial German company led by Bartolomé and Antonio Welser, having their main center of activities at Augsburg (Germany), as well as subsidiaries in Seville and Zaragoza (Spain), where they controlled the market for saffron. While primarily a commercial company, at times the Welsers loaned money to Charles V (emperor of the Holy Roman Empire). In return for one of these loans, the Welsers asked to be granted the right to establish a commercial venture in Venezuela. This was to be considered a local business with the initiative and direction of their factory established in Seville, that had extended its business of importation and exportation, first to Santo Domingo, and later to Venezuela, thus incorporating the New World to their commercial market.[38] In his book *Historia del Protestantismo en América Latina*, Jean-Pierre Bastian recounts the story that, in 1526, to finance his wedding with Isabel, Charles V asked for a loan from the Welsers, his banking company. In exchange, the Welsers asked to be given Venezuela. Charles V accepted the trade and authorized Enrique Ehinger and Jerónimo Sayler for the conquest and colonization of Venezuela. These German bankers then transferred their right to Ambrosio Alfinger and Georg Ehinger in 1528. Alfinger became governor of the colony and Nicolás Federman the vice-governor. Yet, according to most Roman Catholic studies of the epoch, among them Bartolomé de las Casas, this German venture was as unscrupulous as some of the most violent Spanish conquistadores, for their main interest was in gold and in trafficking slaves.[39]

While the slave traffic was indeed an activity carried out by these German settlers, Friede argues that the responsibility for the tragic experiences of this violent conquest and settlement needs to be shared with the Spanish officials that were working for these German leaders. In fact, properly speaking, the government of this colony was not in the hands of Germans because Spaniards were the ones who led the government for longer periods of time. Throughout the twenty-eight years that the colony lasted, Germans ruled for only five; the rest of the time it was ruled by Spanish governors or Spanish officials.[40]

The question of whether this German colony became Lutheran or not has been debated by many scholars. Various distinguished historians, including Jean-Pierre Bastian,[41] Lars P. Qualben,[42] and Pablo Alberto Deiros,[43] argue that these German settlers, originally from the region of Augsburg, had already embraced the ideas of Lutheranism. Others, such as Roberto Huebner and Rodolfo Blank, claim that we lack enough evidence to assume that they had become Lutheran.⁴⁴ To be sure, the fact remains that, given their foreign origins and the suspicion of being Lutheran,⁴⁵ they were exposed, more than others, to the attacks by people at the colony, as well as those coming from colonial chroniclers and other colonial authorities.⁴⁶

EARLY CARIBBEAN LUTHERANS

In his 1987 report on "Lutheranism in the Caribbean," Vernon H. Naffier, the retired pastor and professor of religion and philosophy at Grand View University (Des Moines, Iowa), provides a valuable historical review of Lutheran missions in the Caribbean.⁴⁷ In the report, Naffier claims that while the first Lutheran congregation was established in 1666 by the Danish on Saint Thomas in the Virgin Islands,⁴⁸ the Lutheran expression was also present during the seventeenth and eighteenth centuries in Surinam (1664)⁴⁹ and Guyana (1743).⁵⁰

Although the earliest Dutch settlement in what we now call Guyana was established in 1616,⁵¹ a Lutheran congregation was not organized there until October 15, 1743. In 1664, however, the Austrian-German Lutheran layman, Baron Justinian Ernst von Welz, a native of Chemnitz, Saxony, sailed for Surinam, at that time known as Dutch Guyana, to begin his commitment to mission work. Von Welz's original intention was to have a Lutheran pastor sent as a foreign missionary but having failed to convince his fellow Lutherans in establishing a program of overseas mission, Welz traveled to Holland, became ordained by a Lutheran pastor, and undertook a Lutheran mission in Surinam for a period of four years until his death in 1668.⁵²

In fact, Johann Heinrich Ursinus, the church superintendent at Regensburg, and considered one of the most respected leaders of the Lutheran orthodoxy in his day, reproached Welz for falling prey to self-appointed satanic fallacies, pronounced denunciations upon Welz's opinions, and warned all Christians to avoid being seduced by his ideas, which Ursinus attributed to the encouragement of theosophists, Quakers, and followers of Thomas Müntzer.[53]

According to Scherer, the failure of Welz to receive support from the church and Christian society of the time may be attributed to several causes, among them his personal religious enthusiasm and belief in private spiritual revelations that led him to be considered a pariah by the dominant Lutheran orthodox theologians, his ferocious and irritable attack on the clergy which was naïve and not altogether warranted,[54] and his associations with the young religious enthusiast Johan Georg Gichtel, whom he met at Regensburg, and pastor Friedrich Breckling. They were both already considered religious outcasts and notoriously polemical; they provided Welz with hospitality while in Holland, and it was Breckling who ordained Welz as an "apostle to the heathen." Also influential were Ursinus's strong opposition to Welz's missionary project, the opinion of political authorities that considered Welz's missionary venture as untimely and unviable, and the fact that, while Lutheran orthodoxy was slowly changing, it had not yet been exposed to the influence of spiritual reform, adversely influencing Welz's cause.[55] However, in spite of Welz's inability to convince his own contemporaries to commit to the mission with heathens, and his unsuccessful personal missionary effort on the coast of Surinam, Welz still became a decisive figure in the history of Lutheran and Protestant missions.[56]

On March 30, 1666, Erik Nielsen Smidt, endorsed by the Danish Crown, arrived with his ship and an initial shipload of colonists to the island of Saint Thomas. Also on board the vessel was a Lutheran pastor, Kjeld Jensen Slagelse, who before leaving Denmark had signed an agreement with Smidt to carry out a mission in the colony. Shortly after their arrival, Smidt died and Slagelse became the second governor of the island.[57] After nineteen challenging months, the colony failed, and in 1668 Slagelse returned to Denmark. Historically, the Frederick Lutheran Church traces its beginning to 1666 in Charlotte Amalie, St. Thomas (the town named after Denmark's German-born queen), a few years after the first two congregations were begun on the North American mainland.[58] In 1671, the Danish West India Company emerged and settled in the harbor of Charlotte Amalie. In 1672, Slagelse decided to return to St. Thomas, but, like many aboard the ship, he died during the voyage and was buried at sea.[59]

A number of pastors who led this missionary venture during the early years were less than honorable.[60] However, all Danish people in the island were required to participate in Sunday worship service, otherwise they could be punished with a fine of twenty-five pounds of tobacco.[61]

Slaves were brought to St. Thomas early in the 1700s and sold to other countries. Their fate was to labor as enslaved Africans in agricultural communities producing sugar cane, cotton, and tobacco. Some slaves resisted this burden by rebellion in St. John (1733), and St. Croix (1848).[62] In his book on slave society and slave life in the Danish West Indies, Eddie Donoghue argues that at times resistance to slavery led to *marronage*,[63] or for slaves to find refuge within the caves and thick forests of the colony. When these alternatives were no longer available, slaves turned to the sea to gain freedom.[64]

> For the enslaved on St. John, the narrow straight to Tortola offered a chance of emancipation. For those on St. Croix and St. Thomas, the Spanish island of Puerto Rico was considered the best place to escape from the horrors of Danish slavery.[65]

The Lutheran mission to slaves began only after the Moravians had engaged in such practice during the second half of the eighteenth century.[66] A characteristic of this Lutheran mission was to establish one congregation for the Danes and a separate one for the slaves. Eventually these separate services disappeared.

After incorporating the island of St. John under their governance in 1717, the Danish established Nazareth Lutheran Church in Cruz Bay, St. John. A Lutheran mission in St. Croix began in 1736 with the arrival of Rev. Gunder Thomas Snydermann, after Denmark purchased the island from France in 1733.[67]

In addition to the contribution of pastors, there were some important lay workers such as Sister Emma Francis (1875–1945), who made significant contributions in expanding the Lutheran mission in the Virgin Islands. Sister Francis was the first Black deaconess in the Lutheran Church in the United States. She was born in St. Kitts and trained to be a missionary at the Deaconess Center in Minneapolis, Minnesota. Following her training she was sent to the Danish West Indies to work on the Ebenezer Orphanage in Frederiksted, St. Croix, known today as the Queen Louis Home for Children.[68]

While there were other enclaves of Lutheranism in the Caribbean and Latin America, given the geographical proximity of the Virgin Islands to Puerto Rico, merchants, slaves, and other interested people made their way to the archipelago of Puerto Rico, spreading their Lutheran religious expression openly or in a hidden fashion.

Since our study is focused on the Lutheran mission in Puerto Rico, while the Lutheran presence in the island[69] is usually set in 1898 with the arrival of Gustav Sigfried Swensson, a seminary student from Augustana Seminary in Illinois,[70] more recent studies trace it back to the time of Alonso Manso (1465–1539), the first Roman Catholic bishop in Puerto Rico.[71] In his book, *La Inquisición Española y las supersticiones en el Caribe hispano, siglo XVI* (The Spanish Inquisition and superstitions in the Hispanic Caribbean, XVI century), Pablo L. Crespo Vargas argues that on January 7, 1519, Manuel Alonso was named Inquisitor to the Indies. As inquisitor, Manso attended the case of maestre[72] Juan, probably the first case of Lutheranism prosecuted in the Indies.[73] In his study on the Welsers in Venezuela, Friede agrees with Crespo in declaring that, in his letters to the Spanish authorities in Spain, Bishop Rodrigo de Bastidas (who also became governor of the German venture in Venezuela, and after Alonso Manso bishop in Puerto Rico), informed them of the case of Lutheran heresy raised against the Flemish maestre Juan, who was sent to the inquisitor in San Juan, Puerto Rico because he had been infected with such "leprosy."[74] Two other distinguished historians of the sixteenth century, Vicente Murga Sanz and Alvaro Huerga, support this claim in their studies.[75]

Luis Martínez-Fernández argues that during the early decades of the nineteenth century, immigrants from Protestant Europe, North

America, and the non-Hispanic Caribbean began to practice their faith in Puerto Rico, particularly in the city of Ponce and the island of Vieques. Since exercising their faith openly was banned, they strove to retain or hide it as dispersed collections of individuals. The source and social standing of these immigrants and transitory persons prompted the typical character and orientation of the Protestant groups that first formed in Puerto Rico.[76]

Class, for example, helps explain Protestants' various responses to official Catholic exclusivism. While some individuals pursued crypto-Protestantism (that is, maintaining a low religious profile while privately adhering to their faith), others responded as pseudo-Catholics: remaining Protestants at heart but publicly participating in the sacraments and other ceremonies of the Catholic church. Moreover, geography and demography affected where Protestants settled and thus limited their individual religious options as well as state and church response to their presence.[77]

In terms of the slave community in the Caribbean islands, their resistance to the institution of slavery led to what scholars in this area of studies call *grand marronage*, that is, "the permanent desertion of slave owners." While *grand marronage* took various shapes as discrete communities threatening militarily and economically the plantation system, given their geographical conditions, slaves in the Danish islands of St. Thomas, St. Croix, and St. John were forced into maritime *marronage*, and Puerto Rico became their favored destination, due to the sparse population of the archipelago, and the leniency, if not encouragement, of the authorities for runaways to embrace Catholicism, or to function as auxiliary militia.[78] As Neville A. T. Hall observes, "Eugenio Fernández Méndez has argued that the Spanish acted largely from religious motives. But there was also an element of calculating realpolitik: in addition to providing manpower, maroons were potentially sources of useful intelligence in the event of hostilities."[79]

CONCLUDING REMARKS

In this first chapter, I began by examining some important aspects of the Lutheran identity. Since Martin Luther was not willing to use his name to describe his sixteenth-century challenge to the dominant Christendom experience in Germany, a good way to describe it is as a reformation movement within the Catholic Church. Eventually, Luther's Protestant colleagues and followers adopted the term "Lutheran" to label this movement, a movement that spread rapidly throughout Europe and later all over the world.

Afterwards, I briefly considered what major Lutheran historians have contemplated regarding the notion of mission, from the sixteenth to the nineteenth century. Then I succinctly examined the Lutheran mission that took place in the Caribbean during those centuries. The purpose of this survey is to provide a better understanding of the way most Lutheran leaders, and particularly those from the United States, conceived their missionary involvement in Puerto Rico by the end of the nineteenth century. I concluded the chapter by mentioning some of the challenges foreign Protestant, and in particular the slave, community in the Caribbean islands faced when migrating to Puerto Rico, where the dominant Christian religious expression has been, since the sixteenth century, Roman Catholic.

In the next chapter I will outline the foundational conditions which led the way for the emergence of Protestantism in Puerto Rico.

NOTES

1 To address this difficulty, "In 1976, the U.S. Congress passed a law that mandated the collection and analysis of data for a specific ethnic group: 'Americans of Spanish origin or descent.' The language of that legislation described this group as 'Americans who identify themselves as being of Spanish-speaking background and trace their origin or descent from Mexico, Puerto Rico, Cuba, Central and South America, and other Spanish-speaking countries.' . . . Standards for collecting data on Hispanics were developed by the Office of Management and Budget (OMB) in 1977 and

revised in 1997." Pew Research Center, "Who Is Hispanic?" accessed June 19, 2023, https://www.pewresearch.org/short-reads/2022/09/15/who-is-hispanic/.
2. Raul A. Reyes, "Love It? Hate It? 'Latinx' Points to the Future, Writes Author Ed Morales," NBCNews.com, September 25, 2018, https://www.nbcnews.com/news/latino/love-it-hate-it-latinx-points-future-writes-author-ed-n912581?icid=related.
3. Karl Marx, *Critique of Hegel's Philosophy of Right*, ed. Joseph O'Malley (Cambridge: Cambridge University Press, 1970), 137–39.
4. See for instance the work of Alvin J. Schmidt where he argues, "In 1970, a nationwide representative survey asked Lutherans what they believed as members of the American Lutheran Church (ALC), the Lutheran Church in America (LCA), and the Lutheran Church-Missouri Synod (LCMS), all three bodies representing about nine million Lutherans. Two years later, the survey's finding appeared in 'A Study of Generations.' The study reported that many Lutherans held a number of beliefs incompatible with basic Lutheran theology." Schmidt, *Hallmarks of Lutheran Identity* (St. Louis: Concordia Publishing House, 2017), 9–14.
5. Martin Luther, "The Christian in Society II," in *Luther's Works Vol. 45*, ed. Walther I. Brandt, gen. ed. Helmut T. Lehman (Philadelphia: Muhlenberg Press, 1962), 70–71. For an interesting study of Martin Luther's life and contributions see Bernhard Lohse, *Martin Luther: An Introduction to His Life and Work* (Philadelphia: Fortress Press, 1986), A valuable study of Martin Luther from a Latin American perspective is Walter Altmann, *Lutero e libertação* (São Leopoldo: Editora Sinodal, 2016).
6. James A. Scherer, *Gospel, Church, & Kingdom: Comparative Studies in World Mission Theology* (Minneapolis: Augsburg, 1987), 51–52. An important study of the history of Lutheranism is Eric W. Gritsch, *A History of Lutheranism* (Minneapolis: Fortress Press, 2002). In terms of a description of the development of Lutheranism in North America, see Mark Granquist, *Lutherans in America: A New History* (Minneapolis: Fortress Press, 2015).
7. Eric W. Gritsch, *A History of Lutheranism* (Minneapolis: Fortress Press, 2002), xi.
8. Scherer, *Gospel, Church, & Kingdom*, 51.
9. Scherer, 54. Also Gustav Warneck, *Outline of the History of Protestant Missions from the Reformation to the Present Time*, 10.
10. While "In the period immediately before Pietism Lutherans raised almost insuperable obstacles to the development of a positive missionary tradition, the emergence of the Lutheran pastor Philip Jakob Spener (1635–1705), the 'father of Pietism,' set forth new tasks and goals which prepared the ground for the missionary impulse." Scherer, 70–71. It is valuable to note at this point that the Lutheran Seminary in Philadelphia, along with Augustana Seminary in Rock Island (Illinois), at which the early North American Lutheran missionaries that went to Puerto Rico

made their theological studies, were highly influenced by the University of Halle in their missionary perspective. The pietist incentives mentioned above were further developed by August Hermann Francke at this university.
11 Scherer, 55. See also Otto Hardeland, ed., *Gesschichte der lutherischen Mission nach den Vorträgen des Prof. D. Plitt*, vol. 1 (Leipzig: A. Deichertsche Verlagsbuchandlung, 1894-95). E. Theodore Bachmann and Mercia Brenne Bachmann argue that "Lutherans in Africa trace their beginnings from such scattered starts as the Strand Street Church in Cape Town, founded in the 1780s among German settlers, and the first missionary efforts among the Black people in South Africa in the 1820s. Other Lutheran missionary efforts began in Liberia, Eritrea, Ethiopia and Madagascar in the 1860s, and in Tanzania in the 1880s." Bachmann and Bachmann, *Lutheran Churches in the World*, 48. In China, "the Lutheran mission developed in two stages, and mainly in two regions of the vast nation. First came a succession of missionaries from Germany to Canton and the province of Kwangtung. Pioneers (1846) of the Basel and Rhenish societies were followed by those from Berlin (1850). In 1898 Berlin began work also in the northeast port city of Ch'ing-Tao (Tsingtao) but transferred this undertaking to the United Lutheran Church in America in 1925," Bachmann and Bachmann, *Lutheran Churches in the World*, 160.
12 Scherer, *Gospel, Church, & Kingdom*, 55.
13 See Johannes Aagaard, "Missionary Theology," in *The Lutheran Church Past and Present*, ed. Vilmos Vajta (Minneapolis: Augsburg, 1977), 206-10.
14 Scherer, *Gospel, Church, & Kingdom*, 55-66.
15 For a more thorough analysis of this topic see James Arnold Scherer, "The Relation of Mission and Unity in Lutheranism: A Study in Lutheran Ecumenics," a dissertation submitted in partial fulfillment of the requirements for the degree of Doctor of Theology at Union Theological Seminary in the city of New York (1968), 6-14.
16 Scherer, *Gospel, Church, & Kingdom*, 66.
17 Scherer argues that, according to this practice, "Lutheran princes—especially from Sweden and Denmark -carried out territorial missions in their overseas possessions, sending chaplains to preach the gospel to both Christians and non-Christians," 67.
18 Scherer, 68.
19 Scherer, 69-70. For a more comprehensive analysis of the life, writings, and missionary significance of Justinian Von Welz, see James A. Scherer, *Justinian Welz: Essays by an Early Prophet of Mission* (Grand Rapids, MI: William B. Eerdmans, 1969).
20 "In his programmatic essay, *Pia Desideria* (1675), Spener proposed a more extensive use of the Scriptures by individuals and groups, diligent exercise of the spiritual priesthood of the laity, the view that Christianity consists more of practice (*praxis pietatis*) than of theory, reform in theological

education; and an emphasis on edification rather than erudition in sermons and religious education," Scherer, *Gospel, Church, & Kingdom*, 71.
21 For a good study of this Indian missionary venture, see Peter Vethanayagamony, *It Began in Madras: The Eighteenth-Century Lutheran-Anglican Ecumenical Ventures in Mission and Benjamin Schultze* (Delhi: ISPCK, 2010).
22 For a more detailed analysis of the contribution of Pietism to Lutheran missionary work, as well as the strengths and weaknesses of this effort, see Vethanayagamony, *It Began in Madras*, 71–73. Also, Scherer, "The Relation of Mission and Unity in Lutheranism," 20–32; *Pietists: Selected Writings*, ed. Peter C. Erb (New York, Ramsey, and Toronto: Paulist Press, 1983); Margaret R. Seebach, *An Eagle of the Wilderness the Story of Henry Melchior Muhlenberg* (Philadelphia: The United Lutheran Publication House, 2004).
23 Scherer, *Gospel, Church, & Kingdom*, 73–78. Also, Scherer, "The Relation of Mission and Unity in Lutheranism," 32–53.
24 Scherer, *Gospel, Church, & Kingdom*, 75.
25 Scherer, "The Relation of Mission and Unity in Lutheranism," 37. The impact of this confessional emphasis in the United States was established in The Lutheran Church – Missouri Synod, formed in 1847 by persons connected with the Saxon emigration of 1839 to North America. This specific strand of Lutheranism represented the ultimate development of confessional and separatist principles in Lutheranism. Scherer, 50.
26 However, "Once the framework of confessional propaganda was left behind, missionaries of the Missouri Synod encountered the same tasks of evangelical proclamation and missionary adaptation as other groups did." Scherer, 51. Also, F. D. Lueking, *Mission in the Making. The Missionary Enterprise among Missouri Synod Lutherans, 1346–1963* (St. Louis: Concordia Publishing, 1964), 227.
27 Scherer, "The Relation of Mission and Unity in Lutheranism," 54.
28 Scherer, 79. Also 78–83, 54–88.
29 See note 19 above. See also the valuable study on Protestantism in the Colonial Caribbean, "For God and Nation," in Ennis B. Edmonds and Michelle A. Gonzalez, *Caribbean Religious History: An Introduction* (New York and London: New York University Press, 2010), 65–92.
30 Alicia Mayer, *Lutero en el Paraíso: La Nueva España en el espejo del reformador alemán* (México: Fondo de Cultura Económica, 2008), 20–21.
31 Mayer, *Lutero en el Paraíso*, translation mine. Some of these scholars also maintain that God had granted these lands to the Roman Catholic Church as reparation for the lands lost to them by the Reformation of Martin Luther. See, for example, Bachmann and Bachmann, *Lutheran Churches in the World*, 458.
32 In his study, Jean-Pierre Bastian also mentions the Huguenot colony in Rio de Janeiro (1555–60), their other attempt in Florida (1564–65), and the Calvinist Dutch experience in Brazil (1630–54). Jean-Pierre Bastian,

Historia del Protestantismo en América Latina (Mexico: Casa Unida de Publicaciones, 1986), 46–57.
33   Roberto Blank, *Teología y Misión en America Latina* (St. Louis: Concordia Publishing House, 1996), 7. Luis N. Rivera Pagán makes a similar claim in his book, *Historia de la conquista de América: Evangelización y violencia* (Barcelona: CLIE, 2021), 2.
34   Pablo Alberto Deiros, *Historia del Cristianismo en América Latina* (Florida and Buenos Aires: Fraternidad Teológica Latinoamericana, 1992), 587. In his voluminous work on the conquest of América, Luis N. Rivera Pagán argues that: "The sixteenth-century Spanish debates [regarding the Spanish conquest of America during the sixteenth century] had a peculiarity that the historian has to understand and respect, if they are not to be distorted. They were engaged principally in theological and religious conceptuality. Perhaps the main defect of any modern studies of the age consists in not recognizing the primacy of the theological discourse in sixteenth century ideological production. Truly the Spanish conquerors of the Americas were driven by their quest for God, gold, and glory. But it was the language related to God-*theology* that served to rationalize avarice and ambition, not vice versa. It was religion that attempted to sacralize political dominion and economic exploitation." Luis N. Rivera, *A Violent Evangelism: The Political and Religious Conquest of the Americas* (Louisville, KY: Westminster/John Knox Press, 1992), xv. To support his claim, Rivera makes reference to the works of scholars of the time, such as Antonio León Pinelo (1590–1660), who wrote a book entitled *El Paraíso en el Nuevo Mundo: Comentario apologético, historia natural y peregrina de las Indias Occidentales* (1696), the Franciscan Bernardino de Sahagún (1499–1590), *Historia general de las cosas de Nueva España* (1577), Fray Toribio de Motolina (1489/91–1569), *Historia de los indios de la Nueva España: Relación de los ritos antiguos, idolatrías y sacrificios de los indios de la Nueva España, y de la maravillosa conversión que Dios en ella ha obrado* (1536), and many others.
35   Deiros, *Historia del Cristianismo en América Latina*, 590–91.
36   Juan Friede, *Los Welser en la conquista de Venezuela* (Caracas and Madrid: The commemorative edition of the IV centenary of the death of Bartolomé Welser, leader of the German company from Augsburg, 1961). This German colony in Venezuela seems to be important in German history, given that some contemporary books on German history incorporate it in their narrative. See, for example: "The power of the Welser was based mainly on overseas trade. In 1528 they committed themselves in a treaty with the Spanish Crown to organize the slave trade with America. The first shipment consisted of Negro slaves. In order to accelerate the development of mining in the newly discovered areas, the Welsers brought thirty German miners to America. In Venezuela they even founded their own colony, which they soon had to give up. There was no strong nationally state-oriented monarchy that could have given German companies support on the world market,"

translation mine, *Deutsche Geschichte von den Anfangen bis 1789* (Berlin: VEB Deutscher Verlag der Wissenschaften, 1974), 471.
37   Friede, *Los Welser en la conquista de Venezuela*, 13-25.
38   Friede, 21.
39   Voloida Telelboim's valuable study claims that apparently these German settlers sold more than a million native people as slaves in the markets of Santa Marta, Jamaica, the San Juan islands, and New Spain where the Real Audiencia tribunal was located. Voloida Telelboim, *El amanecer del capitalismo y la conquista de América* (Havana: Casa de las Américas, 1979), 150. For a valuable study on Christianity and slavery in the Caribbean see Armando Lampe, "Christianity and Slavery in the Dutch Caribbean," in *Christianity in the Caribbean: Essays on Church History*, ed. Armando Lampe (Barbados, Jamaica, Trinidad and Tobago: University of the West Indies Press, 2001), 126-52. Also Keith Hunte, "Protestantism and Slavery in the British Caribbean," in Lampe, ed., *Christianity in the Caribbean: Essays on Church History*, 86-125. An earlier and foundational study of this topic is *Escravidao Negra e História da Igreja na América Latina e no Caribe*, ed. J. O. Beozzo (Petrópolis: Vozes, 1987).
40   Friede, *Los Welser en la conquista de Venezuela*, 37-41.
41   Bastian, "Colonial Protestantism, 1492-1808," in *The Church in Latin America 1492-1992*, ed. Enrique Dussel (New York: Orbis Books, 1992), 314.
42   Lars P. Qualben, *A History of the Christian Church* (New York: Thomas Nelson & Sons, 1940), 415n3. M. Baralt argues that the father of Nicolás Federman, vice-governor of the colony, was among those that signed the Augsburg Confessions. M. Baralt, *Historia de Venezuela* (Paris: Desclée de Brower, 1939), 36-37.
43   Deiros, *Historia del Cristianismo en América Latina*, 591-94. Deiros argues that Nicolás Federman (1501-42), who was vice-governor of the German colony along with Ambrosio Alfinger, was the son of Claus Federmann, who cosigned the Augsburg Confession (the foundation of Lutheran doctrine) in 1530. Rafael María Baralt y Pérez (distinguished Venezuelan diplomat and historian) and Sidney Roy also claim that Federman was Lutheran.
44   Blank, *Teología y Misión en America Latina*, 159-60.
45   Friede argues that this suspicion was based, in part, on a questionable neutrality that the Welsers expressed in the religious struggles that tore up Europe at the time, as well as the fact that the Alfinger and Federman families provided forthright support to the reformation movement. Friede, *Los Welser en la conquista de Venezuela*, 23-24.
46   Friede, 7. While some members of the Welser family supported the Roman Catholic cause, others, such as Hans Welser and Ulrich Welser (who represented the city of Augsburg at different times), became strong advocates for the protestant movement. Friede, 82.

47 Vernon H. Naffier, "Historical Sketch of Lutheranism in the Caribbean" (unknown binding), January 1, 1987.
48 Naffier, "Historical Sketch of Lutheranism in the Caribbean," 50–55.
49 Naffier, 21–36.
50 Naffier, 3–20.
51 Naffier, 3.
52 Naffier, 3, 21. Scherer claims that, "There is no record of his activity in Surinam, or of the cause of his death. Phillip Jakob Spener records that Welz was reported to have been torn by wild beasts. A more probable cause of death is malaria. Groessel, the German editor of Welz's writings, comments: 'Thus died Justinian von Welz, lonely and forsaken, a sacrifice to his own self-elected calling, an enlightening model for all times of faithful courage and joyful readiness to give all – even one's own life—for the sake of Christ.'" Scherer, *Gospel, Church, & Kingdom*, 22. Welz's life story is told by W. Grössel in *Justinianus von Weltz, der Vorkämpfer der lutherischen Mission* (Leipzig: Akademische Buchhandlung, 1891); cf. also Grössel, *Die Mission und die evangelische Kirche im 17 Jahrhundert* (Gotha: Perthes 1897), 33–67.
53 Scherer, *Justinianus von Welz*, 20–21, 106–7.
54 In 1664, and in response to the negative reaction that members of the Corpus Evangelicorum expressed at Regensburg to his missionary project, Welz wrote the tract, *A Repeated Loyal and Earnest Reminder and Admonition to Undertake the conversion of Unbelieving Peoples*, where he strongly rebuked the delegates of the Corpus Evangelicorum, and attacked his contemporary clergy, scholars, preachers and rulers. See the translation made of excerpts of this tract by James A. Scherer in *Justinianus von Welz*, 91–96.
55 Scherer, *Justinianus von Welz*, 22–23.
56 For a more detailed analysis of Welz's notable contributions in the history of mission, see "Welz's Place in the History of Missions," in Scherer, *Justinianus von Welz*, 36–46.
57 In a recent article in the *Living Lutheran* (the latest new magazine published by the Evangelical Lutheran Church in America) about this specific topic, the author, Nicolette Peñaranda, claims that Frederick Lutheran Church's parsonage "was intentionally built right next to the governor's house in St. Thomas," because "It was common practice that when the governor was not in St. Thomas, the Lutheran pastor acted in his place." Nicolette Peñaranda, "The Oldest ELCA Church Resides in the US Virgin Islands," *The Living Lutheran* (January/February 2023): 18.
58 Bachmann and Bachmann, "The Lutheran Churches in the World," 487.
59 Bachmann and Bachmann, 487.
60 According to Naffier, "One such pastor was Theodore Christensen Riisbrick who arrived in 1674. He was a heavy drinker who seldom conducted worship services and often quarreled with the governor. After he crippled an officer

in a fight, he was dismissed in 1678. From then until the end of the century, the Lutheran Church in St. Thomas was supplied with a pastor for less than half of the time." Naffier, "Historical Sketch of Lutheranism in the Caribbean," 21.

61 Naffier, 21. Nicolette Peñaranda claims that "the authority of the church was so substantial it had the power to incarcerate those that didn't attend Sunday service. That narrative is present to this day: 'Frederick Church? The one that threw people in jail!' The parsonage also had rooms on the top floor that operated as a jail for enslaved Africans rebuking slavery." Peñaranda, "The Oldest ELCA Church Resides in the US Virgin Islands," 18.

62 Peñaranda, 18–19.

63 Maroon refers to an African or Afro-American person who freed themself from enslavement in the Americas and lived in hidden towns outside of the plantations. Enslaved people used several forms of resistance to fight their imprisonment, everything from work slowdowns and tool damage to full-fledged revolt and flight. Some self-liberated people established permanent or semi-permanent towns for themselves in hidden places not far from the plantations, a process known as *marronage* (sometimes also spelled *maronnage* or *maroonage*). "History and Culture," Thought.co, accessed June 20, 2023, https://www.thoughtco.com/history-and-culture-4133356.

64 Eddie Donoghue, *Negro Slavery: Slave Society and Slave Life in the Danish West Indies* (Bloomington and Milton Keynes: AuthorHouse, 2007), 181–83. See also the interesting report that slaves at Jolly Hill estate intended to create a disturbance on March 29, 1801, in Neville A. T. Hall, *Slave Society in the Danish West Indies* (Mona: The University of the West Indies Press, 1992), 27–28.

65 Donoghue, *Negro Slavery*, 181. Peñaranda claims that, in the case of the island of St. Johns, enslaved Africans were so despairing for their freedom, that on Mary's Point overlooking the Tortola shore, they leapt into the ocean suffering the possibility of death. "Stories continue today about sharks lingering by that cliff where people claim to see red in the water." Peñaranda, "The Oldest ELCA Church Resides in the US Virgin Islands," 19.

66 Naffier argues that "Isolated ministrations to slaves did occur. The first baptism of a slave, performed by Pastor Christian Fischer of the Lutheran Church, took place in 1713." Naffier, "Historical Sketch of Lutheranism in the Caribbean," 51. Another notable exception "was the ministry of the Rev. Hans Jacob Ottesen Stoud, who served congregations in both St. Thomas and St. Croix between 1740 and 1749. Among his many activities, he tutored some fifty slaves in reading and writing." Naffier, 52.

67 Naffier, 51. For an informative article on the type of overseas empire Denmark was characterized by see Lars Jensen, "Postcolonial Denmark:

Beyond the Rot of Colonialism," in *Postcolonial Studies* 18, no. 4 (2015): 440–52. In terms of resistance to colonialism by a Virgin Islands poet and literary scholar, see Edgar O. Lake, "The Role of the Artist in the Liberation Struggle," The Leonard Tim Hector Annual Memorial Lecture, Anglican Cultural Center, St. John's, Antigua, WI, November 7, 2005. For a richer description of the history of Lutheranism in the Virgin Islands by Virgin Islanders see "Redemption Song: Talks at the Desk," season 2, ep. 2, 2023, YouTube, https://youtu.be/aEF21R4Zxv4, where Lutheran leaders speak about the history of Lutheranism in the Virgin Islands.

68 See Catherine B. Herzel, *She Made Many Rich: Sister Emma Francis of the Virgin Island* (Frederiksted: CRIC Productions, 1990).

69 To be sure, there is an island in the Caribbean named Puerto Rico; however, a better geographical term for Puerto Rico is that of an archipelago since the island includes a group of small islands, including Culebra, Vieques, and Isla de Muertos.

70 Alfredo Ostrom, "Principios de la Iglesia Luterana en Puerto Rico," *El Testigo* (The Witness), año VII, 9 and 10: 1, 4. Notwithstanding this claim, in the "Chronology of Protestant Beginnings in Puerto Rico 1598–2011," compiled by Drs. Daryl L. Platt, Clifton L. Holland, and Dorothy Bullón, https://www.ranchocolibri.net/prolades/historical/pri-chron.pdf (last updated on 2 April 2012), the contention is that a Lutheran congregation was formed among Danish immigrants in Puerto Rico by the 1840s.

71 On May 12, 1512, Alonso Manso is named bishop and consecrated in Sevilla in August 23. On November 15, he sails with his entourage to Puerto Rico in the caravel *San Francisco*, and on December 25 lands in Puerto Rico to become the first bishop in the Americas. José Antonio Benito, "Alonso Manso: Primer obispo de América, de Salamanca a Puerto Rico. 500 años de su llegada, accessed June 20, 2023, jabenito.blogspot.com. See also https://www.histopediadepuertorico.com/post/alonso-manso-primer-obispo-de-puerto-rico (accessed July 12, 2023).

72 A man who, after the captain, was responsible for the economic government of merchant ships; on a ship, the person responsible for the provision and distribution of food for seafarers and troops. See Real Academic Española, Spanish Dictionary, accessed June 20, 2023, https://dle.rae.es/maestre.

73 Pablo L. Crespo Vargas, *La Inquisición española y las supersticiones en el Caribe hispano, siglo XVI* (Lajas: Editorial Akelarre, 2013), 151.

74 Vargas, *La Inquisición española y las supersticiones en el Caribe hispano*, 150–51. Also Friede, *Los Welser en la conquista de Venezuela*, 23–24.

75 See Vicente Murga Sanz y Alvaro Huerga, *Episcopologio de Puerto Rico* (Ponce: Universidad Católica de Puerto Rico, 1987), 231–355.

76 Luis Martínez-Fernández, *Protestantism and Political Conflict in the Nineteenth Century Hispanic Caribbean* (New Brunswick, NJ, and London: Rutgers University Press, 2002), 48–71.
77 Martínez-Fernández, *Protestantism and Political Conflict in the Nineteenth Century Hispanic Caribbean*, 48.
78 Neville A. T. Hall, *Slave Society in the Danish West Indies: St. Thomas, St. John, and St. Croix* (Jamaica, Barbados, and Trinidad: The University of the West Indies Press, 1992), 124–38.
79 Hall, *Slave Society in the Danish West Indies*, 127.

CHAPTER 2

Setting the Stage for an Emerging Protestantism

While a seminary student at the Lutheran School of Theology at Chicago, I was often asked if I became Lutheran while in the United States, given the general assumption that Puerto Rico, being a colony of Spain since the sixteenth century, was a Roman Catholic country. My usual answer was that, while it is true that during the sixteenth century Spain's empire made Puerto Rico one of its many American colonies, during the end of the nineteenth century, and as a consequence of losing the Spanish–American War, the United States took Puerto Rico as a booty of war territory from Spain. Following the United States military invasion of Puerto Rico, most Protestant denominations came from North America to divide the archipelago among themselves. In other words, the type of Protestantism characteristic of the sixteenth-century European Reformation has been in Puerto Rico since the end of the nineteenth century, including the Lutheran mission. However, a more insightful scholarly investigation of this topic may find its presence even at an earlier time.

EARLY MILITARY VENTURES

In his important research about the Protestant presence in Puerto Rico during the Spanish period, Rev. Dr. Angel Luis Gutiérrez argues that, as early as 1554, the city of San German was attacked by Lutheran corsairs and later by the English, who destroyed all the images in the church while leaving behind some Bibles in Spanish. In 1559, King Phillip II wrote to the region's prelates about the need to punish rigorously anyone embracing the Lutheran heresy, authorizing them to collect Lutheran writings and all other books forbidden by the church. In May 1585, the English under the leadership of Sir Richard Grenville came to Puerto Rico, landing in the south of the island. There they tried unsuccessfully to receive the support of Puerto Ricans, and after taking from them all they had, left them some Bibles in an attempt to convince them of their Protestant religious perspectives. In September 1625, the Dutch Balduino Enrico entered San Juan, the capital of the island, but Spanish soldiers, under the leadership of Governor Juan de Haro, forced them to abandon the city. Prior to their departure, the Dutch soldiers took the bells of the cathedral, which ended up at the first temple-church built in the city of New York.[1] There was another later attempt by the British to invade Puerto Rico. On April 17, 1797, after conquering Trinidad, British troops led by General Ralph Abercromby and Admiral Henry Harvey landed in the coast of Loiza, in front of Punta de Cangrejos (today's Piñones). Despite the enormity of the invading force (63 British war ships along with 14,000 soldiers and sailors), in two weeks the British force left the island defeated—disease offered an effective defense.[2]

The North American (1775–83) and French (1789–99) revolutions that fought against dominant European monarchies at the end of the eighteenth century provided a broad impetus for political reform influencing Spain and its American colonies. In Spain, this spirit of political reform led in 1810 to the constitution of the Spanish Cortes to govern the country. The American colonies, which since 1809 had been part of the Spanish territory, sent delegates to the Cortes, who, despite supporting Catholicism as the state religion of Spain and its territories, facilitated a political openness to this policy leading to a tolerance of dissident religious expressions in their own context. This weakening of the church's influence was further advanced with the arrival of the printing press in the Americas,[3] which provided the foundation for a journalistic tradition of mass communication disseminating a plethora of ideas worldwide, both in support of and against the Catholic faith. Ideas influenced by the North American and French revolutions nurtured in Puerto Rico a nationalist sentiment against the Spanish colonial government, along with a drive for the eradication of slavery.[4]

EARLY PROTESTANT COMMUNITIES IN PUERTO RICO

In 1868, following the liberal revolution in Spain, freedom of religious gatherings was extended to their Caribbean territories. Motivated by this governmental legislation, in 1869 the Protestant communities of Ponce, Aguadilla, and Vieques publicly organized their congregations, legalizing their condition, and building their schools and chapels.[5] While the first authorized Protestant worship service was celebrated on November 28, 1869, at Ponce in the house of Mr. Thomas G. Solomons,[6] the first Protestant church building was inaugurated in the same city on July 23, 1874, assisting approximately four hundred persons.[7]

The religious, political, and social impact of this emerging Protestant community in the island became highly significant. During this century, Protestants and Freemasons were perceived by the post–French Revolution Catholic Church as leading the movement toward revolution, independence, and the equality of human beings, including the abolition of slavery and the burial of non-Catholic believers in available cemeteries. Puerto Rican intellectual and political leaders of this epoch sympathized with many of these Protestant ideas. However, it was not until the military invasion by the United States of the island in 1898,[8] and the subsequent arrival of missionaries from a variety of Protestant denominations, that Protestantism began to have a strong presence in Puerto Rico.

It is important to point out that up until then, the initial Protestant community in Ponce was organized by wealthy foreigners, and the extension of the Protestant mission to Spanish-speaking Puerto Ricans or Spaniards became a controversial matter. There, the increased prominence of West Indians of color in its membership led many of its initial white founders to resent their presence and withdraw their support from the congregation.[9]

In Vieques, however, given its unique history and proximity to the British and Danish Virgin Islands, the island also attracted a large number of Protestant Black contract laborers from the British West Indies, as well as escaped slaves from the islands of St. Croix and St. Thomas. As Luis Martínez-Fernández claims,

> Although a Protestant population may have existed on the island since 1840s and there is some sign of organized Protestant activity by the late 1860s, a formal community did not emerge until 1880.[10]

Yet, to be sure, it was the early work of these Protestant communities and their foreign and native leaders, such as don Eduardo Heyliger (1812–1900), don Antonio Badillo (1827–89), and the group called Los Bíblicos ("believers in the word"), in this labor that smoothed the influence and progress of Protestantism in the island for later centuries.[11]

It is notable that the two pioneers of Protestantism in Puerto Rico mentioned above had a significant impact in social and political life on the island. Both were connected to the revolutionary movement leading to El Grito de Lares. They were very active in their respective regional social organizations, used their wealth to contribute to the building of schools and hospitals, and struggled for the eradication of slavery.[12]

Don Eduardo Heyliger is considered one of the earliest Protestants in Puerto Rico during the nineteenth century because it is suspected both now and by his contemporaries that he brought the first Protestant Bible to the region or "barrio" La Montaña in Aguadilla.[13] He was a descendant of Johannes Heyliger, governor of San Estaquio Island in the Caribbean (1717–19, 1721), heir of Guillaume Heyleger and Unna Rodward, who were originally from the German states.[14] Citing official documents from the city of Aguadillas, Gutiérrez notes that Don Eduardo was born in Danish Saint Croix in 1812 to Don Guillermo and Doña María Isabel Heyliger.[15]

Don Eduardo came to Puerto Rico in the middle of the nineteenth century, becoming first a landowner in St. Croix, Virgin Islands, then moving to Mayaguez and later to Isabela, in the region that includes what is called today "La Bajura" or "Playa," adjoining the eastern part of Playa Guajataca Hills, in the town of Quebradillas. In 1848, his name appears in *La Gaceta de Puerto Rico* as contributing to a private fund for immigrants from the French Antilles.[16] He and Doña Isabel Riquelme had five children, Guillermo, Cornelio, Eduardo, Maria Isabel, and Cesar Augusto.[17] In Isabela he was a justice of the peace and established a sugar cane farm called "La Hacienda del Moro" [the Moor farm] (probably given his Protestant ideas in a Roman Catholic and Spanish land). He was arrested on October 10, 1868, by the Puerto Rican government for his active participation in the Grito de Lares insurrection, but was later freed on October 25 by General Jose Laureano Sanz, who gave amnesty to all political prisoners related to the Lares insurrection. After being released from prison, Don Eduardo moved to the city of Mayaguez.[18] According to his great grandson, Eduardo Heyliger Barnes, given his experience of persecution during the first years of the 1890s, Don Eduardo Heyliger fled the city of Mayaguez to Saint Croix, but after the military invasion of Puerto Rico by the United States, he returned to the island.[19]

While some sources trace his religious affiliation to the Presbyterian church,[20] my estimation is that he was Lutheran since, according to one of his descendants, Don Eduardo Heyliger came from a German family, and from St. Croix, which was ruled by the Lutheran Danish Government at that time. However, the fact is that Protestant groups in Puerto Rico prior to the establishment of an

Episcopal (Anglican) church in Ponce or Vieques came from various Protestant denominations developing a type of nondenominational ecumenical Protestantism, resisting the Roman Catholic Spanish religious tradition.[21]

In a recent article Sarahí Rivera Martínez, a Puerto Rican medical technologist presently studying for her PhD in theology at the Ibero-American Institute of Sciences and Humanities (INIBERCIH) in Peru (South America), describes this early Protestant experience as follows:

> The name of "Los Bíblicos," derived from the strong impression that their home meetings had around the reading of the sacred Scriptures. In fact, this identity feature dissolved any other denominational, doctrinal distinction, or sectorial qualifying within the Protestant field. Badillo as well as his companions favored a religious Society of "brothers" gathered in the simplicity of the domestic life around the Biblical text, prayer, the congregational singing, along with the fraternal bonds and mutual help.[22]

For Rivera Martínez, the beginning of Protestantism in Puerto Rico comprehends two principal stages. The first is the period from 1860 up to 1870, a phase characterized by a Protestant movement recruiting among communities of significant diversity incorporating foreigners, free slaves, and residents, but overall an autochthonous Protestantism taking roots among the creole element, identified by a piety that turned around the Holy Scriptures, simple and spontaneous prayers, congregational singing, and solidary mutual assistance. Such societies were also characterized by establishing coalitions with anti-Catholic and anti-Spanish liberal sectors of society in encouraging an array of causes including autonomy, abolitionism, freedom of conscience, religious tolerance, separation of church and state, secularization of cemeteries, popular education, and so on.[23]

The second stage, covering the period from 1898 to 1920, while it continued maintaining the core features of the same piety, and its social ethics retained a progressive ideology in a reformist form, nevertheless left behind its previous role of resistance and support for a historical project for the emancipation of the colonial power to become an instrument for "Americanization," collaboration in the neocolonial project of the island by the United States of America.[24] Yet, the history of resistance by Protestant religious leaders in Puerto Rico against established structures of the island's colonial society cannot be limited to Spanish colonial interests. While it is true that Protestant sectors of Puerto Rico welcomed US intervention in the island in 1898, considering the Spanish–American War as a great prospect to increase its missionary efforts and even joining anti-Spanish guerilla activities, political and religious leaders soon grew increasingly discontented with US control and cultural influence.[25] In a publication sponsored by the West Indies Mission Board of the United Lutheran Church in America with the title *The Isles of the Sea* (1936), as it addresses the obstacles facing the Lutheran mission in Puerto Rico, you find the following statement:

> A third obstacle has been the conduct of many tourists and American residents who by their life and conversation would never lead anyone to think that America was a Christian nation. By their mad pursuit of pleasure and their utter indifference to the church and its standards of morality, such Americans have prejudiced the minds of many natives against everything American, including missionaries.[26]

In an article written by Rubén Arrieta Vilá and published in the "Sunday Journal" of the Puerto Rican newspaper *El Nuevo Día* addressing the relationship between politics and religion, Francisco L. Sosa, then Lutheran Bishop of the Caribbean Synod, claimed that faithfulness to the Word of God led the early Lutheran missionaries in Puerto Rico to focus on the needs of the population instead of supporting the imperial military expansion of the United States in the Caribbean.[27]

Scholar Ángel Santiago-Vendrell claims that while the Americanizing motif was part of the evangelistic efforts of some missionaries, new evidence shows that a minority of missionaries, among them Presbyterians James A. McAllister and Judson Underwood, had a clear vision of indigenization/contextualization for the emerging church based on language (Spanish) and culture (Puerto Rican). This investigation also claims that the assumption that native Christians would follow the missionaries in their quest to Americanize Puerto Rico is more nuanced and complicated than previous research on the Americanization process of Puerto Rico has shown. The ministry of some Puerto Rican protestant leaders (such as Adela Sousa and other Bible women, as well as the one of Miguel Martínez in the Presbyterian church) offer examples where Puerto Ricans were not in the same place as the missionaries when it came to issues of Americanization. They never equated the gospel with Americanization. They believed in the God of the Bible who sent Jesus Christ to redeem the world from sin. Their new pastors' ministry as local evangelists showed them as committed to the gospel and not to a political ideology. For these pastors all the technological, cultural, and social advances in Western civilization remained byproducts of the wisdom of the gospel of Jesus Christ. The initial success of their ministry showed the centrality of native agency in the spread and establishment of the gospel in Puerto Rico.[28] In this regard, I agree with Sarahí Rivera Martínez when she argues that, in spite of the ambiguous expression of early Protestantism in Puerto Rico (both the one of resistance against the Spanish dominant religion and colonial dominance characteristic of the 1860 to 1897 period, and the one that emerged after the invasion of the island by the United States in 1898 which supported the "Americanization" of the island), it will still be possible today to retrieve the Protestant function of resistance in a new historical project against the neocolonialism characteristic of the present relationship between Puerto Rico and the United States.[29]

SETTING THE STAGE FOR AN EMERGING PROTESTANTISM

THE US MILITARY AND THE PROCESS OF "AMERICANIZING" THE PEOPLE

For many scholars of Puerto Rican history, the United States military played an important role in addressing the efforts to "Americanize" the people of Puerto Rico after the Spanish–American War. To be sure, most scholars of North American empire-building expansion tend to focus on the political, economic, and cultural aspects of US interventionism in Puerto Rico—as, indeed, did contemporary US journalists and other commentators.[30] Harry Franqui-Rivera argues that, as the island of Puerto Rico experienced a transition from Spanish to United States colonial rule, Puerto Rican national identities underwent a strong and complicated change, producing a liberal, popular, and broad definition of *Puertorriqueñidad.*

> In this study, I analyze the impact of military service on the converging sociocultural and political histories of Puerto Rico. . . . The analysis centers on patterns of inclusion/exclusion within the military and how they transformed into socioeconomic and political disenfranchisement or enfranchisement. . . . I rely on an intersectional analysis of gender, race, and class to understand modernity projects driving nation-state building and identity formation processes via military service taking place in a colonial setting under two empires.[31]

Since my research focuses on the Lutheran mission in Puerto Rico, my approach will concentrate on the role of military chaplains arriving in Puerto Rico after the Spanish–American War. The reason for this effort lies in my conviction that in various ways these chaplains, whether Protestants or Roman Catholics, embodied the Christian and civilizing missionary influence of North American values to the Puerto Rican culture.[32] To begin, it is important to consider that Christianity in the United States strongly supported the United States' declaration of war against Spain in 1898. Some

Protestant groups saw the Spanish colonies in the Americas as oppressed by Spanish colonial rule, and the war as an opportunity to liberate them from this burden. Roman Catholics, on the other hand, urged a hardline foreign policy against Spain, assuming that political pressure could sway Spain toward a more benign treatment of its American possessions. However, with the sinking of the *USS Maine* those church groups contesting the war or not favoring the military curbed their objections, allowing for overwhelming support for the declaration of war.[33]

> Prominent Protestant leaders in America expounded a type of American Imperialism with Christian evangelism and the spreading of Anglo-Saxon civilization. Missionaries called for government support in the evangelization of heathens, ignoring the fact that Cuba, Puerto Rico, and the Philippines had been under Roman Catholic control for centuries. After the declaration of war, many Protestant churches rationalized the war into a religious crusade, blending the expansion of Americanism and Christendom.[34]

THE SPANISH AMERICAN WAR FROM THE PERSPECTIVE OF GEORGE G. KING

A valuable narrative about the war comes from the letters of George Glen King, a North American soldier who served in the Puerto Rican campaign.[35] The letters, written home, describe him enlisting as a volunteer at the break of the war in the Sixth Regiment of Infantry formed in Concord, Massachusetts. He ascended promptly to the rank of sergeant. King provides a fairly specific rendering of his life as a soldier during the war, starting with his departure from Concord to Camp Dewey, at Framingham, Massachusetts, only fourteen miles away, on May 11, 1898, to undergo a physical examination:

The physical examinations, which we anticipated with a considerable amount of apprehension, were of two kinds. We became familiar with the process through the experiences of other companies in camp. The first test was an eye test. The general physical examination followed; it was hasty and superficial, but a certain amount of stress was laid on the matter of weight. This was in accordance with the stereotyped regulations of the regular army.[36]

On May 12, 1898, King was mustered into the United States Army, and on May 23, he was moved to Camp Alger at Falls Church, Virginia. It was here that he first learned that Puerto Rico might be the eventual destination of his unit. From Camp Alger his detachment was sent to Charleston to embark on the ship *Yale* and set sail for Cuba on July 11, 1898. The *Yale* was the temporary headquarters of General Miles, commanding the army. The trip on the *Yale* brought some challenges and opportunities. Not being a transport, the war vessel was crowded and had no accommodations for the troop, so sleeping took place in the floor of the steerage and the deck. Since the training camp had not provided much time to learn to fire weapons, "off the Bahamas we had desultory rifle practice, shooting at boxes thrown overboard. It was surprising to discover men who had never fired a gun. This was the only rifle practice we had in the service."[37]

On July 23, after a short time in Cuba, the *Yale* set course for Puerto Rico. In his letters, King provides a negative perspective on the nature of the Spanish and Puerto Rican people he encountered during his time on the archipelago. The assigned task for King's regiment was to establish a base of supplies in the archipelago for a force of about thirty-five hundred soldiers that would follow to do the fighting. On July 27, King and his troops camped on the plain of the village of Guánica within a quarter of a mile of the shore. Soon afterward, the soldiers had the first encounter with the enemy:

There was slight resistance at first; but the marines and the Gloucester's guns cleared the shore. Our company was detailed to guard stores and prisoners—that is, until last evening. The first and second battalions had a little skirmishing in the hills, and a few men were slightly wounded. Last night word came of a possible night attack from San Juan, and we went out with all the others. My squad was on picket line—the best we could do was to kill a horse that proved to be riderless when we got closer. There were a few Spaniards round, but no real fighting. There won't be. We outnumber them, and they won't ever face us. I am actually enjoying the life here.[38]

King's first encounter with Puerto Ricans in Guánica showed quite a negative empathy: "The inhabitants had fled at first, and are just beginning to come back, shouting 'Viva Americanos,' and doing their best to be subservient. They are a servile, lazy-looking lot, all dressed in linen and straw hats, and all smoking incessant cigarettes."[39] Later, when in Yauco, twelve miles away from Ponce, King complained about Puerto Ricans who, while longing for North American rule, were just after North American money.[40] While King called attention to the fact that soldiers hired Puerto Ricans to render the army efficient and valuable service as drivers of ox-cart vehicles, he also complained that "they use an ox-goad, dialect, and profanity—all in profusion. They seem never happy unless they are jabbing the flank of a bull and yelling 'ow-amo carajo' at the top of their lungs."[41]

In his letters, King gives a fairly broad description of the location and circumstances the soldiers were experiencing: rivers as wide as in Concord, beautiful valleys "green and luxuriant, and shut in on all sides by steep mountains, covered with dense tropical foliage," yet he complains about the constant rains that, given the dog tents provided by the army for sleeping, caused many soldiers colds and other health-related problems.[42] While pausing for the peace negotiations to take place, King provided specific description of places where the troop lay ready and waiting:

Utuado is a little inland city between Ponce and Arecibo, and in the valley between the north and south ranges. We are waiting here, apparently, until peace negotiations are brought to a result. We don't know anything, but persistent rumors, and what we read from newspapers a couple of weeks old, convince us that the end is not far off. We know that a truce has been declared—our outposts are protected by a flag of truce, and we are awaiting its suspension so that we can advance.[43]

King also wrote about the spiritual care of the soldiers. In one of his letters, he mentions that it took a new officer, Col. Rice, to take command of his regiment for Sunday church services to take place on a regular fashion, "We hadn't had church or a chaplain for a month, but there was a Y.M.C.A. man along with us—a charming man, by the way—who was to conduct the services."[44]

Some scholars argue that military chaplains have been part of the history of the Americas from the times when the early European explorers came to these lands, up to the present.[45] Others trace this experience all through history.[46] However, the crucial time of its delineation as a professional organization with its own identity was the period between 1860 and 1920.[47] One of the controversial issues of military chaplains related to their responsibilities.[48]

Jacqueline E. Whitt[49] argues, that in 1882, when the United States signed the Geneva Convention, Articles I and II of the original convention defined the role of chaplains as noncombatants, as long as they restricted their task as assigned to ambulances and hospitals. However, the participation of a few chaplains near the front during the Spanish–American War set a new pattern of ministering to wounded soldiers in the battlefield itself, leading many chaplains to decide during the twentieth century that their rightful place was in combat, rather than in the rear, at headquarters, or in a hospital.[50]

Chaplains' activities were wide-ranging at the regular army and militia training camps preparing forces for invading Puerto Rico. They included military funerals, conducting religious services, and counseling soldiers at a time of anxiety and uncertainty.

Chaplain William F. Dusseault (Unitarian Universalist) of the 6th Massachusetts Volunteer Infantry, who later served in Puerto Rico, coordinated wholesome activities for the soldiers with the Salvation Army and the YMCA. In May 1898, at age forty-five, he joined the 6th Massachusetts Volunteers as the chaplain to serve deploying soldiers in the Spanish–American War. The unit was actively engaged against the Spanish at Utuado and in various skirmishes. The 6th Massachusetts had four men wounded in combat, none killed, and twenty-five men who died of disease. Amidst controversy, Chaplain Dusseault resigned from the unit while on Puerto Rico and returned to Massachusetts. After the war, Rev. Dusseault returned to his full-time civilian ministry as a pastor in Acton, Massachusetts.[51]

Two other chaplains, James Carl Schindel (Lutheran) of the 4th Ohio Volunteer Infantry Regiment,[52] and Edward H. Smith (Methodist) of the 2nd Wisconsin Volunteer Infantry Regiment,[53] joined Chaplain Dusseault in Puerto Rico. While at Camp Thomas in Georgia, the former insisted on the regular observation of Sunday worship, conducted mid-week Bible studies, and sponsored a temperance society. The latter distributed free religious literature, formed the men into religious societies, and preached several times each Sunday.[54]

Chaplain Schindel was a Lutheran pastor in Circleville, Ohio, when he joined the 4th Ohio USV to fight in the Spanish–American War. During the Spanish–American War, Chaplain Schindel and the 4th Ohio US Volunteers mustered in Columbus, Ohio, and then trained at Camp Thomas, Georgia. His unit landed in Arroyo, Puerto Rico, on August 3, and successfully fought its only major skirmish at Guayama several days later. Frequently irritated by Spanish snipers, the unit celebrated the August 12 armistice and departed the island on October 29, 1898. Chaplain Schindel was busy performing funerals for his Ohio soldiers, as fourteen troops died in Puerto Rico and four died at sea, all of disease.[55] Unfortunately, I have as yet found no evidence that he contributed to developing the Lutheran mission in Puerto Rico.

Chaplain Smith joined the 2nd US Volunteers of the Wisconsin National Guard in 1892 and served in Puerto Rico during the Spanish–American War. While at Camp Thomas in Georgia, Chaplain Smith created a national controversy by stating that "good beer is better than bad water," in reference to the diseased water that affected US troops in the camp. Smith enlisted on April 28, 1898, as a chaplain captain in the 2nd Wisconsin US Volunteers for two years of service. He mustered out on November 15, 1898.[56]

On July 21, 1898, as the US Army moved from Cuba to Puerto Rico in a huge naval convoy,[57] the death of Corporal Charles F. Parker led Chaplain Dusseault to perform a burial service liturgy at sea within sight of Puerto Rico.[58] During their travel, soldiers were tended by army and navy chaplains. On board the flagship *USS Massachusetts*, army chaplains Dusseault and John W. Ferris[59] (United Methodist) of the 6th Illinois US Volunteers comforted and prayed with the soldiers. Rev. Walter G. Isaacs (Methodist),[60] the senior navy chaplain on board who served from 1888 through 1926, ministered for the four days of travel to a military congregation that included the senior army commander Major General Nelson Miles, along with the interim division general officers Brigadier General Guy Henry and Brigadier General Henry Garretson.

After the war, army chaplains serving in the Puerto Rico campaign came mostly from volunteer units of their state militia. Their performance, such as holding religious services, counseling soldiers, and providing recreational activities for the troops, was regulated by their state. These chaplains had invaluable experience as civilian pastors, but hardly any training as active-duty military chaplains. In total eight US volunteer regimental Protestant chaplains served in Puerto Rico: Walter B. Lowry (Episcopal) of the 16th Pennsylvania USV;[61] Edward H. Smith; Charles E. Butters (Methodist) of the 3rd Wisconsin USV;[62] Dusseault; Ferris; Schindel; George A. Knerr (United Evangelical Church) of the 4th Pennsylvania USV;[63] and Delivan Daniel Odell (Baptist) of the 3rd Illinois USV.[64] Rev. Lawry mustered into the 16th Pennsylvania on May 10 and served through December 28, 1898. Chaplain Lowry served his troops in Puerto Rico under Major

General Wilson's command in the southern campaign to capture Ponce, Coamo, and Aibonito. At the battle of Coamo, the unit had one soldier killed in combat and six wounded. He stayed on Puerto Rico for a few months after the armistice was signed to minister to US troops in hospitals on the island.[65] Chaplain Butters was a Methodist clergyman who graduated from Northwestern Theological School in 1891. He served as a pastor for almost twenty years, his pastoral work interrupted by the Spanish–American War. As chaplain of the 3rd Wisconsin during the war, he ministered to soldiers during the sharp engagement at Coamo and along the sniper-filled road to Aibonito. The regiment lost two men killed in combat, two men wounded, and forty-one who died from disease.[66] Chaplain Knerr of the 4th Pennsylvania USV, caught up in the patriotic and missionary spirit of the time, mustered into the unit on May 10 and mustered out on November 16, 1898. Apart from his several months' service in the Spanish–American War, Knerr rarely traveled outside Pennsylvania. On Puerto Rico, the 4th Pennsylvania saw its only major action at Guayama and was pestered by skirmishers around Ponce. Only a few weeks after returning home, Rev. Knerr performed the funeral service for a soldier who returned home sick and died.[67] Chaplain Odell served in the 3rd Illinois Volunteers USV from August 1, 1898, through January 24, 1899. "In the war the 3rd Illinois fought skirmishes and was in supporting roles in Arroyo, Guayama, and at Guamani. There were over 1,300 soldiers in the 3rd Illinois. The unit suffered 43 deaths in Puerto Rico, all from disease."[68]

In volume 2 of his *Documentos históricos de la iglesia Episcopal en Puerto Rico*, Father Jorge Juan Rivera Torres, a Puerto Rican Episcopal historian, informs us that, during August 1898, Rev. M. Sutherland (Episcopal), chaplain of the United States Army (19th infantry regiment) celebrated at Holy Trinity Episcopal Church (Ponce) a memorial service for the soldiers that died during the Spanish–American War. Chaplain Sutherland also conducted a special Christmas service at the church that same year.[69] In addition, that year the General Convention of the Episcopal Church in the United States met in the city of Chicago and appointed a special commission to address the increasing responsibilities in its mission and ministry. In March 1899, the report of this commission included a charge for the bishop in Chicago to study the possibility of developing missionary work in Puerto Rico. The bishop authorized Rev. Henry A. Brown, who was earlier chaplain to the "Rough Riders," and by that time chaplain of the regular United States Army in Puerto Rico, to promptly begin this task.[70]

In Vieques, when people became aware of the arrival of the US military, they were fearful that these foreign soldiers were coming to burn the town and kill the people, including those recently born. Joseph Bean, the parish priest of All Saints Episcopal Church, contacted a colonel from the US Army and invited him to the island. The US colonel accepted the invitation. He arrived in Vieques with his troops and the parish priest dedicated the US flag in the altar of the church with prayers. As soon as the US military took over the island, the priest began to receive a salary, contributing to help him in his last days without financial worries or impediments by the government.[71]

While by 1898 there were four Black regiments in the regular army, with many Black units in the militia, in the Spanish–American War Black regiments served in Cuba and not in Puerto Rico. Despite this fact, Company L of the 6th Massachusetts US Volunteers, consisting of 109 Black soldiers, did fight in Puerto Rico. The chaplain of this Black unit was the white Chaplain Dusseault.[72]

> The Black soldiers of Company L in Puerto Rico came under enemy fire at Guánica, Yauco, and Adjuntas. They endured long hours of picket duty, and marched day and night in rain and intense heat under threat of Spanish snipers. Senior officers in the 6th Massachusetts USV had no complaints about the men of Company L.[73]

Very little is known regarding the soldiers wounded or injured in Company L.[74] In any case, what is known is that none of them died. A woeful incident took place on July 25, 1898, when Company

L became part of the invasion force at Guánica. Their commander, Colonel Charles Woodward, stayed behind sick[75] on board the *Yale*. While he was not able to link up with his troops in the short-term skirmish at Guánica, the next day he joined his troops in the trenches. After the battle, when the company marched from Guánica to Ponce, numerous men crumpled from fatigue and lack of food. These incidents reflected poorly on the leadership of the senior officers of the unit, and Major General Miles called a board of inquiry to press charges against Colonel Woodward, Lieutenant Colonel George H. Chaffin, Major George Taylor, and Captain U. A. Goodell. All four officers resigned their commissions and returned home, despite their defense by Chaplain Dusseault. Believing that an injustice had been done to these officers by Brigadier General Henry Garretson with the endorsement of Major General Miles, Chaplain Dusseault also resigned.[76]

It is interesting to note that in a campaign that relied on state-based units, these invading army Protestant chaplains were originally clergy with civilian congregations who volunteered to serve as a chaplain with their state's troops. At the end of the war, they returned home with their detachments, so their impact was limited compared to the civilian clergy who arrived or were sent by their respective denominational boards in the United States to establish missions to serve Puerto Rican congregations. In fact, only one of these chaplains (James C. Schindel), was Lutheran, and as a minister in the Missouri Synod he came from a different strand of North American Lutheranism to the bodies that eventually established the Lutheran mission in Puerto Rico.

POSTWAR US PRESENCE

After the war, army chaplains continued their ministry in Puerto Rico. Two of them merit special recognition: US volunteer chaplain Thomas E. Sherman and regular army chaplain Edward J. Vattmann. The first was the oldest son of General William T. Sherman. A highly intelligent young man, he graduated from Georgetown University at age eighteen. Two years later, he earned a law degree from Yale

University. Despite his famous father's Protestantism, he unexpectedly felt a calling for the priesthood and was ordained a Jesuit in Philadelphia in 1889. He taught at Saint Louis University in Missouri, Jesuit colleges in Detroit and St. Louis, and gave numerous public lectures on religion. His strong commitment to parish work and his itinerant lecture schedule drove him to exhaustion, and he was ordered to rest. Although born in San Francisco, Father Sherman bore great appreciation for the state of Missouri, and when the 4th Missouri US Volunteers marshaled into the Spanish–American War on May 14, 1989, he enlisted as their chaplain.[77]

Chaplain Sherman traveled all over Puerto Rico saying mass, hearing confessions, establishing wholesome recreational activities, visiting soldiers in the hospitals, and ministering to the troops. One distinctive dimension of his chaplain experience was his attachment to the personal staff of General Ulysses S. Grant III as a special observer for the War Department. In this position he traveled extensively, documenting copious features of the culture and local landscape that later helped US investors and developers. In September 1898, on one of his traveling ministries, he paused in Adjuntas and later reflected on his experience:[78]

> I stayed a night at Adjuntas, a town nestled among the mountains, where I found a small detachment of Massachusetts men, half of whom turned out to be Catholics, glad to see a chaplain. At the tavern where I put up, my character caused a lively debate among the guests, one of who had seen me in the pulpit at Ponce and declared that I was a Catholic priest, much to the consternation of the rest who found it hard to admit that an American chaplain could be a priest. They have been taught to think down here that the advent of Americans means the downfall of Catholicism. The truth is that there is so little religion among Porto [sic] Ricans that it cannot sink much lower than it now is.[79]

After his departure from Puerto Rico in September 1898, Chaplain Sherman became a parish priest at the Holy Family Church in

Chicago and a successful speaker. He later experienced midlife depression and left the Jesuit order. He returned to the West Coast, becoming an active priest with an assignment in Santa Barbara from 1924 to 1929. In 1929 his health declined and he applied for a Spanish–American War veteran's pension. When his family learned of Father Sherman's poor health condition, his wealthy aunt, Eleanor Sherman Fitch, relocated her ailing nephew to a sanatorium in New Orleans where he lingered for a few years. Shortly before his death in 1933, he restored his vow as a Jesuit.[80]

Chaplain Vattmann was another leader who demonstrated his ability in diplomacy. Father Vattmann was perhaps the principal Roman Catholic chaplain commanding these endeavors.[81] Vattmann was born in Westphalia,[82] but spent most of his life in the United States. He was selected for chaplaincy by President Harrison and participated with the United States troops in the Indian wars.[83] In February of 1891, at the end the campaign that followed the battle of Wounded Knee, he registered for duty at Fort Meade in South Dakota. As a polyglot, Chaplain Vattmann was able to understand Hebrew and Greek, and speak in Latin, German, French, and Italian, which made him able to speak to soldiers and civilians of foreign extraction who could not communicate in the English language.[84] At the beginning of the Spanish–American War, he was appointed to serve at Fort Thomas, Kentucky, and later in the Philippines and Puerto Rico.[85]

While the motivations of US chaplains regarding the Spanish–American War differed, they joined the troops for war—with the militia units' chaplains volunteering. In his study of this topic, Stover argues that army chaplains shared in their concerns for the war against Spain similar influences as their fellow countrymen, including revenge. This was the position of Chaplain Allen Allensworth and Chaplain Henry Swift. However, other chaplains, like Theophilus G. Steward and William D. McKinnon, countered this attitude by "explaining that the enemy was human and deserved compassion."[86] In the case of Chaplain Vattmann, his friendship with six North American presidents (Hayes, Garfield, McKinley, Taft, Roosevelt, and

Wilson), led to his establishing a close relationship with President Roosevelt, and the latter's political plans to be instituted in the island.[87] This relationship was so important that, when a problem regarding the position of Catholic bishop James Blenk[88] on public schools in Puerto Rico emerged,[89] President Roosevelt requested Chaplain Vattmann's assistance to find an adequate solution for the crisis.[90] Stover also notes that:

> When Vattmann retired from the Army in 1905, the Chief of the Bureau of Insular Affairs offered him the position of Assistant Superintendent of Filipino Students in the United States, apparently in recognition of his success in resolving Church and State problems in Puerto Rico and the Philippines. Vattmann accepted the position and served in it until he resigned eight years later.[91]

The US military chaplains' presence in Puerto Rico was not limited to the Spanish–American War. In the first page of the September 1922 edition of *El Testigo*, there is a description of a new missionary joining the Lutheran mission in the island. On August 24, 1922, Rev. C. F. Knoll, a chaplain in the United States Army, and his wife, arrived in Puerto Rico to serve as pastor of the First Lutheran congregation. Rev. Knoll was ordained in 1901. His first pastorate took place at a Lutheran congregation in South Dakota. He later moved to a church in Saint Paul, Minnesota, where he also completed his studies for a PhD at the University of Minnesota. From there, he went to a church in Seattle, Washington. He enlisted in the US Army at the beginning of World War II, serving as chaplain at the War Prison Camp in Salt Lake City, Utah. His task at the camp was to provide spiritual guidance to the German prisoners. After the war, he taught at Wagner College in New York and concurrently served at a church in Brooklyn, before accepting a call to a pastorship in Puerto Rico.[92]

The United States military chaplaincy was transformed for all time by the Spanish–American War. Theodore Roosevelt established a high standard for chaplains. On June 10, 1902, as secretary of war and secretary of the navy, he gave his standards on the expectations of a good chaplain:[93]

> I want to see hereafter no chaplain is appointed in the Army [and Navy] who is not a first-class man—a man who by education and training will be fitted to associate with his fellow officers, and yet had in him the zeal and the practical sense which will enable him to do genuine work for the enlisted men. Above all, I want chaplains who will go in to do this work just as the best officers of the line or staff or medical profession go in to do their work. I want to see that, if possible, we never appoint a man who desires the position as a soft job.[94]

UNFORTUNATE OUTCOMES FOR PUERTO RICANS

For the people of Puerto Rico, the US victory over Spain in the Spanish–American War resulted in the establishment of a military government[95] that later shifted to a civil government led by North American governors appointed by the president of the United States.[96] For a brief time (June 25–September 11, 1939), Puerto Rican-born José E. Colom became acting governor of Puerto Rico, after the previous governor, Blanton C. Winship, was removed from office by President Franklin D. Roosevelt for abusing his authority in depriving the people of Puerto Rico of their civil rights.[97] On September 2, 1946 the Puerto Rican Jesús T. Piñeiro was appointed governor of Puerto Rico under the US colonial administration. It was only on January 2, 1949, that the people of Puerto Rico were able to elect their first governor, Luis Muñoz Marín.[98] Yet, given the recent indiscriminate decision of the US Congress and President Barack Obama in establishing on June 30, 2016, the Financial Oversight and Management Board for Puerto Rico without the consent of its people,[99] it seems that the colonial administration of Puerto Rico by the United States continues to be a great burden to the Puerto Rican people in the archipelago.[100]

SETTING THE STAGE FOR AN EMERGING PROTESTANTISM

CONCLUDING REMARKS

As we have seen throughout this chapter, Protestant incursions in the Puerto Rican archipelago have been led by Lutheran corsairs and the military assaults of countries like Great Britain and the Netherlands since the sixteenth century, when Puerto Rico became an American colony of the Spanish Empire. By the end of the nineteenth century, the US military invasion of the archipelago established Puerto Rico as a territory of the United States of America. While two important Protestant churches of foreign immigrants were first established in Ponce (1869) and Vieques (1880), along with the emerging Protestant offshoot movement of Los Bíblicos led by Eduardo Heyliger and Antonio Badillo, enduring expressions of Protestantism in Puerto Rico were established with the arrival of North American Protestant denominations in the late nineteenth century. In other words, Christianity, in its twofold expressions of Roman Catholicism[101] and Protestantism, was brought to Puerto Rico following violent military advances, clearing the way for institutionalizing the Christian church in the archipelago. In these ventures, and those of Protestants after the end of the Spanish–American War in 1898, this chapter has made clear the important role of military chaplains in fostering the process of the "Americanization" of the people in the archipelago.

Yet, as the social and political policies of these foreign empires negatively affected Puerto Ricans, local resistance was also experienced and led by representatives of the various Christian denominations, along with non-Christian Puerto Rican groups, as an effort to protect the Latin American identity of Puerto Ricans in the Caribbean, as well as the immigrant Puerto Rican community on the US mainland.

In the next chapter I will describe the beginning of the Lutheran mission in Puerto Rico that was later established as the Caribbean Synod of the United Lutheran Church in America in 1952.

NOTES

1 Ángel Luis Gutiérrez, *Evangélicos en Puerto Rico en la época española* (Guaynabo: Editorial Chari, 1997), 9–13.
2 See "English Invasion and Creole Victory of 1797," EnciclopediaPR, April 3, 2022, https://enciclopediapr.org/content/invasion-inglesa-de-1797/.
3 While no one really knows when the first printing press was invented, the oldest known printed text came out of China during the first millennium CE; "Printing Press," History Channel, October 10, 2019, https://www.history.com/topics/inventions/printing-press. The printing press in the Americas was established in Mexico City in 1539 by the Spaniards; "American Printing," Cambridge Historical Society, 2012, https://historycambridge.org/innovation/American%20Printing.html. In Puerto Rico, the first printing press arrived from Mexico in 1806. The first book was written by Juan Rodríguez Calderón (a Spaniard) that same year, with the title *Ocios de la juventud*; "Puerto Rican Literature," Wikipedia, accessed June 20, 2023, https://en.wikipedia.org/wiki/Puerto_Rican_literature. See also https://tinyurl.com/3p6ujas4 (accessed July 12, 2023).
4 Gutiérrez, *Evangélicos en Puerto Rico en la época española*, 17–26.
5 Samuel Silva Gotay, *Protestantismo y política en Puerto Rico 1898–1930: Hacia una historia del protestantismo evangélico en Puerto Rico* (San Juan: Editorial de la Universidad de Puerto Rico, 1997), 6–8.
6 Gutiérrez, *Evangélicos en Puerto Rico en la época española*, 49. The author claims that the preacher was Rev. Allen from the Reformed church in St. Thomas and that there were approximately two hundred people present. Mr. Solomons was a British merchant doing business in Puerto Rico. See Father Jorge Juan Rivera Torres, *Documentos de la Iglesia Episcopal puertorriqueña*, vol. II (Ponce: Taller Episcográfico, 2006), 11.
7 Silva Gotay, *Protestantismo y política en Puerto Rico 1898–1930*, 7. According to the author, at that time the city of Ponce was wrapped up with the international sugar business, and by the end of the century it reported four hundred foreigners coming from Protestant countries, among which 216 were from Lutheran Denmark and 143 from Anglican Britain. Silva Gotay, 7. For a more extended description of these Protestant ministries in Ponce and Vieques, see Luis Martínez-Fernández, *Protestantism and Political Conflict in the Nineteenth-Century Hispanic Caribbean* (New Brunswick, NJ: Rutgers University Press, 2002), 91–115.
8 For information about the Spanish–American War of 1898, see Henry Watterson, *History of the Spanish–American War* (New York, Akron, and Chicago: The Werner Company, 1898); Ángel Rivero, *Crónica de la Guerra Hispanoamericana en Puerto Rico* (Río Piedras: Editorial Edil, 1998). For a detailed description of the preparation of the US military forces, their landing, and follow-on campaign for the invasion of Puerto Rico, see Kenneth E. Lawson, *With Courage and Confidence: The US Army*

Chaplaincy and the Puerto Rico Campaign of 1898 (Ft. Buchanan, PR: Installation Chaplain's Office, 2008), 15–36, 49–74.
9 Martínez-Fernández, *Protestantism and Political Conflict in the Nineteenth-Century Hispanic Caribbean*, 110.
10 Martínez-Fernández, 111. See also Eddie Donoghue, *Negro Slavery: Slave Society and Slave Life in the Danish West Indies* (Bloomington and Milton Keynes: Authorhouse, 2007), 181–83.
11 For a more detailed description of the contributions of these leaders see Gutiérrez, *Evangélicos en Puerto Rico en la época española*, 27–38.
12 El Grito de Lares, also described as Lares's uprising, rebellion, or revolution, became the first major uprising against the Spanish colonial government in Puerto Rico. The insurgency was organized by Ramón Emeterio Betances and Segundo Ruiz Belvis, and began on September 23, 1868; "El Grito de Lares 1868," EnciclopediaPR, April 21, 2021, https://enciclopediapr.org/content/el-grito-de-lares-1868/.
13 The city of Aguadilla is in the northwest of Puerto Rico. Its name comes from the native word "guadilla," or "guayida" meaning garden. While the date of its foundation was 1775, it was not until 1780 that it was officially established. "Municipality of Aguadilla," EnciclopediaPR, February 9, 2010, https://enciclopediapr.org/content/municipio-de-aguadilla/. While there had been Bibles smuggled to Puerto Rico by pirates and corsairs during the sixteenth century, the Bible brought by Heyliger was used to convert Antonio Badillo and a group of Puerto Ricans later called "Los Bíblicos," that became the seed for a later development of Protestantism in the archipelago.
14 Papo Vives, "La familia Heyliger," QuebradillasPR.org, June 15, 2008, http://quebradillaspr.blogspot.com/2008/06/la-famila-heyliger-por-papo-vives.html. The official name of Papo Vives is Dr. Miguel Angel Vives Heyliger. See "Doctor Miguel (Papo) Vives," QuebradillasPR.org, July 2, 2013, http://quebradillaspr.blogspot.com/2013/.
15 Gutiérrez, *Evangélicos en Puerto Rico en la época española*, 31. AGPR, Fondo Protocolos Notariales Aguadilla Pueblo: Isabela Su Testamento Escribiente José Román y Gallardo, Caja 1359, año 1866.
16 Gutiérrez, 31.
17 Gutiérrez, 33. Also AGPR, FDN, Isabela, Caja 1359, año 1866.
18 Gutiérrez, 35. The distance between Lares and Mayagüez is about 30 kilometers. It is interesting to note that the Danish vice-consul Juan Alfondes writes to the Puerto Rican governor referring to the Danish citizenship of Don Eduardo alleging his innocence, but these claims were rescinded. Gutiérrez, 34–35.
19 Papo Vives, "La familia Heyliger." Gutiérrez, *Evangélicos en Puerto Rico en la época española*, 34. In his valuable narrative on the Protestant pioneers in Puerto Rico, Edward A. Odell, a North American Presbyterian missionary in Puerto Rico claims that "when a small pox epidemic broke

out in Aguadilla and the surrounding countryside they [Heyliger and Badillo] made available their houses for the care of the sick. Heyliger fell ill with the infection and died, but after his death Badillo carried on." See Edward A. Odell, *It Came to Pass* (New York: The Board of National Missions of the Presbyterian Church in the United States of America, 1952), 14.

20 See Rev. Dr. Pablo E. Rojas Banuchi, "Los Bíblicos 1860–1898," in *Didaskalos: Teología para Formar, Capacitar, y Transformar* (blog), May 22, 2011, https://didskalosteologaparaformarycapacitar.blogspot.com/2011/05/.

21 In his book *Accidental Pluralism: America and the Religious Politics of English Expansion, 1497–1662*, Evan Haefeli argues that the pluralist characteristics of North American religious settlements during the colonial era were a product of the political and social conflicts and resolutions in Europe, showing the ways in which the codifications of relationships among states, churches, and publics were endlessly contested. This provocative argument may shed some light on the type of Protestantism that originally came to Puerto Rico before the takeover by the United States at the end of the nineteenth century. It seems that this early Protestantism must have been of a generic or eclectic type, similar to the one which emerged during the sixteenth century in Europe, particularly in the emerging cities and in rural areas. Evan Haefeli, *Accidental Pluralism: America and the Religious Politics of English Expansion, 1497–1662* (Chicago: University of Chicago Press, 2021). However, as Kristie Patricia Flannery claims in her review of Haefeli's book, in his study the place of native American or enslaved Africans is very limited (mostly confined to the first chapter), and since the incipient Protestantism in Puerto Rico prior to 1898 appeared mostly among poor native Puerto Ricans, Afro-Caribbean sectors in the West Indies, and the small population of foreign descent in the island, Haefeli's book has serious limits in helping us understand the early Protestantism that developed in Puerto Rico prior to the US military invasion of the island. Kristie Patricia Flannery, "Review of *Accidental Pluralism, America and the Religious Politics of English Expansion, 1497–1662* by Evan Haefeli," *Australasian Journal of American Studies* 40, no. 1 (July 2021): 121–23.

22 Sarahí Rivera Martínez, "La difusión del protestantismo en Puerto Rico (1860–1920): Claves identitarias para la misión actual," *Teología y Cultura*, año 19, 24, no. 1 (May 2022): 65, translation mine.

23 Martínez, "La difusión del protestantismo en Puerto Rico," 62.

24 Martínez.

25 Martínez-Fernández, *Protestantism and Political Conflict in the Nineteenth-Century Hispanic Caribbean*, 162–63. See also Ellen Walsh, "The Not-So-Docile Puerto Rican: Students Resist Americanization, 1930," *Centro Journal* 26, no. I (Spring 2014): 148–71.

26 *The Isles of the Sea* (a publication by the West Indies Mission Board of the United Lutheran Church in America, 1936), 14.

27 Rubén Arrieta Vilá, "A distancia la política y la religión," *El Nuevo Día*, "Sunday Journal," October 28, 2001, 17. Bishop Sosa's comments in this interview were not aimed at expressing the Protestant tendency to maintain a clear separation between "church and state," but rather to establish a distance between the position of the Lutheran Church and those other conservative Protestant groups in Puerto Rico which at that time were supporting the ideological and political preference for statehood.

28 See Ángel Santiago-Vendrell, "Give Them Christ: Native Agency in the Evangelization of Puerto Rico, 1900 to 1917," *Religions* 12, no. 3 (2021): 196, https://doi.org/10.3390/rel12030196.

29 Sarahí Rivera Martínez, "La difusión del protestantismo en Puerto Rico (1860–1920)," 80–81.

30 María E. Estados Font, *La presencia militar de Estados Unidos en Puerto Rico: 1898-1918* (Río Piedras: Editorial Universitaria, Universidad de Puerto Rico, 1986); José López Baral, *The Policy of the United States towards Its Territories with Special Reference to Puerto Rico* (San Juan: Editorial de la Universidad de Puerto Rico, 1999); Kal Wagenheim and Olga Jiménez de Wagenheim, *The Puerto Ricans: A Documentary History*, rev. ed. (Princeton, NJ: Markus Weiner, 2002).

31 Harry Franqui-Rivera, *Soldiers of the Nation: Military Service and Modern Puerto Rico, 1898-1952* (Lincoln and London: University of Nebraska Press, 2018), xv–xvi.

32 For a study of the emergence and expansion of the US chaplaincy, see Richard M. Budd, *Serving Two Masters: The Development of American Military Chaplaincy, 1860-1920* (Lincoln and London: University of Nebraska Press, 2000). Also, the thorough study of the emergence and expansion of the US chaplaincy provided in the five-volume series of the US chaplaincy produced by the US Army Chaplain Center and School, particularly volume 3, written by the United Methodist Church chaplain Earl F. Stover, *Up from Handymen: The United States Army Chaplaincy 1865-1920*, vol. 3 (Washington, DC: Office of the Chief of Chaplains Department of the Army, 1977).

33 See Stover, *Up from Handymen*, 107–8.

34 Lawson, *With Courage and Confidence*, 8.

35 The letters were later published as a book, George Glenn King, *Letters of a Volunteer in the Spanish–American War* (Chicago: Hawkins and Loomis, 1929). In the book, "King describes in some detail the life of a soldier during the war, including the kind and extent of training received, and the lean diet and physical hardships of campaigning in Puerto Rico. King's letters are interspersed with notes and explanatory commentary that puts his letters in perspective. Some of his letters and commentaries describe the interrelationships between American soldiers and the inhabitants of Puerto Rico during the War. He pointed out, for example, that the Americans hired native Puerto Ricans, who rendered the army efficient and

valuable service as mounted scouts." https://www.loc.gov/item/30012858/ (accessed July 12, 2023). Also, https://tile.loc.gov/storage-services/service/gdc/lhbpr1/12858/12858.pdf (accessed July 12, 2023).
36 King, *Letters of a Volunteer in the Spanish-American War*, 6.
37 King, 45.
38 King, 54.
39 King, 56.
40 King, 62.
41 King, 68.
42 King, 73.
43 King, 72.
44 King, 77.
45 Budd, *Serving Two Masters*, xi.
46 For Roy J. Honeywell (Colonel, Ret., USAR, and Professor of History at Boston University [1920–1933], a chaplain since July 5, 1918), "The influence of religious faith upon fighting men and military events is conspicuous through all history." Roy J. Honeywell, Chaplains of the United States Army (Washington, DC: Office of the Chief of Chaplains, Department of the Army, 1958), 1–9.
47 "Lone Ranger chaplains who were accustomed to working with little or no supervision or help from anyone at the beginning of this era found themselves by the end of the First World War much more a part of an organizational structure with definite powers and controls over how they conducted ministry." Budd, *Serving Two Masters*, 1.
48 "As the evidence makes clear, it was no coincidence that when the army and navy chaplains finally got organizations of their own, each with a chaplain at its head, the chaplaincy reached previously unattained levels of professional standards and efficiency. Only then were chaplains' rights and responsibilities clearly delineated, and only then did military chaplaincy attain the degree of bureaucratic leverage within the military organization that most chaplains had long sought." Budd, 1.
49 Dr. Jacqueline Earline Whitt is an assistant professor in Department of History at the US Military Academy. She earned her BA at Hollins University, Virginia, and her MA and PhD at the University of North Carolina at Chapel Hill.
50 Jacqueline E. Whitt, "Dangerous Liaisons: The Context and Consequences of Operationalizing Military Chaplains," *Military Review* (March–April 2012): 55.
51 "Chaplain William F. Dusseault (1853–1937) was a lifelong resident of Massachusetts and a graduate of Tufts College. He was a Unitarian Universalist clergyman. From 1899–1920 he reenlisted and then maintained his part-time position as chaplain with the 6th Massachusetts, retiring with the rank of Lieutenant Colonel in the National Guard. He was well-respected in the Unitarian Universalist Society in Massachusetts. In his later years

he served a church in Lynn, MA. He died in January 1937." Lawson, *With Courage and Confidence*, 43.

52 Chaplain James C. Schindel was born in Pennsylvania and subsequently lived in Ohio, Missouri, and California. After the war, Rev. Schindel returned to his Lutheran parish in Circleville, Ohio. In July 1901 Schindel left Circleville for a larger parish at Newark, Ohio. Rev. Schindel served at Saint Paul's Lutheran Church in Newark from 1901 to 1906. Lawson, 47.

53 "Chaplain Edward H. Smith (1842–1931) of the 2nd Wisconsin USV was born on 14 December 1842 in Cheshire, England. He studied theology at New College and pastored a Congregational Church in Abergavenny, Monmouth Shire. He immigrated to the US in the late 1860s. He did his postgraduate work at Yale and then moved west to pastor the New England Congregational Church of Chicago around 1873. Rev. Smith then pastored a church in Morrison, Illinois for seven years: and came to Oshkosh, WI in 1886 and pastored the First Congregational Church for 27 years." Lawson, 45–46.

54 Lawson, 15–19.

55 "After the war, Rev. Schindel returned to his Lutheran parish in Circleville, Ohio. Rev. Schindel served at Saint Paul's Lutheran Church in Newark from 1901–1906. He created a Lutheran mission church on the other side of Newark and was popular as a musician, a preacher, and administrator. Schindel died on 6 January 1932 at age 69. As a veteran he was buried in the Los Angeles National Cemetery. On his tombstone it states that Rev. James C. Schindel was the chaplain of the 4th Ohio Infantry in the Spanish American War." Lawson, 47–48.

56 Lawson, 45–46.

57 "The Landing in Guánica," 1898: La Guerra Hispanico American en Puerto Rico (website), accessed June 20, 2023, http://home.coqui.net/sarrasin/desembarco.guanica.htm.

58 "On the morning of the 23d [July 1898], Corp. Charles F. Parker died [aboard the U.S.S. YALE, heading from Cuba to Puerto Rico], and was buried at sea the same day. Chaplain Dusseault read the burial service, and a squad of twelve men fired the customary three volleys." Frank E. Edwards, *The '98 Campaign of the 6th Massachusetts, USV* (Boston, 1899), 70. "Corp Charles F. Parker (1872–1898)," Find A Grave Memorial, accessed June 20, 2023, https://tinyurl.com/mwcdmdxz.

59 John W. Ferris, a United Methodist clergyman, was born in 1871. He was appointed Chaplain of the 6th Illinois US Volunteers and was the pastor of a flourishing church at Abingdon, Illinois when the Spanish–American War broke out. Ferris died on March 21, 1931, in Tampa, Florida, where he and his wife Nettie G. Ferris were spending the winter, given his failing health. He is buried at Abingdon Cemetery, Abingdon, Knox County, Illinois. "John W. Ferris (1871–1931)," Find A Grave Memorial, accessed June 20, 2023, https://www.findagrave.com/memorial/8050454/john-w-ferris.

60 "Navy Chaplain Walter G. Isaacs became a chaplain in 1888. Chaplain Isaacs conducted religious services, prayer meetings, and counseled ill soldiers on board the USS Massachusetts. He served as Navy chaplain until 1926, when he retired with the rank of Captain at age 66." Lawson, *With Courage and Confidence*, 34.

61 "Chaplain Walter B. Lowry of the 16th Pennsylvania USV (Episcopal) was born in Philadelphia and became a deacon in 1890. The 1898 *Protestant Episcopal Church Clerical Directory* lists Walter B. Lowry as a resident of Corry, Pennsylvania." Lawson, 44–45.

62 "Chaplain Charles E. Butters (1868–1930) of the 3rd Wisconsin USV was a Methodist clergyman who graduated from Northwestern Theological School in 1891. In 1917 he deployed to Europe with the 32nd Infantry Division to France for over two years of service as Quartermaster with the rank of Captain. After the war, from 1919 to 1930 he was a successful Wisconsin banker and a Major in the Wisconsin National Guard (1919–1928). At age 62 he died at his home in Nakoma, survived by his wife Fanny (Blythe) Butters." Lawson, 42.

63 "He was born and raised in Mahanoy, PA, the son of an evangelical minister. It is interesting to note that the gravestone marker for George Knerr does not mention his 40 or so years of civilian ministry, but rather highlights his few months' service as a chaplain in the Spanish American War." Lawson, 43–44. Also, "Rev George A. Knerr (1862–1926)," Find a Grave Memorial, accessed June 20, 2023, https://www.findagrave.com/memorial/60363567/george-a-knerr.

64 "At the start of the Spanish American War, he was the pastor of the First Baptist Church of Peoria, Illinois. After the war his residence in 1900 was in Joliet, Illinois." Lawson, 41–42. "Delivan Daniel O'Dell 1853–1902," Ancestry.com, accessed June 20, 2023, https://www.ancestry.com/genealogy/records/delivan-daniel-o-dell-24-22zwwf0.

65 Lawson, 44.

66 Lawson, 42.

67 Lawson, 43.

68 Lawson, 41.

69 Jorge Juan Rivera-Torres, "La Iglesia Episcopal en Puerto Rico—Documentos Históricos de la . . .," Yumpu.com, accessed June 20, 2023, https://www.yumpu.com/es/document/read/13162590/la-iglesia-episcopal-en-puerto-rico-documentos-historicos-de-la-, 13.

70 Rivera-Torres, "La Iglesia Episcopal en Puerto Rico," 5–6.

71 Rivera-Torres, 6–7.

72 Lawson, *With Courage and Confidence*, 75–78.

73 Lawson, 77.

74 "A few of the wounded from the skirmish at Guánica were Corporal H.J. Pryor, who was wounded in the hand; and Private F.B. Bostic, who was wounded in the right arm." Lawson, 77.

75 "Colonel Charles F. Woodward experienced an enduring intestinal ailment, and his health had deteriorated in the Military training camps, and on board of the USS *Yale*." Lawson, 79.
76 Lawson, 79–84. "After the war, Rev. William Dusseault returned to the civilian pastorate and retained his status as Chaplain of the 6th Massachusetts. He served with the 6th during World War I, but did not leave Massachusetts as the unit was not deployed. He retired from the National Guard in July, 1920 at age 57 with the rank of Lieutenant Colonel. Continuing to reside in Massachusetts as a civilian pastor, he died on January 14, 1937 at age 84." Lawson, 83–84.
77 Lawson, 97–98.
78 Lawson, 98–99.
79 Lawson, 99.
80 Lawson, 100–101.
81 Rt. Rev. Msgr. Edward J. Vattmann, "served in several Indian campaigns as a chaplain and was sent to the Philippines in 1903. . . . At the outbreak of World War I, Father Vattmann rejoined the Army and was appointed to a major and sent to Fort Sheridan to serve as chaplain, where he stayed until his health compelled him to relinquish all activities. He died in 1919." See the newspaper *Wilmette Life* (Wilmette, Illinois), June 27, 1974, p. 38, accessed July 12, 2023, https://history.wilmettelibrary.info/1419519/data. Also, see "Armistice Day in Wilmette, 1918," Wilmette Historical Museum blog, November 10, 2018, https://wilmettehistory.org/blog/armistice-day-in-wilmette-1918/.
82 A historical region of northwestern Germany, comprising a large part of the present federal *Land* (state) of North Rhine–Westphalia. See Britannica.com, accessed June 20, 2023, https://www.britannica.com/place/Westphalia.
83 See "American-Indian Wars," History.com, August 24, 2022, https://www.history.com/topics/native-american-history/american-indian-wars. For an interesting account of Vattmann's ministry in this context see Stover, *Up from Handymen*, 40–43. In 1894, Vattmann also participated in the Pullman strike in South Chicago. Stover, 85–86. In regard to the pacification policy of the United States in the Philippines, see Stover, 128, 131–133, 144, 151, 175n3.
84 See US Army Chaplain Corps Facebook page, accessed June 20, 2023, https://www.facebook.com/ArmyChaplainCorps/posts/608153409260024.
85 See *The Sacred Heart Review* 57, no. 10 (February 17, 1917), https://newspapers.bc.edu/?a=d&d=BOSTONSH19170217-01&e=-------en-20--1--txt-txIN-------.
86 Stover, *Up from Handymen*, 108–23.
87 See the letter from Robert H. Todd Wells (mayor of San Juan, Puerto Rico) to Theodore Roosevelt of March 25, 1904, in which Todd declares he has spoken to Chaplain Vattmann on issues related to Puerto Rico as President Roosevelt requested, and suggesting to the president to continue that

conversation with the chaplain. "Letter from Robert H. Todd to Theodore Roosevelt," Theodore Roosevelt Center, accessed June 20, 2023, https://www.theodorerooseveltcenter.org/Research/Digital-Library/Record/ImageViewer?libID=044759. See also the letter sent by Regis Henri Post to Theodore Roosevelt on March 7, 1904, praising Father Edward J. Vattmann's contributions in Puerto Rico, expecting the chaplain's return to the island in the next year. "Letter from Regis Henri Post to Theodore Roosevelt," accessed June 20, 2023, https://www.theodorerooseveltcenter.org/Research/Digital-Library/Record/ImageViewer?libID=044522. Regis Henri Post was, "appointed by President Theodore Roosevelt as Auditor of Puerto Rico in 1903, as Secretary of Puerto Rico in 1904, and as Governor in 1907. Post held the office of Governor from April 18, 1907 to November 5, 1909. His governorship was extremely controversial, as his frequent disagreements with the Puerto Rico Legislature led to the Legislature's failure to pass any budget in 1909, resulting in a political crisis on the island and passage of the Olmsted Amendment at the request of President William Howard Taft." Regis Henri Post Life, accessed June 20, 2023, https://www.liquisearch.com/regis_henri_post/life.

88 See Sister Miriam Terese O'Brien, "Puerto Rico's First American Bishop," Records of the American Catholic Historical Society of Philadelphia 91, nos. 1/4 (March–December 1980): 3–5, 7–37.

89 See the unbelievable display of intolerance of a North American prelate in Puerto Rico, "Bishop Blenk Opposes Official Education, Inconceivable Display of Intolerance in a North American Prelate," Theodore Roosevelt Center, accessed June 20, 2023, https://www.theodorerooseveltcenter.org/Research/Digital-Library/Record/ImageViewer?libID=042397&imageNo=1. Also, the letter from William Henry Hunt (appointed by Theodore Roosevelt as governor in Puerto Rico from September 15, 1901, to July 4, 1904) to Theodore Roosevelt of October 6, 1905. "Letter from William Henry Hunt to Theodore Roosevelt," Theodore Roosevelt Centre, accessed June 20, 2023, https://www.theodorerooseveltcenter.org/Research/Digital-Library/Record/ImageViewer?libID=042390&imageNo=1.

90 See "Letter from Theodore Roosevelt to Elihu Root," Theodore Roosevelt Center, accessed June 20, 2023, https://www.theodorerooseveltcenter.org/Research/Digital-Library/Record/ImageViewer?libID=0186841. By advising a way of settling matters between the government and the church, Vattmann resolved the "misunderstanding" between the governor and Bishop James E. Blenk. "The bishop extolled him for his 'intelligence and disinterestedness,' as did the governor, who called him 'a power for permanent good.'" Stover, *Up from Handymen*, 144.

91 Stover, n145.

92 *El Testigo*, año VI, no. 4 (September 1922): 1.

93 Lawson, *With Courage and Confidence*, 106.

94 Lawson, 106.

95 General Nelson Miles was the first appointed military governor of Puerto Rico. On October 18, 1898, General John Brooke became governor but relinquished his authority to General Guy Henry. "Military Government in Puerto Rico –The World of 1898: The Spanish–American War," Hispanic Division, Library of Congress, accessed June 20, 2023, https://www.loc.gov/rr/hispanic/1898/milgovt.html.

96 The first US civil governor appointed by President William McKinley in Puerto Rico was Charles Herbert Allen on May 1, 1900. "Puerto Rico Governors (under US Colonial Administration)," geni.com, accessed June 20, 2023, https://www.geni.com/projects/Puerto-Rico-Governors-under-U-S-colonial-administration/24973.

97 "About: José E. Colom," dbpedia.org, accessed June 20, 2023, https://dbpedia.org/page/Jos%C3%A9_E._Colom.

98 "About: José E. Colom."

99 "President Obama Announces the Appointment of Seven Individuals to the Financial Oversight and Management Board for Puerto Rico," whitehouse.gov, August 31, 2016, https://obamawhitehouse.archives.gov/the-press-office/2016/08/31/president-obama-announces-appointment-seven-individuals-financial.

100 "Puerto Rico's New Phase: People Resist Financial Junta," Workers World, July 6, 2016, https://www.workers.org/2016/07/26048/.

101 For a study of the Roman Catholic evangelization during the sixteenth century, see Pagán, *Historia de la conquista de América*.

CHAPTER 3

Lutherans Begin Their Mission in Puerto Rico

At the turn of the nineteenth century the social and economic conditions in Puerto Rico were somber. The four hundred years of Spanish rule had left a crisis in its educational, economic, and political expressions. Only 15 percent of the total population could read and write, the unhealthy living conditions were such that the death rate between 1887 and 1899 averaged 31.4 per thousand population, and religiously, the people were not ministered to adequately.[1]

> Towards the end of the 1880s, the island population suffered from a severe economic crisis. The local monopoly of Spanish merchants fueled resentment and led to the establishment of secret societies—organizations promoting the boycott of Spanish merchants and greater support for local business. There were many violent incidents against Spanish commercial establishments, particularly looting and arson. The government and its Civil Guard responded with a series of raids and imprisonments, applying severe torture measures which became known as "compontes." The social conditions of the island were also critical during this period. In addition to a lack of civil liberties, approximately 85 per cent of the population remained illiterate.

Malnutrition and extreme poverty were widespread throughout most of the countryside.[2]

In 1899, a year after the US military invasion of Puerto Rico, an important section in the report of the General Council's Board of Foreign Missions of the Evangelical Lutheran Church in North America provides a summary of the mission work in other countries. This includes an invitation received by the board in 1898 to send delegates to a New York convention of representatives from various Protestant Mission Boards to consider the question of sending missionaries to Cuba, Puerto Rico, and the Philippines.[3]

While the invitation was rescinded and Lutherans were not represented at the meeting, reports about the convention in secular and religious publications, information received about the willingness of a Lutheran congregation to offer a contribution to support the Lutheran work in Puerto Rico, and the interest of two Lutheran seminary students in Philadelphia (both preparing to graduate in 1899) in receiving a call to serve in Puerto Rico, led the board to give serious consideration to this opportunity. It was at this meeting that the name of Gustav Sigfried Swensson, a young student of Augustana College and Seminary, first surfaced as a result of his initiative of having recently started, without any institutional or individual support, Lutheran work in Puerto Rico.[4] Rev. Dr. C. A. Blomgren, a member of the board and seminary professor at the Augustana seminary, shared with his colleagues at the board a letter sent to him by Swensson dated March 13, 1899. In the letter, Swensson describes the state of Protestant initiatives in the island, yearns for the board's support of this mission field, and suggests specific plans for developing Lutheran missionary work in Puerto Rico.[5] After vital discussions of the matter and additional meetings with other parties to clarify contesting issues and concerns, on August 31, 1899, the board resolved to extend a call to Rev. Benjamin F. Hankey and Rev. Herbert F. Richards to go to Puerto Rico to begin mission work.[6]

This seed sprouted. In October 1901, the General Council of the Evangelical Lutheran Church in North America authorized the creation of a Porto Rico Mission Board for the administration of Lutheran missionary work in Puerto Rico. In its first report to the General Council in 1903, this board provided a description of the conditions of this labor and the challenges posed, along with a valuable account of the work carried out from 1901 up to 1903 by Rev. Richards.[7]

The story of the Lutheran mission in Puerto Rico cannot be reduced to the decision of the General Council of the Evangelical Lutheran Church in North America in 1899,[8] nor the arduous work of pastors Hankey and Richards who arrived in Puerto Rico on October 29, 1899, to begin work there.[9] To be sure, institutional support by a Lutheran Church body and the resilient contribution of these two ordained Lutheran pastors gave an important official standing to the work of the Lutheran Church in the island. However, our claim in this study is that the initiative and dynamic force of this mission, given its particular denominational identity, was and continues to be the product of different and complex elements that come together to expand the geographical boundaries of the Lutheran mission in Caribbean history.

BIBLES AND VISITORS

In previous sections of this study, we have mentioned the religious and devout but ambiguous efforts of various European immigrants, including Lutherans, who, along with introducing their Protestant convictions in America since the sixteenth century, also expressed their greed, along with their racial and cultural prejudice, violently. Prominent among these initiatives were those of religious leaders closely related to the Reformation movement led by Martin Luther during the sixteenth century in Germany. This seems to have been the case of the Welsers' colony in Venezuela, led by Enrique Ehinger and Jerónimo Sayler in 1526. As we have seen, however, the contribution of Eduardo Heyliger, who originally came from the Lutheran Danish Virgin Islands to Puerto Rico and contributed to preparing the way for the institutional establishment of Protestantism on the island during the nineteenth century with the valuable support of Los Bíblicos ("believers in the word"), provides a different picture.

The first Bibles were introduced in Puerto Rico by pirates, corsairs, smugglers, and British, French, Danish, and Dutch merchants.[10] Saint Croix and Saint Thomas were islands strategically positioned to introduce Bibles into Puerto Rico and the Dominican Republic. During the first two decades of the twentieth century, a partnership between the British and American Bible Society led the way for the introduction of Protestant religious literature in the Hispanic Caribbean. In 1934, James Thomson, a representative of the British Biblical Society who was dedicated to distributing Bibles throughout Central and South America as well as the Caribbean, arrived in Puerto Rico with the intention of introducing Bibles and religious literature to the island. While Thomson's plans were frustrated by custom agents who denied such entry,[11] the presence of Protestants on the island continued to increase. This growing community influenced government organisms such as the Junta de Comercio y Fomento to review the Leyes de Gracia, legislation previously established which required foreigners to profess the Catholic faith as a condition for their settlement in the island, to eliminate such an obligation. Despite the numerous efforts by the church and government to control Protestant growth, these heterodox religious expressions and practices continued their increasing presence on the island.[12]

Another important contribution came, as we mentioned earlier, from the initiative of Gustav Sigfried Swensson, a Swedish American Lutheran theological student from Augustana College and Seminary at Rock Island, Illinois. Swensson arrived on the island of Puerto Rico on October 13, 1898. His arrival occurred approximately three months after the US military had occupied Puerto Rico on July 25, two months following the armistice between Spain and the United States on August 12, and two months prior to the Treaty of Paris on December 10, 1898, that ended the Spanish–American War.[13]

Swensson held the first Lutheran service in San Juan on November 14, 1898. Lacking institutional financial support from any Lutheran body, he first began teaching English to private students and later became supervisor of government schools in the Carolina district. A year later, on October 29, 1899, pastors Hankey and Richards traveled to San Juan to carry out mission work on behalf of the Evangelical Lutheran Church in North America. While Swensson continued his volunteer work to support this missionary effort, by 1900 he returned to Augustana Seminary to complete his seminary studies. Two congregations were then formally organized by pastors Hankey and Richards: the First English Evangelical Church of San Juan on January 1, 1900, and San Pablo Lutheran Church, a Spanish-speaking congregation, on April 15, 1900. After the arrival of Pastor Alfred Ostrom in 1903, further missionaries came to Puerto Rico, and new congregations were also organized.[14]

READING THE BIBLE IN SPANISH

As mentioned earlier in the introduction of this study, my goal is to use a Caribbeanist historiography to investigate the emergence of the Lutheran mission in Puerto Rico, rather than employing an antiquarian or traditional Rankean approach[15] to the subject. In so doing, I also aim to include a postcolonial perspective in my effort to provide, as Carlos Cardoza Orlandi claims, "tools that will help Christian communities be in mission without losing the awareness that we are both *objects and subjects of mission*."[16]

In his introduction to Alejandro (Alex) García-Rivera's *St. Martín de Porres: The "Little Stories" and the Semiotics of Culture*, Robert Schreiter describes the author's contribution to current research in postcolonial studies as follows:

> In contemporary postcolonial writing, formerly subjugated peoples are trying to reconstruct their identities, not simply by imagining a precolonial past, but by coming to terms with the many strands of culture in which they participate. With the unprecedented migration of peoples around the planet, as well

as the impact of global communication technologies and circulation of cultural images in music and video, nearly everyone everywhere is part of a great cultural churning. This creolization of hybridization of cultures, undercuts long-held assumptions about cultures being enclosed, integrated wholes. García-Rivera adds to that discussion with his expanded concept of mestizaje, especially to the role of human agency as it encounters the power of the conqueror.[17]

In my research I want to move these efforts forward by exploring the historical significance of several stories recalled about the Lutheran mission in Puerto Rico. These stories are produced in the process of integrating the witness of Lutheran missionaries along with the testimony of North American and Puerto Rican church leaders; but mostly, these stories derive from an attempt to recover the experience and beliefs of those early Puerto Rican converts emerging from traditionally underrepresented communities and sectors of society. My goal is to pursue and bring to light what Orlando O. Espín has called the *faith of the people*, that is, the faith and beliefs of indigenous Lutheranism in the Caribbean Synod;[18] or from a Protestant perspective, that which Justo L. González, the prominent Cuban American church historian has described as *reading the Bible in Spanish*.[19] His proposal is not a chauvinistic appeal for Latinx to give up biblical research based on the historical-critical method. Nor does he argue for using just a Spanish translation of the text. His point is to recover a central feature in the Protestant tradition of making the Bible available to the people in their *vernacular*. For González, the emphasis of this approach is to read the Scriptures as presenting a history of the people of God *beyond innocence*, in contrast to the characteristics of the dominant culture; that is, to view biblical history as *responsible remembrance*, leading to *responsible action*. Such an approach provides an interpretation of the Bible compatible with our own history, riddled with ambiguity, joys and failures. When the Bible turns into a resource accessible to the people, and the people discover in the Bible their own particular perspective, then the Bible becomes the people's book, a subversive book no longer under the control of the dominant groups in society.[20]

Vítor Westhelle, a fellow professor of systematic theology at the Lutheran School of Theology at Chicago, contended that one of Martin Luther's most significant contributions was providing a language to give voice to the voiceless of his time. The reformer's importance for the normative nature of the German language is generally recognized. Yet, his contribution in providing a means of communication capable of constituting knowledge for empowering the aspirations and desires of the common people in sixteenth-century European society, has received very little attention.[21] My research intends to provide an example of the significant impact of the contribution of these scholars for a better understanding of the relationship between culture and religion in developing the Lutheran mission in Puerto Rico. At this point I also want to indicate that my account of this mission will make reference to the Puerto Rican journal *El Testigo* (The Witness), for it was the main vehicle used by the leadership of the mission.[22]

The Lutheran Church in Puerto Rico began the publication of *El Testigo* in June 1917.[23] The goal of this publication was to become a resource for the catechetical formation of its members, provide studies of the Bible for the use of congregational leaders, along with articles about the history of the Lutheran Church around the world. It also published editorials on a variety of topics, and news about the missionary field in Puerto Rico and in other parts of the world.[24]

The first story for the launching of the mission takes place at the end of the nineteenth century. The narrative is better told by incorporating it in the context of a biblical narrative that has a special significance to the Puerto Rican people. The Scripture account comes from the gospel of Matthew. It is the story of the Magi. The impact of this story on Puerto Ricans has been so great that for a long time, prior to the North American presence in the island, it was celebrated as a national holy day.

In his book *Christmas Inspirations*, Fulton Sheen explains that G. K. Chesterton wrote an essay on three modern Wise Men. They journeyed to a city of peace, a new Bethlehem. They wanted to enter this city and offered their gifts as passport of admission. The first put forth gold and suggested it could buy the pleasures of the earth. The second, instead of frankincense, brought the modern scent of chemistry. This scent has the power to drug the mind, seed the soil, and control the population. The third brought myrrh in the shape of a split atom. It was the symbol of death for anyone who opposed the way of peace. When they arrived at the palace of peace, they met Saint Joseph. He refused them entrance. They protested, "What more could we possibly need to assure peace? We have the means to provide affluence, control nature, and destroy enemies." St. Joseph whispered in the ear of each individually. They went away sad.[25]

LUTHERAN FOUNDATIONS IN UNEXPECTED PLACES

As I've become acquainted with the late nineteenth-century Protestant expansion into the Catholic Caribbean, it has become clear that one of the prominent features driving the spirit of the initial North American missionaries was their struggle against the Spanish religious and sociopolitical rule of the region. In the case of Lutheranism, this combative spirit was powerfully expressed in the life of Swensson, at the time a second-year student for the ministry who had dropped out of seminary; he was working as a clerk in the newly secured American territory of Puerto Rico when he was invited to preach. Swensson's missionary-driven initiative contributed to establishing the main present Lutheran work in Puerto Rico.[26] He expressed this missionary zeal in an article written shortly after his return from the island to the United States:

> The development of the war I followed closely. Finally, Puerto Rico was ceded to the United States. I saw the Puerto Ricans as people in misery, ignorance, superstition and fatal errors. There I could see and learn what the Catholic church is and what fruits she has produced when not influenced by any other church.[27]

He was right. The early North American missionaries viewed their role as a transforming institution. As the modern Wise Men of the story of Chesterton, the Protestant missionaries came to Puerto Rico to bring education, health, and a new social order to lift up the standards of life of our people. The significant impact of this contribution for the economic, cultural, and political life of Puerto Ricans was so impressive that it is difficult to deny. Yet, as in the case of the modern Wise Men, these North American missionaries forgot the child. Their passion to spread the gospel and benefits of the Protestant nation blinded them to the fact that this process was imposed by a military rule. Their unfortunate tendency to confuse the gospel with the ideological, social, and political structure of the North American way of life prevented them from resisting the imposition and colonial interests of this military rule.

The Magi were engaged in the very important pursuit of the Messiah. Yet, they lacked precise directions and could not travel by daylight. A star led them, a tiny point in the sky. Their quest was mainly in darkness and minimal light. The success of their quest depended not just on their best resources, but on their trust in the divine initiative coming always from the most unexpected places. Hence:

> On 3 December, 1898 Gustav Sigfried Swensson was walking along a San Juan Street when a voice called out in English from the doorway of a tailor shop across the street: "Can you preach? You look like a man of God." A student for the Lutheran ministry, forced by lack of money to give up his theological education temporarily, young Mr. Swensson could rely in the affirmative—he had been doing lay preaching for several years. And he had long felt the call to be a man of God. It was his keen missionary zeal that had brought him to Puerto Rico in October. Forthwith he crossed the street and entered into a conversation that founded the Lutheran church in an island where, for four hundred years, Lutheranism had been denied the right to raise

its voice and its representatives, at one time, had to answer the so-called "Holy Inquisition."[28]

Searching for the Messiah has never been an easy task. For the Magi in the gospel story it took not just a long and costly search, but the crossing of national and cultural borders; and the willingness to be led, in trust, by a star and the initiative of others. The experience of Lutheran missionaries in Puerto Rico followed a similar path. The visionary initiative of young Swensson had failed to receive the support of his own denomination. Critically short of cash, he withdrew from his college studies, borrowed money from a friend and, at his arrival in Puerto Rico, looked for a teaching job expecting to begin a new mission field on the island.

Swensson was hardly alone in this impulse. Other North American Lutheran missionaries to Puerto Rico would follow a similar self-giving ministry by giving up good and stable salaries on the mainland, risking tropical diseases, and depriving themselves and their families of many other comforts. An article narrating the early years of the Lutheran mission in Puerto Rico eloquently describes the sacrifices and resilience characteristic of these early missionaries.

> Their faith was greater than that of the Church which failed to support them, so that one of these pioneers were compelled to accept the hospitality of the United States Navy and come home in a transport because no money was forthcoming either for salary or passage. The burning words of his report awakened many to the great task which lay before our church *in the new possessions* of the United States, and support was secured for the missionaries who remained in the field. Later on, other missionaries were sent, but meager support compelled these self-sacrificing workers to hold services and to live in woefully unsuitable and inadequate quarters. Unfalteringly they persevered, and with more adequate support in later years a work was established of which the church need not be ashamed.[29]

More importantly, this was also the call to which Gabriela Cuervo (1905–13),[30] Demetrio Texidor (1908–20; 1923–27),[31] Eduardo Roig (1903–91),[32] and a host of other Puerto Rican men and women from a variety of social backgrounds responded, pioneering with their conviction and initiative new models of lay and ordained ministry throughout these one-hundred-plus years of Lutheran evangelism in Puerto Rico.

The gospel story shows the Magi finding the messiah in the most unexpected place. When they arrived in Palestine, their background and common sense led them to Herod's palace. Yet, they were to find the newborn Messiah in Bethlehem lying in a manger among lowly folk, celebrating the disclosure of God's self-revelation in history.

I've always been bewildered by the scandalous[33] nature of God's manifestation in our midst; a presence that, following the witness of Scripture, takes place in the least expected places. Luther's narrative of the reaction of the Wise Men upon finding the newborn Jesus is illuminating.

> Let us observe how these Wise Men took no offence at the mean state of the Babe and his parents that we also may not be offended in the mean state of our neighbor but rather see Christ in him, since the kingdom of Christ is to be found among the lowly and despised, in persecution, misery and the holy cross. . . . Those who seek Christ anywhere else, find him not. The Wise Men discovered him not at Herod's court, nor with the high priests, not in the great city of Jerusalem, but in Bethlehem, in the stable, with lowly folk, with Mary and Joseph. In a word, they found him where one could least expect it.[34]

Swensson had a similar shocking experience as he went along his task of establishing a Lutheran mission in Puerto Rico:

> It happened that on the 3rd of December, 1898, when I was walking home from one of my classes that coming up Sol Street

an English Negro from Jamaica was standing in the window at number 87 and as he beheld my insignificant being passing by, he said to me, "How do you do! You look like a man of God. Can't you preach?" I stopped and returned greetings and although the Negro, with whom I was not acquainted, did not look very dignified, yet I advanced toward him and with a blush on my face such as I never felt before.... After I conversed with Mr. Browne, for that was the Negro's name, I promised him to come again on the morrow, Sunday, and conduct a meeting at 9:30 AM. Sunday, the 4th of December, 1898 came, and the 1st Protestant meeting was held in San Juan. In the morning about 8 attended and in the evening about 30—[military]officers, and English-speaking Negroes.[35]

In establishing the foundations of the Lutheran mission in Puerto Rico, this young and enthusiastic lay missionary from a Swedish American background, born, brought up, and educated in the Lutheran tradition, as well as the men and women that followed him to Puerto Rico, all had to overcome the social, economic, cultural, and ethnic prejudices and biases of their epoch. To his credit, Swensson was willing to be led by a humble African Caribbean tailor, who provided the location, recruited most of the people that participated in the initial worship service, and identified the preacher to hold the first Protestant service in the city of San Juan. The full name of this tailor was John Christopher Owen Browne, a Jamaican African Caribbean of Protestant background who had been in Saint Thomas, where he formed a decided liking for the Lutheran Church. On learning that Mr. Swensson was a Lutheran, he offered his tailor shop as a meeting place for services.[36] In an article written by Alfred Ostrom about the Lutheran mission in Puerto Rico in the *Journal of Augustana College and Theological Seminary* in June 1909, he claims that Mr. Browne lived with another Afro-Caribbean from the island of Antigua where the latter, Mr. Jarvis, had been in the service of the Christian Alliance.[37] Both Mr. Browne and Mr. Jarvis provided faithful and loyal support to Mr. Swensson, yet, unknown to Swensson, they planned to turn over the whole mission along with its two organs and hymn books, to the Christian Alliance of New York City. These plans were then totally forestalled by the arrival of the General Council missionaries, Revs. Hankey and Richards on October 29, 1899.[38] To be sure, these first two ordained Lutheran pastors of the mission, as well as others who followed, had to overcome these same racial prejudices.[39] These are the local foundations on which the successful Lutheran mission was founded.

In a parallel that the early Lutheran missionaries in Puerto Rico did not chose to evoke, in the Virgin Islands, it was originally an African slave by the name of Anthony (a slave at the service of Count Lauverig), transported from the Virgin Islands to Copenhagen, who met Count Zinzendorf there and pleaded for someone to go to the Virgin Islands to teach his sister and others the Christian way of salvation. Zinzendorf encouraged two men, Leonhard Dober, a porter by trade, and David Nitschmann, a carpenter, to go to the Virgin Islands to preach the gospel. Financially supported by the family of King Christian VI, who paid their fare and purchased the tools needed to carry on their trade, on October 1, 1732, they sailed from Holland to St. Thomas. There they found the sister of Anthony and other slaves, who cheerfully responded as they learned that the gospel was not limited to white people but was also for them. "In thus financing these brethren, Denmark became pioneer in sending the Gospel to the West Indies as well to the East Indies."[40]

One of the first records of the Lutheran initiative in Puerto Rico is documented in The Lutheran magazine, where the author mentions Swensson's initiative, and the plans for developing it as a Lutheran mission.[41] In the *Lutheran* issue of February 8, 1900, appeared one of the first and most interesting descriptions of the experience of the first two ordained Lutheran pastors as they entered the service of the Lutheran mission in Puerto Rico.[42]

The Lutheran mission in Puerto Rico was mostly focused among the humble sectors of society.[43] In a publication by the West Indies Mission Board of the United Lutheran Church in America already mentioned, congregations read:

Because of the meagre support, our missionaries could only labor among the humblest class and while they made slow progress their labors had a mighty influence which was never realized until in later years. A prominent member of the House of Representatives of Porto Rico said to Executive Secretary Corbe: "Your church has done a marvelous work. Without knowing the power of class prejudice in Porto Rico you started work at the bottom with the lowest class of society and by helping them to improve their condition you compelled every other higher class to move up a notch in order to maintain their supremacy. The result has been that your work among the lowliest has had a remarkable effect and has unconsciously influenced the very highest class of society in Porto Rico."[44]

CONCLUDING REMARKS

This chapter has outlined the early developments of the General Council's Board of Foreign Missions of the Evangelical Lutheran Church in North America in its support for the Lutheran mission in Puerto Rico. This includes a letter dated March 13, 1899, sent by Gustav Sigfried Swensson to Rev. Dr. C. A. Blomgren, a member of the board and a seminary professor at the Augustana Seminary, which he shared with his colleagues at the board. Swensson's letter described the state of Protestant initiatives in the archipelago, yearned for the board's support of this mission field, and suggested specific plans for developing a Lutheran missionary work in Puerto Rico. The positive response to this letter marked the beginning of financial support to the Lutheran mission in Puerto Rico. I have also provided, by the use of short accounts, an approach to the development of this mission that expresses both positive and negative attitudes and concerns conveyed by these pioneer Lutheran North American missionaries as they engaged in this venture. Last, but not least, I identified some of the early Puerto Rican leaders that emerged in support of this mission.

One of the most interesting features in the history of this Lutheran mission was the encounter of these white North American Lutheran missionaries with people from African Caribbean heritage. The early encounter of Gustav Sigfried Swensson with the Jamaican tailor John Christopher Browne, as well as the engagement of the first ordained Lutheran pastors with Lutherans from the Virgin Islands residing in Puerto Rico, was surely controversial given the racial prejudices of the time. Certainly, the scant financial support received by the boards of North American Lutheran bodies, the numerous health-related conditions affecting the people in Puerto Rico, and the scarce number of ordained pastors and lay leaders available to support and develop new congregations were also difficult challenges to address. However, the willingness to overcome these attitudes by the front-runners of the mission led eventually to the success of their labor.

In the next chapters I will describe the ensuing stages in this mission, up to the organization of the Caribbean Synod in 1952.

NOTES

1 Michael Saenz, "Economic Aspects of Church Development in Puerto Rico: A Study of the Financial Policies and Procedures of the Major Protestant Church Groups in Puerto Rico from 1898 to 1957" (a dissertation in economics to the Faculty of the Graduate School of Arts and Sciences of the University of Pennsylvania, 1961), 20–21. Also, Howard B. Grose, *Advance in the Antilles* (New York: Literature Department, Presbyterian Home Missions, 1910), 196, 200.

2 Marisabel Bras, "The Changing of the Guard: Puerto Rico in 1898," Library of Congress, accessed June 20, 2023, https://loc.gov/rr/hispanic/1898/bras.html.

3 While the work of the Board of Foreign Missions had been mostly focused on India, at this meeting, the question of expanding this work to other countries continued to be given serious consideration by its members. *Report of the Board of Foreign Missions to the General Council of the Evangelical Lutheran Church in North America, 1899*, 52. In any case, in the following pages I will describe the arrival of Gustav Sigfried Swensson, a Swedish American Lutheran theological student from Augustana College and Seminary at Rock Island Illinois, who arrived in Puerto Rico in October,

1898. His arrival on the island is generally considered as having initiated the Lutheran work in Puerto Rico.
4 In the book Mark A. Granquist edited to provide seventy-five stories about Lutherans throughout the world from 1517 to the present, he offers a short yet valuable account of Swensson's journey to Puerto Rico at the end of the nineteenth century. The narrative, while brief, incorporates additional information regarding the Lutheran mission in Latin America. Mark A. Granquist, "Lutherans Go Latin: Hispanic Lutheranism," in *Most Certainly True: Lutheran History at a Glance: 75 Stories about Lutherans since 1517*, ed. Mark A. Granquist (Minneapolis: Lutheran University Press, 2017), 157–59.
5 "Report of the Board of Foreign Missions to the General Council," 50–51. Swensson's letter can be accessed in the 1899 "Report of the Board of Foreign Missions General Council," 50–51.
6 "Report of the Board of Foreign Missions General Council," 51–52.
7 "First Report of the Board of Porto Rico Missions to the General Council of the Evangelical Lutheran Church in North America" (October 1903). The most important challenges facing the Lutheran mission at that time were securing permanent missionaries/helpers and financial support. The report seems to claim that the reason for these challenges laid in the poor response of pastors and churches for this appeal. *First Report of the Board of Porto Rico Missions*, 2. In a later publication prepared by the Board of American Missions and the Women's Missionary Society in October 1930, Dr. Zenan M. Corbe argues that this poor response was due to the divided condition of the Lutheran Church in North America. Dr. Zenan M. Corbe, *In the Land of Unending Summer* (Philadelphia: Prepared by the Board of American Missions and the Women's Missionary Society of the United Lutheran Church in America, October 1930).
8 It is important to observe that, at the assembly, two main contesting issues regarding the mission to Puerto Rico were raised by Dr. Spaeth from the Philadelphia seminary and Dr. Gerberding from the seminary at Chicago. They opposed tenaciously the project because Puerto Ricans had already been Christianized, even if by name only, and the venture had a bold imperialist mindset. While the plan was eventually approved, the project would only be funded by monies received for that purpose. Given the few contributions received, the project was poorly financially supported. *El Testigo*, año XXII, no. 11 (April 1939): 3.
9 *Report of the Board of Foreign Mission to the General Council of the Evangelical Lutheran Church in North America, 1901*, 30.
10 Gutiérrez, *Evangélicos en Puerto Rico en la época española*, 8.
11 These were Protestant Bibles. Their content did not include the apocryphal or deuterocanonical books that were included in the Roman Catholic Bibles. Besides, most Bibles, even those translated from the Latin, followed the

Latin (Vulgate) version. The Protestant Bibles were usually translations from the original languages (Hebrew and Greek) by the sixteenth-century European reformers.

12 Gutiérrez, *Evangélicos en Puerto Rico en la época española*, 21–26.
13 Raquel Reichard, "Why Isn't Puerto Rico a State?" History.com, October 4, 2021, https://www.history.com/news/puerto-rico-statehood.
14 Official nonpublished document produced by the Caribbean Synod of the Lutheran Church in America, developed in 1969 and revised in 1983, 1–2. It is interesting to point out that, according to Mark A. Granquist, the Lutheran presence in the Caribbean and Latin America had been there for centuries. However, this presence was characterized by developing communities of faith among European Lutheran immigrants themselves in their own immigrant languages. "Though they lived in countries that spoke Spanish or Portuguese, they did not initially consider an outreach to their neighbors who used those languages." This changed in the twentieth century with Swensson, when the Lutheran mission in the region began to make the transition to the use of the Spanish language or the vernacular of the local populations. Granquist, "Lutherans Go Latin," 157.
15 This notion refers to the use of the historiography proposed by Leopold von Ranke, one of the founding fathers of the modern source-based history science. See http://scihi.org/leopold-von-ranke-science-history/ (accessed July 12, 2023).
16 Orlandi, *Mission* (Nashville: Abingdon Press, 2002), 12, emphasis original.
17 Alex García-Rivera, *St. Martín de Porres: The "Little Stories" and the Semiotics of Culture* (New York: Orbis Books, 1995), xiv.
18 For a further understanding of this concept, see Orlando Espín, *The Faith of the People: Theological Reflections on Popular Catholicism* (New York: Orbis Books, 1997).
19 In my estimation, since the term is basically used as a hermeneutical approach, it can equally be used for history, literature, and other areas of research. Justo L. Gonzalez, *Mañana: Christian Theology from a Hispanic Perspective* (Nashville: Abingdon Press, 1990), 75–87.
20 Justo L. Gonzalez, *Mañana* (Nashville: Abingdon Press, 1990), 75–87.
21 Vítor Westhelle, "Communication and the Transgression of Language in Luther," *Lutheran Quarterly* 17, no. 1 (Spring 2003), 1–27. Another valuable study exploring the impact of Martin Luther's understanding of the *vernacular* for the transmission of ideas in the Lutheran Reformation is Helga Robinson-Hammerstein, "The Lutheran Reformation and Its Music," in *The Transmission of Ideas in the Lutheran Reformation*, ed. Helga Robinson-Hammerstein (Dublin: Irish Academic Press, 1989), 141–71.
22 An important reason to choose this journal for my research is that, far more than the official correspondence and minutes of meetings contained in the administrative reports held in the archives of the Evangelical Lutheran

Church in America, *El Testigo* can seize the enthusiasm/zeal/excitement of the early congregation members and their pastor in their account of the story of this Lutheran mission.
23 See *El Testigo*, año I, no. 1 (June 1917). At that time, this was the only journal published by the Lutheran Church in Puerto Rico.
24 *El Testigo*, año XXI, no. 1 (June 1937): 17. Those interested in learning further about the emergence and development of this important Lutheran journal from 1917 up to 1937 should refer to W. G. Arbaugh, "Witnessing through Twenty Years," in *El Testigo*, año X X I, no. 2 (July 1937): 11–12. The first director/editor of *El Testigo* was the US Lutheran missionary Rev. Alfred Olstrom.
25 Fulton Sheen, *Christmas Inspirations* (New York: Maco Publications, 1966), 32.
26 In addition to the Lutheran mission that is the focus of my research, other Lutheran bodies in North America, such as the Lutheran Church–Missouri Synod, have also ventured in developing a Lutheran mission in the archipelago. See Rev. James and Deaconess Christel Neuendorf, the Lutheran Church–Missouri Synod, accessed June 20, 2023, https://www.lcms.org/neuendorf.
27 Gustav Sigfried Swensson, "I Went to Puerto Rico," in *El Testigo*, año XXXII, no. 5 (October 1948): 16. The article was found among the papers of the late pastor Gustav Sigfried Swensson. He wrote it shortly after his return to the United States in 1900. It was sent for publication by William G. Arbaugh.
28 William G. Arbaugh, "Because He Looked Like a Man of God," in *El Testigo*, año XXXI, no. 11 (April 1948): 16.
29 Rev. Lewis R. Fox, "The Lutheran Church in Puerto Rico," in *El Testigo*, año XIX, no. 12 (May 1936): 11, translation mine. Given that the Roman Catholic Church came to Puerto Rico in 1493, it became the religious expression of the ruling and dominating class. Therefore, Protestants' missionary efforts at the turn of the nineteenth century in Puerto Rico could only be directed to the humbler sectors of society.
30 The first Puerto Rican Lutheran missionary in the island.
31 Along with Salustiano Hernández and Guillermo Marrero, they were among the early Puerto Rican Lutherans to be ordained in the field.
32 The first Puerto Rican ordained to the ministry of Word and Sacrament.
33 Here I am using the adjective in the title of one of my colleagues' books, Vítor Westhelle's *The Scandalous God: The Use and Abuse of the Cross* (Minneapolis: Fortress Press, 2006).
34 Quoted in Roland Bainton, *The Martin Luther Christmas Book* (Philadelphia: The Westminster Press, 1948), 64. This section is taken from one of Luther's sermons, "The Gospel for the Festival of the Epiphany, Matthew 2:1–12 (1527)," in *Luther's Works*, ed. Jaroslav Pelican and Helmut T. Leheman, 55 vols. (Philadelphia: Fortress Press, 1955), vol. 52: 159–286.
35 Swensson, "I Went to Puerto Rico," 16. In my research on the Lutheran missionary expansion to Puerto Rico, I have a debt of gratitude to Rev.

Ronald Will for providing me with a number of important documents. These were sent for the celebration of the centennial of Lutheranism in Puerto Rico. One of these documents, written by Rev. William G. Arbaugh after visiting with Pastor Swensson in Detroit, Michigan in 1948 argues that, (i) it was in November, about a month after Swensson's arrival in San Juan, that he was confronted by Mr. Browne; (ii) Mr. Browne's tailor shop was at 11 Luna Street; (iii) while the exact date of the Lutheran service in Puerto Rico is uncertain, Arbaugh favors as the most probable the date of November 11, 1898. William G. Arbaugh, "Gustav Sigfried Swensson and the Puerto Rico Lutheran Mission" (this essay was written on March 22, 1948 and mimeographed for distribution at Frederick Lutheran Church, St. Croix, Virgin Islands during the 1960s).

36 Arbaugh, "Because He Looked Like a Man from God," 16.
37 The Christian Missionary Alliance emerged in 1881, when Pastor Albert Benjamin Simpson left the Presbyterian Church to organized a small group of followers devoted to experiencing Jesus in his fullness and making him known to New York City's marginalized dock workers. Christian and Missionary Alliance, "Who We Are," accessed June 20, 2023, https://cmalliance.org/who-we-are/.
38 Alfred Ostrom, "Our Porto Rico Mission," in *The Journal of Augustana College and Seminary* (June 1909): 186–87.
39 On November 30, 1899, an article published in *The Lutheran* magazine written by R. E. McDaniel informs its readers that, on October 31, the Puerto Rican English daily newspaper *San Juan News* reported that on Sunday of that week both pastors held a Lutheran worship service at the meeting-room of the Christian Missionary Alliance, where Swensson had held the first Lutheran worship service in the city of San Juan. *The Lutheran* IV, no. 9 (November 30, 1899): 3. The *Lutheran Magazine* was and continues to be one of the official organs of the United Lutheran Church in America aimed at keeping the Lutheran constituency informed about news relating to its ministry and mission.
40 Rev. G. W. Critchlow, "The Virgin Isles' First Missionary Effort," *The Lutheran* May 8 (1919): 4.
41 *The Lutheran* IV, no. 8 (November 9, 1899): 5.
42 *The Lutheran* IV, no. 19 (February 8, 1900): 6.
43 In spite of this fact, there were some members that were professionals, such as Dr. John S. Browne and his family from Jamaica. See *El Mundo* (April 18, 1922): 6, Library of Congress, https://chroniclingamerica.loc.gov/lccn/sn86077151/1922-04-18/ed-1/. *El Mundo* (San Juan, Puerto Rico) printed its first issue on February 17, 1919. This Spanish-language publication self-identified as the "Diario de la mañana" ("the daily"). In its first years, *El Mundo*'s content primarily focused on providing information from the Americas and Europe, frequently including news services from the United States.
44 *The Isles of the Sea*, 12.

CHAPTER 4

The Mission and Its Trailblazers

In 1997 I had the great opportunity to work together with my friend Loida I. Martell-Otero in producing a book, gathering some remarkable Latinx theologians to provide an introduction to the main teachings of the Christian faith from a Latinx Protestant perspective. The book's title was *Teología en conjunto*[1]: *A Collaborative Hispanic Protestant Theology*. It became one of the earliest publications of the Asociación de Educación Teológica Hispana (AETH).[2] In the introduction, Martell-Otero and I stated that the title was intentionally chosen to emphasize two fundamental aspects describing the nature of Latinx theology: its rich diversity and its primary collaborative spirit.[3] These two important elements also seem to characterize the emergence of the Lutheran mission in Puerto Rico.

In 1917, sponsored by the Co-operative Literature Committee of the Woman's Missionary Societies of the Lutheran Church, Mrs. Elsie Singmaster Lewars wrote a book recounting the story of Lutheran missions. In the book, she described the shallow nature of religion in the people of South America by arguing that "the natives have many crosses but no true cross, many saints but few true believers in Christ." She depicted a similar condition in Puerto Rico, arguing that:

> The experience of the General Council in Puerto Rico has been that of all workers in Latin America. They have discovered that

the Roman Catholic Church has lost its hold on the people and that thousands are longing for a better way.[4]

This reproach about the work of the Roman Catholic Church served as prelude to describe the successful work of the Lutheran Church in Puerto Rico:

> Here the General Council has had a mission since 1899. It has in all nine congregations and twelve stations with more than five hundred communicant members. Among its stations are Cataño, San Juan and Bayamón where it owns fine church properties and has excellent schools. In Cataño there is a kindergarten in connection with the parroquial school to which Miss May Mellander has given years of devoted service. In Cataño the missionaries instruct native teachers.[5]

Later on, an article written by Leopoldo Cabán[6] in the journal *El Testigo*[7] provides a summary of the important developments of the Lutheran mission in Puerto Rico from the time of the arrival of Gustav Sigfried Swensson on October 5, 1898, up to May 1937. In the article we find the arrival of missionaries from the United States.[8] Cabán also mentions pastors from other countries that joined the Lutheran mission.[9] The men in the list functioned as pastors of congregations. The women were deaconesses, teachers, or health professionals (nurses). It is also important to highlight the contribution of the wives of these pastors to the work of the mission. This body of missionaries led the way for the emergence of native lay workers and pastors,[10] and also of Puerto Rican women teachers and missionaries.[11]

Given the precarious conditions of the time, the lack of adequate financial resources, the exposure to perilous climate conditions (hurricanes, cyclones, earthquakes, etc.), along with the variety of diseases that affected many of them (in some cases requiring a return to their country of origin), their work was arduous and challenging, yet a valiant witness to their commitment of faith and courageous response to their Christian calling.

EARLY MISSIONARY WORK AND THE CATHOLIC RESPONSE

On their arrival in San Juan on October 29, 1899, Rev. Herbert F. Richards and Rev. Benjamin F. Hankey were received by Mr. Gustav S. Swensson, who proceeded to hand over to them the work he had started, along with the rented facilities where the missionary activities were being held.[12] In December, they moved to a new location in the second floor of a building in front of a small plaza next to the Roman Catholic cathedral, with a rental contract for three years. The new place was rearranged to provide a bigger and more adequate space for the sanctuary. Swensson brought a small organ that he already owned. At the entrance of the building there were two rooms on the first floor that the missionaries rented out to cover the costs for the rental of the building. It was at this location that the First Evangelical Lutheran Church was formally organized on January 1, 1900, with twenty-three members.[13] At that time ministerial activities were also held in San Juan (Sunday school, worship services, catechetic classes, etc.) and Cataño by the same two missionaries.[14] The missionaries employed many hours visiting prospective members and learning Spanish, which kept them busy as well as joyful.[15]

Financial resources for the mission were short and, with these commitments becoming reduced, the pastors decided that one of them should return to North America to increase the interest of the General Council in the mission field. Given that Pastor Hankey had become ill with malaria, he was chosen for the trip, in the hope that the voyage would help him recover.[16] Since money was not available, Dr. Stimson, a physician who originally came to the island with the US Army, found Hankey a special fare for indigents in a military transport.[17] Pastor Hankey returned to North America in May 1900 and did not return as a missionary, though his interest in the Puerto Rican mission remained. Instead, after a fruitful ministry in the west of Pennsylvania, he became secretary of the Board of Missions for Puerto Rico and Latin America at the General Council, and later as a member of the Board of Missions for the West Indies of the United Lutheran Church in America, he visited Puerto Rico, accompanying Dr. Zenan M. Corbé, in the summer of 1919.[18]

Pastor Richards married Miss Lillian Ainslay McDavid, a teacher in the United States who had been a missionary in Saltillo, Mexico, on July 3, 1901. During the summer of 1902, the couple went for two months' vacation in the United States. To make this possible, the board employed for the summer the services of Mr. Swensson, who brought with him several copies of Martin Luther's *Small Catechism* in Spanish published by Augustana's Book Concern and translated by Swensson himself.[19] Prior to his return to Augustana College to resume his studies in September 1900, Swensson prepared the first class of catechumens and, on April 15, four young women were confirmed: Gabriela Cuervos, Eufemia Flores, Belén Martínez, and Pascuala Pantojas.[20] This group led to the development of the Iglesia de San Pablo, which took the date of the first confirmation as the time of its foundation.

In his valuable study on the history of Protestantism in Puerto Rico, Samuel Silva Gotay provides an important description of the reaction of Roman Catholic leaders to what he calls "the invasion of Protestantism in Puerto Rico."[21] Given their experience of losing the support and budget provided by the state, along with the exodus of the majority of priests, their exclusion from the educational system they had formerly dominated, and the expropriation of properties constructed with state funds, the remaining leaders of the Roman Catholic Church in Puerto Rico were aggressive in confronting the forceful Protestant militancy of the new regime.[22] From its first edition of August 15, 1899, *El Ideal Católico* became the Roman Catholic journal of combat against Protestantism,[23] challenging its Christian nature, branding it as socialist or revolutionary, and considering it a heresy, a diabolic sect invented by the devil to have souls deceived—the last a long-established anti-Lutheran trope that went back to the sixteenth century.[24] Regarding Martin Luther, the journal argued against the Reformer's doctrine of salvation by faith alone using the Catholic epistle of James 2:14–18,[25] and described Luther as "an opportunist monk interested in marrying a nun and leading the world to believe in anything they wanted and doing whatever they willed."[26] In choosing to locate their new congregation across from the Catholic cathedral, the new Lutheran mission faced off against a shaken but still hostile and defiant Catholic Church.

However, it is interesting to note that in a later study already anticipated in his book on Protestantism in Puerto Rico, Silva Gotay argues that, with the invasion by the United States in 1898, the Roman Catholic Church had to, among other things, insert itself in the United States' "Americanization" agenda, in order to survive in the new colonial system imposed in Puerto Rico. For the author, this was a shift led by the Holy See to have the bishops as well as the Apostolic delegates in the island lead the "Americanization" of the Puerto Rican Roman Catholic Church, to prove the loyalty of the United States Catholics to their own government. To reinforce his claim, Silva Gotay argues that Pope Leon XIII chose Monsignor Placide Louise Chapelle[27] and Monsignor James Hubert Herbert Blenk[28] to configure the Roman Catholic Church to the style of the one in the United States.[29]

To be sure, this last claim of Silva Gotay became a controversial issue among scholars of the history of Puerto Rico. Most of these historians agree that, with the United States' military invasion of Puerto Rico, the Roman Catholic Church, which was already experiencing a crisis, suffered a deeper predicament.[30] Nevertheless, others, like Gerardo Alberto Hernández Aponte,[31] argued that becoming aware that, contrary to the North American democratic tradition, Puerto Rico was not to be annexed but become a colony of the United States, the Roman Catholic Church devised a plan to maintain Puerto Rico's Hispanic-American profile by trying to conciliate the loyalty of the new prelates to the United States by selecting North American pastors. Thus, the presence of Monsignor Blenk in Puerto Rico, rather than expressing an "Americanization" policy, became a diplomatic pastoral action from the Holy See to preserve its Puerto Rican Roman Catholic constituents.[32]

In any case, as time went by, the confrontational attitude of some sectors of the Roman Catholic Church in Puerto Rico began to change, recognizing its decreasing social importance as the Protestant movement continued to strengthen in the island. A generation later, in December 1949, William C. Arbaugh claimed in a letter sent to his friends that:

> In Puerto Rico the Roman Church has become relatively impotent. Here the bishop's blessings are mainly for the new breweries and casinos. Endorsement by a bishop is the kiss of death to a politician's election hopes. There are about as many people in Protestant services as at Roman masses. We have full religious liberty and personal security.[33]

THE FIRST LUTHERAN CHURCH BUILDING AND THE CONTINUING WORK OF US MISSIONARIES

In 1902, Rev. Charles H. Hemsath was sent to the island to supervise the construction of a church building. The building was funded by the Board of Porto Rico Missions of the General Council of the Evangelical Lutheran Church in North America and completed by 1903. On August 30 of that year the Divino Salvador Lutheran church was established. While the work in Cataño was slow in developing, once the building was constructed, the church grew rapidly.[34] In the First Report of the Board of Porto Rico Mission, Rev. D. H. Geissinger, president of the board, informed readers that the total cost of the church, including the lot ($300), the construction of the building, and the expenses related to sending Rev. Hemsath to Puerto

Rico, was $3,111.63. The board paid for these expenses in order to have a dedication service of the church without debt.[35]

In San Juan, however, the rental contract for the property was due to come to an end on December 31, 1902. When the property went on sale, the board tried to purchase it, but learned that the Episcopal Church had already bought it and was not considering surrendering it.[36] After this, the church's activities were first moved to the second floor of a house located on the crossroads between Cristo and San Francisco, and later to the second floor of number 20 Cruz Street. In the early summer it moved again, to the corner of San Francisco and O'Donnel streets. By September 1903, the mission had eighty-eight adult members in all: fifty-one at the First (English) in San Juan, twenty-eight in San Pablo, and nine in Divino Salvador, Cataño.[37]

Rev. Alfred Ostrom and his wife Betty Ostrom arrived in Puerto Rico as missionaries on April 12, 1905. On May 1, Pastor Richards handed over responsibility for the mission to Rev. Ostrom and left for the United States on May 9. The mission's new head, Rev. Ostrom, was born in Degerfors, Vesterbotten, Sweden, on April 18, 1868. His family had moved to Lockport, Illinois in 1869. After graduating from Augustana College in 1893, Ostrom served at Salem Lutheran Church in Chicago, teaching Sunday School, playing the organ, and developing a choir. In 1897, he graduated from Augustana Theological Seminary, was ordained, and began his ministry as pastor in a church in La Grange, Illinois. On April 17, 1901, he married Betty Olson from Sioux City, Iowa, and in 1902 became pastor of the church in Aurora, Illinois, from where he left to go to Puerto Rico.[38] Ostrom, who came from the Augustana Synod, became an important leader in the mission. Although he and his wife initially experienced health-related problems while on the island that led them to take a six-month furlough for treatment in the United States, both returned to continue their work in Puerto Rico until 1920.[39] In November 1905, given her poor health, Miss Annette Wahlstedt was forced to leave the island. With the assistance of Miss Clara Hazelgreen, a Lutheran missionary from the United States, Pastor Ostrom and his wife moved forward the work of the mission. Their labor led to the expansion of the mission to communities close to San Juan, as well as the recruitment of the first "native workers."[40]

At the time of Pastor Ostrom's arrival in Puerto Rico, there were three congregations: the First English Lutheran Church, Iglesia Luterana San Pablo (both in the city of San Juan), and Iglesia Luterana Divino Salvador in Cataño.[41] While the first Lutheran worship service in the city of Bayamón took place on October 28, 1906, the Iglesia Luterana Santísima Trinidad was established on July 15, 1908. In Monacillos, one of the eighteen barrios in the municipality of San Juan, the first worship service took place on April 1, 1906, and the Iglesia Luterana Betania was organized on June 30, 1911.[42] The first worship service in Toa Baja[43] was held on August 17, 1908, and the Iglesia Luterana San Pedro was established on June 29, 1909. The first worship service in Dorado took place on August 24, 1908, and the Iglesia Luterana Getsemaní was established on June 25, 1911.[44] In Palo Seco, the first worship service was held on October 19, 1906, and the church was established on December 9, 1912.[45] In Bayamón, the first worship service was celebrated at Comerío Street on Thanksgiving Day 1907. A chapel was dedicated on January 15, 1909, and the Iglesia Luterana Sión was established on April 27, 1913.[46] During 1912 regular worship services were held in Campanilla, Sardinera, Maracayo, and Higuillar; however, the work in the first two locations was later discontinued. The first worship service in Maracayo was held on September 13, 1912, but the Bethel church was not established until December 11, 1920. In Higuillar, the first worship service took place on April 6, 1913, but the San Juan church was not established until June 26, 1931.[47] In Palo Seco, the first worship service was held on October 19, 1906, and the church was established on December 9, 1912. In Juan Domingo, a rural community close to Monacillos, the Iglesia Luterana Nuestro Salvador was established on September 6, 1920.[48] Finally, on April 29, 1917, the First English Lutheran Church and the Iglesia San Pablo moved to Puerta de Tierra, where a building was constructed, bringing an end to the previous rental of locations.[49]

THE MISSION AND ITS TRAILBLAZERS

While the Lutheran Church in Puerto Rico was smaller in membership when compared to other Protestant denominations, it is interesting to note that the congregation in San Juan became one with increasing attendance. In its edition of December 27, 1919, the newspaper *El Mundo* reported that, at the funeral of the mother of José Álvarez, a distinguished officer of the municipal jail, held at San Pablo Lutheran church on December 26, the attendance was enormous.[50]

On April 26, 1907, Rev. Axel Peter Gabriel Anderson arrived in Puerto Rico and established his residence in the town of Bayamón.[51] In March 26, 1910, he married Miss Augusta C. Hohansen. Miss Hohansen was a young teacher of Swedish origin with musical training whom Pastor Anderson met when he was on vacation in the United States during the summer of 1909. Pastors Ostrom and Anderson came from the Augustana Synod, and during their tenure the synod increased its allocation for the mission. That allowed for two additional missionaries to be added to the staff on the island, Miss May Mellander on September 26, 1906, and Miss Noemi Anderson (sister of Pastor Anderson) on October 24, 1907. With this increase in the labor force, the social initiatives originally established by the Lutheran mission were improved, expanding educational and health-related programs for Puerto Rican children, and addressing the needs of people on the Virgin Islands.[52] In addition, Miss Emma R. Schmid came to Puerto Rico on March 18, 1914 (she married Pastor Hans Naether in November 30, 1921), Miss Nanca Schoen arrived on July 16, 1917, and Miss Sofía Probst on September 2, 1914.[53] However, Schoen also had to request a furlough because of illness that required hospital treatment. While in Puerto Rico, she oversaw the missionaries' educational work among children, as well as the Queen Louise Home for sick and neglected babies in Christiansted, St. Croix (Virgin Islands).[54] After a successful surgery Schoen returned to the Lutheran Mission in Puerto Rico to supervise all educational activities in the various islands, devoting special attention to the training of kindergarten teachers.[55]

TENSIONS OVER INDIGENOUS LEADERSHIP

Offering a broader indication of effectiveness, a number of Puerto Rican lay workers were added to the missionary body, including Manuel Hidalgo (1906), Lorenzo Hurtado (1909), Jaime Más (1908), Pascual López (1909), Juan Zambrana (1911), Alfredo Cosme Mercado (1911), and Dionisio Miranda (1915). The following Puerto Rican women were also added: Gabriela Cuervos (1906), María C. González (1909), Dolores Quidgley Martínez (1910), Genoveva Fernández 1913), (Matilde Llanes (1913), Concepción González (1914), Dolores Rosado (1917), and Serafina Parrilla (1919).[56] Given the significant expansion of the mission field, a good part of the labor was taken care of by lay workers, who were known as "lay pastors." They led worship services, but did not wear clergy vestments. They preached and led catechetic classes, but did not administer the sacraments. They could celebrate funerals, but not weddings. Their assignments to congregations were decided by considering the needs of these lay workers and the congregations in which they were appointed.

Among the important stories in the development of the Lutheran mission in Puerto Rico, some recount the struggles experienced by Indigenous leaders in their formation for the various ministries of the church. For most North American Protestant missionaries, the idea of integrating these native leaders in the missionary project consisted first of all of becoming assistants in congregational tasks, or responding to the social needs of the people of the island. For this purpose, the early Puerto Rican leaders served as readers of the Bible in worship services, lay congregational workers, preachers, and so on.[57]

To prepare capable and competent Puerto Rican leaders, in 1908 North American missionaries established a seminary located at Divino Salvador Lutheran church in the city of Cataño. According to Rev. Arbaugh, the lay preachers had been under the impression that their studies at the seminary would eventually prepare them as candidates for the ordained ministry of Word and Sacrament. Living costs had risen sharply and had seriously aggravated the chronic financial plight of the workers and of their growing families. The North American missionaries, on the other hand, had selected three young men to train and instruct them at the "seminary for native helpers," with the goal of making them efficient collaborators in the missionary work. Ironically, three-fourths of the preaching, with nearly all the catechizing and other pastoral work, was performed by the lay assistants, who were not permitted to perform such pastoral functions as the administration of the sacraments, confirmation, and marriage. In addition, the salaries of the lay preachers were never sufficient to allow their families a decent standard of living.[58] The missionaries were obviously thinking of their own immediate needs and not of the implications as to the future status of the student assistants. In following this procedure our Lutheran missionaries were doing exactly what most other Protestant missionaries were doing all over the world. They probably did not seriously consider the possibility that these "helpers" would eventually stand in line for ordination.[59] They did not stop to think that the situation in 1918 was not in harmony with the best Lutheran practice. At this time the Lutheran mission was mostly focused on the poorer sectors of Puerto Rican society, leading to the neglect of the need to develop a more rigorous educational program for the formation of native helpers to work in this setting. The consequences of this attitude soon became apparent. The first of these students, Manuel Hidalgo, left the work after two years. The next two students, Lorenzo Hurtado and Pascual López, left within one year.[60]

It is important to note that recent reviews of the experience of other Protestant missionary groups in the formation of native Puerto Rican leaders showed some exceptions. In an article mentioned earlier, Ángel Santiago-Vendrell argues that, as a result of the academic formation of Presbyterian missionaries Judson Underwood and James McAllister, they opened a Seminario Teológico de Mayaguez (STM) on October 1, 1906, in the town of Mayaguez. The United Brethren joined the Presbyterian training school in 1912, which changed its name to Seminario Teológico Puertoricense, adding one faculty member to the previous three missionary teachers. The missionaries planned a course of study that would last six years: two years of preparatory studies for students with no prior education, and four years of combined college and seminary work. The seminary developed a winter and summer program designed for students to work with a missionary supervisor in the areas of preaching, evangelizing rural communities, and organizing Sunday schools. In 1914, James McAllister's article "Un Ministerio Nativo Bien Preparado" in *Puerto Rico Evangélico* described what he meant by training a well-educated minister. First, ministers were the religious guides of people on pilgrimage to heaven. Second, the best agent to proclaim the gospel to her/his own people should be a native minister. Finally, native ministers were to be educated for the task of preaching the gospel. McAllister pointed out,

> For ministers to be successful as spiritual guides of people they must be educated because they are the ones leading people in the midst of a world in need. A native minister without education would be a catastrophe. The educational norms for native ministers should be equal to the norms in the United States.[61]

To be sure, we need to acknowledge the great contribution of North American Protestant missionaries for the expansion of Protestantism in Puerto Rico.[62] At the same time, we need to point out that this expression of the gospel was strongly influenced by the prejudices in the dominant culture of their country of origin, against recruiting our people in the mission field. Swensson, to whom the establishment of Lutheranism in Puerto Rico has been attributed by many, once mentioned in a published article that, "I saw the Puerto Ricans as a people in misery, ignorance, superstition and fatal errors."[63] He and the cohort of North American missionaries who followed him were slow in recognizing the potential of native leaders' contributions for the new mission.

Arbaugh states that, eventually, the native lay preachers studying at the seminary in Cataño were able to successfully complete the requirements established for ordination. Seventeen years after its establishment and,

> In the presence of a large congregation at San Pablo Lutheran church in San Juan, Demetrio Texidor, Guillermo E. Marrero and Salustiano Hernández were ordained to the ministry of the gospel on Sunday July 10th, 1926.[64]

The first generation of the Lutheran mission in Puerto Rico would remain dominated by North American-trained pastors.

EXPANSION AND ALLIANCE BETWEEN MISSIONARIES AND PUERTO RICAN MINISTERS

In a summary of Protestant missions' statistics in Puerto Rico in 1912, published by the *Puerto Rico Evangélico* in 1913, the Lutheran Church reported having eight pastors, two teachers, one lay worker, eighteen points of preaching, 401 communing members, eleven Bible schools, nine hundred members of Bible schools, two daily schools, ninety members of daily schools, seventy-five members of societies for young people, three church buildings and chapels, and three other buildings, with a value of $16,000, and a total of $618.68 collected that year.[65] This information indicated the slow but still important growth of Protestantism in the island. The early years had been dedicated to occupying the territory, while the last two were focused on giving attention to the inner life of the churches and increasing their financial contributions.[66]

In 1915, while there were still only eight ordained pastors and two teachers, the number of lay workers grew to three; there was also an increase in communing members to 455, fifteen Bible schools, 1,500 members of Bible Schools, 120 members of societies for young people, four church buildings and chapels, four other buildings with a value of $32,000, and the amount of $835.97 of offerings collected that year.[67]

By 1918, the membership of the Lutheran mission had increased to 542. Given the illness of his spouse, Pastor Axel Peter Gabriel Anderson was forced to leave the island on August 16, 1918, and one week before his departure Pastor Fred W. Lindke arrived to substitute him.[68] Pastor Lindke studied at the Weidner Institute and Carthage College, moving on to receive his theological formation from the Lutheran Seminary in Chicago where he graduated on April 24, 1918. He accepted a call as a missionary in Puerto Rico and was ordained at Trinity Lutheran church in Fort Wayne, Indiana, on June 16, 1918, by the Chicago Synod. He married Miss Orpha Rothenberger, a peer at Weidner Institute, and both left Brooklyn on August 3 in the steamship *Coamo*. During that time, German submarines were sinking ships in American coastal areas. Two hours after the *Coamo* passed Cape Hateras, the ship *Faro* was torpedoed in the same region, but Pastor Lindke and his wife arrived safely in San Juan on August 9. They were received at the loading dock by Pastor Ostrom, who took them the next day to the house in Bayamón that would become available with the departure of Pastor Anderson.[69]

As in the case of previous missionaries, Pastor Lindke and his wife had to learn Spanish in Puerto Rico[70] for their work to be effective, and they were diligent in this task. He was responsible for the congregations in the field, with the exception of San Juan and Cataño. Given his strong academic and administrative background, he also had to offer some courses at the "seminary" in Cataño as part of his initial assignment. With the organization of the United Lutheran Church in America in the United States, the Board of Missions of the West Indies took over control of the work. In 1919, Pastor Lindke was appointed superintendent of buildings and points of mission. On April 17, 1923, while in New York recovering from an illness, Pastor Lindke was appointed superintendent of the field. It is also important to mention that on Tuesday May 15, 1923, Rev. Lindke received, from the executive secretary of the Puerto Rican government, a certificate registering the West Indies Mission Board of the

United Lutheran Church in America, Inc. to direct and foment the work of the Lutheran Church in Puerto Rico.[71] Meanwhile, Pastor Ostrom served the congregations in the Virgin Islands when they were transferred to the United Lutheran Church in America in 1917.[72] In 1923, in the book *El Libro de Puerto Rico* (The book of Porto Rico), edited by E. Fernández García, Rev. Philo W. Drury[73] describes the standing of the Lutheran Church as follows:

> Superintendent, Rev. Alfred Ostrom. . . . Towns occupied: Bayamón, Cataño, Dorado, San Juan, and Toa Baja. This mission in addition of its evangelistic activities directs a school for works in Cataño, two "kindergartens," three daily schools along with three industrial classes. Six daily and Vacation Bible schools were held the past summer. The mission publishes a monthly periodical "El Testigo."
>
> The Lutherans have 11 organized churches with 608 members; 22 biblical schools with 2,220 registered; 20 church buildings, all valued at $96,850. Contributions in 1921, $1,276.[74]

By the 1920s the mission's need for Puerto Rican ordained ministers became evident to everyone. The first step in this direction was taken by Rev. Hans Naether, a German-born missionary and the child of German immigrants who arrived in Puerto Rico on October 26, 1920, starting a vigorous ministry in Cataño. He recommended that Eduardo Roig, one of the young men recently converted, be sent to the United States to pursue a college and seminary education. However, since the conflict of lay workers aspiring to be ordained led authorities at the Lutheran mission, as well as the board, to hesitate in establishing precedents, they gave no regard to the suggestion of Pastor Naether, who had only just arrived on the island. In spite of the apathy of the authorities, Pastor Naether convinced Roig's parents of his project, and, on January 1922, Mr. Roig left for the United States, registering at Wartburg College in Waverly, Iowa. From there, he moved to the Lutheran Seminary in Philadelphia, graduating in

1926. Having married Miss Rosario Esteves during his studies in Philadelphia, Roig was later ordained by the New York Synod. On June 14, 1926, they arrived in Puerto Rico, where Rev. Roig became the pastor of the Iglesia Luterana San Pablo in San Juan.[75]

During the early 1920s, Gustav K. Huf went as a Lutheran missionary to Puerto Rico. As a young man, Huf was confirmed by Dr. Zenan M. Corbé at the Iglesia de la Transfiguración in New York. After his graduation from the Lutheran Seminary in Philadelphia and his ordination by the Ministry of Pennsylvania in 1924, Pastor Huf was added to the missionary body in Puerto Rico. He arrived in Puerto Rico with his wife in July of that year to become the pastor of the Iglesia Luterana Santísima Trinidad in Bayamón. Along with Pastor Lindke, he began to advocate for a Puerto Rican Lutheran mission owned and supported by Puerto Ricans themselves. To achieve this objective, on June 1, 1926, Guillermo Marrero, who along with Salustiano Hernández and Demetrio Texidor was a native worker ordained in the mission, and had also worked with Pastor Huff in the congregations of Santísima Trinidad and Sion in Bayamón, was installed as pastor of the Iglesia Sión. Salustiano Hernández, who had served as lay preacher in the Divino Salvador church in Cataño, became pastor of that congregation on July 1. At the same time, Demetrio Texidor, who earlier had served the Iglesia Luterana San Pablo, became pastor of the congregations San Pedro Lutheran Church in Toa Baja and Getsemaní Lutheran Church in Dorado. These congregations, whose prior financial support had only come from abroad, were now encouraged to start building their self-sufficiency, and began contributing to the salary of their pastors, the costs of their buildings, ministry programs, and financial support for the church abroad.[76]

During this period, the effort to provide aid to the social needs of the community continued, with the support of the pastor's spouses along with the valuable leadership of Miss Emma Schmidt, who arrived from the United States on March 18, 1914, and married Pastor Naether on December 1, 1921. Other missionaries, such as Miss

Sophia Probst and Miss Nancy Schoen, both of whom came from the United States and were sponsored by the Women's Missionary Society, engaged in the educational work of kindergartens in the urban congregations of Puerto Rico and the Virgin Islands. Miss Frieda M. Hoh (RN) and Miss Florence Hines arrived in Puerto Rico from the United States in 1925, sponsored by the same Women's Missionary Society. The first began to work in health-related matters and continued by developing choirs and improving congregational worship music. The latter joined other Puerto Rican women as teachers in local kindergarten programs.[77]

The year 1928 saw important developments in the Lutheran mission. On February 7, Rev. Franklin F. Fry, executive secretary for American Missions (a new organization that absorbed the earlier West Indies Mission Board), along with his wife, began his annual visit to Puerto Rico. On July 4, Rev. Lindke left Puerto Rico after ten years of service. On September 6, another local recruit, Mr. Balbino González, embarked for the United States to study at a Lutheran seminary, and on November 12, Rev. William G. Arbaugh became the pastor of the First Evangelical Lutheran Church of San Juan. The next year, Balbino González returned to Puerto Rico as an ordained pastor, and the young Leopoldo Cabán received his Bachelor of Arts degree with honors from Gettysburg College. On July 29, the new congregation Villa Betania was inaugurated and in August Rev. Balbino González was appointed director of *El Testigo*, succeeding Rev. Alfred Ostrom and becoming the first locally born missionary to edit the journal.

From 1930 to 1937 other notable events took place at the mission and beyond. In August 1930, Francisco Agostini entered the University of Puerto Rico to begin his training to become an ordained minister. The United Lutheran Synod of New York, the Board of Missions, and members of the congregation formally extended a call (an invitation made by a congregation to a candidate to serve as their pastor) to the Argentinian Jaime Soler, a seminary student who had received his degree from the Lutheran Seminary in

Philadelphia. This church (a Spanish-language congregation in the city of New York) had initially been established by Rev. Dr. Ostrom, Rev. Lindke, and a group of twenty-five Lutheran immigrants from Puerto Rico on May 3, 1924. The original intention of the Board of Missions was to provide services to students completing their theological studies at the Lutheran Seminary in Philadelphia.[78] Given his illness, another long-serving founder, Rev. Ostrom, left the missionary field in June 1932, and in August Francisco Molina entered the University of Puerto Rico to begin his studies for the ministry. On May 2, 1932, Alfredo Ortiz graduated from Hamma Divinity School in Springfield, Ohio. Leopoldo Cabán assumed the direction of *El Testigo* in February 1935 and, in December 1935, the Administrative Missionary Committee of the Lutheran Church in Puerto Rico was appointed to take charge of the responsibilities of the former position of superintendent of the mission. In January 1937, Evaristo Falcó Esteves was presented to the annual assembly of the Lutheran Church and, on May 14, the *El Testigo* celebrated twenty years as the official organ of the Lutheran Church in Puerto Rico.[79]

GROWTH OF A PUERTO RICAN CHURCH

While there are more stories that I will explore in other chapters of this study, it is important to restate at this point that in 1926 Eduardo Roig became the first Puerto Rican ordained a pastor. As already mentioned, other native leaders followed Pastor Roig, including Demetrio Texidor, Guillermo Marrero, and Salustiano Hernández. The contribution of these Indigenous frontrunners became an important stimulus for the development of the Lutheran mission in Puerto Rico. Local women missionaries and parish workers were added to the staff and private elementary schools with Puerto Rican head teachers were organized in various urban congregations. Other Puerto Rican pastors later serving in the mission were Sergio Cobián,[80] Salustiano Hernández Ruiz, José N. Cabán, Balbino González, Alfredo Ortiz,

THE MISSION AND ITS TRAILBLAZERS

Leopoldo Cabán, Francisco J. Agostini,[81] and Francisco Molina.[82] At this point, most pastors in the mission were native Puerto Ricans.

As stated earlier, the Lutheran mission developed from San Juan to Cataño, Palo Seco, Dorado, Toa Baja, Bayamón, Monacillos, and Río Piedras. It also established a theological seminary in Cataño (1908). Puerto Ricans welcomed the publication of Martin Luther's *Small Catechism* in Spanish and other translations of Lutheran works in 1901 and 1908. A valuable contribution of Lutherans from the Puerto Rican mission came in developing the Transfiguración Spanish-language Lutheran church in New York. Similarly, the missionary work of the Lutheran Church in the region of Rio Grande in the south of the United States owes a great deal to Puerto Rican missionaries, including Sergio Cobián, Andrés Meléndez, Demetrio Texidor, and Germán Vásquez, who, along with their spouses, decided to set their tents there to propel the presence of the gospel.[83] It is also important to add that North American and Puerto Rican missionaries ministered regularly to the lepers on the island in San Juan Harbor, and Pastor Critchlow regularly ministered to the inmates of the leper colony on the island of St. Croix.[84] It is interesting to note that the development of the Lutheran mission was also celebrated by other Protestant denominations in the island. In one of the most prominent journals of Protestantism in Puerto Rico, *Puerto Rico Evangélico*, we find the following note,

> On February 9–10, our Lutheran brothers [and sisters] celebrated their second annual Conference in the neighborhood of Monacillo. At the same time, they inaugurated a new chapel in the same place. We congratulate these brothers [and sisters] for their progress.[85]

To be sure, by 1936 the Lutheran mission in Puerto Rico had extended its field of work from San Juan to other towns in the metropolitan area; created a number of private elementary schools;[86] led a project to meet the needs of those experiencing leprosy in a colony in San Juan and another one in St. Croix;[87] developed a center for the theological formation of its Puerto Rican leaders; provided Spanish-language literature for its members; constructed church facilities in a number of places; contributed to the development of a Spanish-language congregation in the city of New York and in the region of Río Grande; provided financially for the domestic and international work of the Lutheran Church;[88] and explored the possibility of establishing a Lutheran mission in Santo Domingo.[89] A report published in *El Testigo* outlining the Lutheran missionary work which had taken place in Puerto Rico by 1936 claimed that

> The Lutheran field is small but is strategically located in the capital city and nearby communities. There are now 13 congregations with 872 confirmed members, 6 other preaching stations, 22 Sunday schools with 2,000 scholars, and 5 kindergartens with 180 pupils. There are 14 senior Luther Leagues with 388 members, 10 women societies with 207 members, and other organizations in proportion. The active missionary staff is composed of 8 ordained ministers, a lay reader, 6 kindergarten workers, a trained nurse, and a parish visitor. Of this staff Pastor and Mrs. William Arbaugh, Pastor Lewis R. Fox and Miss Frieda M. Hoh, R.N. are the only missionaries from the States. The others are all competent, trained Puerto Ricans. Two recent graduates of the University of Puerto Rico are now studying at the Philadelphia Seminary. Field contributions in 1935 were $3,702.41.[90]

The enthusiasm shown by Lutheran leaders about the development of their mission is also shared by other Protestant leaders on the island.[91] It is also remarkable to note the great interest shown by a number of Lutheran pastors in the United States about working in the Puerto Rican mission. In the March 18, 1920, edition of *The Lutheran* magazine, there is a report that a pastor traveled 4,400 miles to have a six-hour conference with the officers of the Executive Committee of the West Indies Mission Board of the Lutheran Church in New York to determine if he possessed the qualifications for a call to the Puerto Rican mission field which had been offered to him.[92]

CONCLUDING REMARKS

In this part of my study, I have provided a broad view of the North American and Puerto Rican forerunners of the Lutheran mission in Puerto Rico, their contributions, and some primary challenges they faced in moving forward with this project. Their resilience in facing hazardous climate conditions, tropical illness, and inadequate financial resources, along with a hostile and combative attitude from Roman Catholic leaders in the archipelago, was a testimony to their calling and faithful convictions.

Eventually, appropriate provision was received from North American Lutheran sources to rent, and later construct, buildings for emerging congregations in support of their evangelistic ministry and social concern programs. More North American missionaries joined the mission, along with Puerto Rican lay workers, increasing the Lutheran presence in the archipelago. Efforts to provide for the theological formation of Indigenous leaders were initiated, with positive and negative consequences, ultimately making progress toward developing well-educated pastors to lead congregations and their ministry.

While the first generation of leaders in the Lutheran mission remained North American missionaries, by the 1920s an emerging number of Puerto Rican candidates for ordination surfaced, fulfilling their theological formation in Lutheran seminaries in North America and then returning to their birth place to begin their ministry. As the Lutheran mission extended its field of work to other cities in the metropolitan area, and representatives of the Lutheran mission migrated to the United States, Lutheran congregations were established in the city of New York and the state of Texas. Finally, despite the fact that the Lutheran mission in Puerto Rico remained smaller than other Protestant denominations, the passion and convictions displayed by Lutheran leaders regarding the progress of their mission was acknowledged and shared by other Protestant leaders.

NOTES

1. This section of the title translated into English literally means "'in conjunction,' or 'conjoined in,' implying not only the coming together but also the integration and intimacy involved in such a sharing. It is reminiscent of the human body, whose various joints, tendons, muscles, and bones must be conjoined in order for it to function in an adequate way." José David Rodríguez and Loida I. Martell-Otero, *Teología en conjunto: A Collaborative Hispanic Protestant Theology* (Louisville, KY: Westminster John Knox Press, 1997), 1.
2. The Association for Hispanic Theological Education (AETH) is a network of people and institutions that, since 1992, works in the United States, Canada, Puerto Rico, and more recently in Latin America and the Caribbean, dedicated to the promotion and improvement of theological education and its impact on the lives of individuals, churches, and communities. See https://aeth.info/en/ (accessed January 19, 2023).
3. Rodríguez and Martell-Otero, *Teología en conjunto*, 1.
4. Elsie Singmaster Lewars, *The Story of Lutheran Missions* (Columbia: Survey Publishing Co., 1917), 207.
5. Singmaster Lewars, *The Story of Lutheran Missions*, 207.
6. Leopoldo Cabán was a Puerto Rican native who received his bachelor's degree with honors at Gettysburg College and who, after being ordained, was installed as pastor of a Lutheran congregation in Bayamón, Puerto Rico on February 8, 1933. In February 1935, he became editor of the journal *El Testigo*. Cabán also became an important Lutheran pastor in San Antonio, Texas. In 1926, the leading Protestant journal *Puerto Rico Evangélico* published an extensive review of his ministry in San Antonio along with Cabán's perspective on the religious work in that city. See *Puerto Rico Evangélico*, año XV, no. 14 (October 9, 1926): 11–12.
7. In addition to Caban's article, *El Testigo* published in Spanish and English a more detailed and comprehensive account of the Lutheran mission from its origins up to 1928 written by William G. Arbaugh. See "Principios de la iglesia luterana en Puerto Rico," *El Testigo*, año XIX, no. 12 (February and March 1924): 1, 4; "Los primeros tiempos de la misión luterana en PR," *El Testigo*, año XXXII, no. 4 (September 1948): 4–7, 14; "Alfredo Ostrom y la era de expansión: Historia de la misión luterana en Puerto Rico desde 1905 hasta 1918," *El Testigo* (December 1948): 5–6, 14; "Fred W. Lindke y

la era de transición: Historia de la misión luterana en Puerto Rico desde 1918 hasta 1928," *El Testigo* (January 1949): 4-7, 9-10, 12. You can find the English versions of these articles in "History of the Lutheran Mission," *El Testigo*, año XXIII, no. 7 (December 1939): 11-12; "How the Puerto Rico Mission was Organized," *El Testigo*, año XXXII, no. 3 (August 1948): 15-16; "Alfred Ostrom and the Era of Expansion," *El Testigo*, año XXXII, no. 7 (December 1948): 15-16; "Fred W. Lindke and the Era of Transition," *El Testigo*, año XXXII, no. 8 (January 1949): 13-16. As early as 1929, Raymond C. Swensson, a senior student at a seminar on church history offered by Professor Adolf Hult at Augustana Seminary, wrote a paper about Lutheran missions in the world including a section on the "Porto Rican Mission." See Raymond C. Swensson, "Lutheran Missions in the World," (paper written for the seminar on church history at Augustana Seminary, 1929), 6-7. For another valuable history of the development of Lutheranism from 1898 up to 1983, see the article by Beverly Peterson, "The first 500 years," *Sunday San Juan Star Magazine* (November 6, 1983): 2-4.

8 Benjamin F. Hankey (1899-1900), Herbert F. Richards (1899-1905), Alfred Ostrom (1905-31), Axel Peter Gabriel Anderson (1907-18), Fred W. Lindke (1918-28), Hans Naether (1920-22), C. F. Knoll (1922), J. C. Pedersen (1923-27), Alberto Ell (1927-29), Gustav K. Huf (1924-32), William G. Arbaugh (1928-58), Lewis R. Fox (1935-36), P. E. Schoenemann (1936-37), Ms. Annete Wahlstedt (1900-5), Leonor Shaw (1909-10), Naomi Anderson (1907-9), Clara Hazelgreen (1904-7), May Mellander (1906-17), Emma Schmid (1914-22), Sofia Probst (1914-24), Nanca Schoen (1917-19), Frieda M. Hoh (1925-40), Florence Hines (1925-26), and Mary Markley (1929-30).

9 The former Roman Catholic priests Marciano López de Alda (1912-16), Evaristo Falcó Esteves from Venezuela (1937-70), Dionisio Miranda (1915-20), and Paul E. West (1915-19) from St. Croix, Virgin Islands.

10 Demetrio Texidor (1908-20; 1923-27), Guillermo Marrero (1911-64), Sergio Cobián (1914-62), Salustiano Hernández (1917-49), Eduardo Roig (1926-91), Alfredo Ortiz (1932-47), Balbino González (1927-35), and Leopoldo Cabán (1933-93).

11 Gabriela Cuervos (1905-13), Leonor Shaw (1909-10), María E. González (1909-10), Dolores Q. de Martínez (1910-14), Matilde Llanes (1912-17), Dolores Rosado (1917-18), Catalina Zambrana (1918-43), Nicolasa González (1920-22), Rosario Ojeda (1926-79), Berta Casos (1921-33), Rosa C. González (1922-23), Carmen M. Rosario (1919-21), Antonia Santana (1922-26), Rosa C. Miró de Cobián (1920-24), Demetria Sánchez (1913-14), Concepción González (1914-20), Genoveva Fernández (1913-17), Carmen Froilán (1913), Aurora Lomeña (1917-19), Mariana Ojeda (1917-20), Carmen L. de Hernández (1920-21), Ramona Sotomayor (1920-30), Marina Agostini (1927-33), Nieves Villarini (1926-29), Francisca Ayala (1930-35), Ana L. Sáenz (1926-31), Carmen M. Villarini (1930-93), Ana L. Domínguez (1931-34), Ofelia Baldorioty (1931-38), and Angélica Martínez (1931-36).

12 At this time these facilities were located on the second floor at the northeast corner of Luna and Tanca streets, next to the old "Escalerillas de San Francisco." *El Testigo*, año XXXII, no. 4 (September 1948): 4. At the beginning, these meetings were called "La Alianza Cristiana," but Mr. Swensson's intention was to develop a Lutheran mission. *El Testigo*, año XXII, no. 11 (April 1939): 8.
13 The members were: Mary J. Adams, S.R. van Beverhoudt, Mrs. Ana Louise van Beverhoudt, John F. Büdinger, Gildfort M. Crawford, Amelia E. Cummings, Susan Mathilda Simpson, Mrs. Anabelle A. O'Mahoney, James C. George, Rebecca A. George, Augusta Godfrey, Teresalia A. Hunt, Mary Jennsen, Erik Kilthoff, William Merkman, H. W. Meyer, Mrs. H. W. Meyer, Anna Moriah Peterson, Dr. R. M. Stimpson, Mrs. Emma H. Stimpson, Gusav S. Swensson, and Carl Thomson. The congregation included Anglicans, Moravians, and Wesleyans, but the majority were Lutherans. *El Testigo*, año XXII, no. 11 (April 1939): 4–5. The Spanish-language congregation of San Pablo was organized when the mission changed its location to a house in front of the Santo Cristo Street, and therefore was in front of the Roman Catholic cathedral in San Juan. *El Testigo*, año XXII, no. 11 (April 1939): 23. For a detailed history of the pastors of this congregation from its origin in 1900 up to 1940, see "Memorial Program: Fortieth Anniversary of the First Lutheran Congregation Organized in Puerto Rico," a January 1940 English supplement to *El Testigo*.
14 The distance between San Juan and Cataño is two miles. Instead of going by horseback, they took a ferry.
15 *El Testigo*, año XXII, no. 11 (April 1939): 5.
16 According to Luis Martínez-Fernández, "For decades, before the tolerance decrees of the late 1860s and early 1870s, thousands of Protestants from Europe, North America and the Caribbean found their way into Cuba and Puerto Rico. . . . Unacclimated immigrants and transient from higher altitudes, many of them Protestants were particularly vulnerable to the onslaught of tropical diseases so prevalent in the Spanish Caribbean. . . . The most dreaded foe of the unacclimated foreigner was yellow fever, a virus transmitted by mosquitoes that thrive in stagnant water." See Luis Martínez-Fernández, "'Don't Die Here': The Death and Burial of Protestants in the Hispanic Caribbean, 1840–1885," in *The Americas* XLVIV, no. I (July 1992): 26–28. In the November 1899 edition of a Roman Catholic journal, an article written by Mark W. Harrington concurred with Martínez-Fernandez's assessment by claiming, "it has the serious drawbacks of a tropical climate; always unfavorable for people from the temperate zone, and especially unfavorable, as history shows, to the great race called Anglo-Saxon, to which Americans generally belong." Mark W. Harrington, "Porto Rico and the Portorricans," *Catholic World* 70, no. 416 (November 1899): 164.
17 Stimpson and Brown, a fellow doctor that participated in the mission, were originally from Jamaica. *El Testigo*, año XXII, no. 11 (April 1939): 8.

18 *El Testigo*, año XXII, no. 11 (April 1939): 8. Rev. Hankey later died in Pittsburgh on November 5, 1930. "Rev Benjamin Franklin Hankey (1866–1930)," Find a Grave Memorial, accessed June 21, 2023, https://www.findagrave.com/memorial/115914529/benjamin-franklin-hankey.
19 *El Testigo*, año XXII, no. 11 (April 1939): 5–6.
20 Mr. Swensson also provided catechetical instruction in English to two young women who were later confirmed by the ordained pastors. *El Testigo*, año XXII, no. 11 (April 1939): 5.
21 Silva Gotay, *Protestantismo y política en Puerto Rico 1898-1930*, 167–71.
22 Following the direction of Bishop Joseph Blenk (the first North American bishop), the Roman Catholic Church struggled to regain its properties and establish a system of Roman Catholic schools. *El Ideal Católico*, año I, no. 3 (August 26, 1899), 17–19. For a detailed description of Bishop James Hubert Blenk's life and actions in Puerto Rico, see Sister Miriam Therese O'Brian, "Puerto Rico's First American Bishop," in *Records of the American Catholic Historical Society of Philadelphia* 91, no. 1/4 (March–December 1980): 3–37.
23 *El Ideal Católico*, año I, no. 1 (August 15, 1899): 1–2. For a distinction between the Roman Catholic faith and that of Protestants in Puerto Rico, see the satiric conversation between the imaginary young man Pepillo and his friend in *El Ideal Católico*, año I, no. 9 (October 6, 1899): 68.
24 Silva Gotay, *Protestantismo y política en Puerto Rico*, 168. Also, *El Ideal Católico*, año II, no. 8 (October 6, 1900): 77; *El Ideal Católico*, año II, no. 10 (October 20, 1900): 106; *El Ideal Católico*, año II, no. 11 (October 27, 1900): 120; *El Ideal Católico*, año I, no. 16 (November 25, 1899): 125.
25 *El Ideal Católico*, año I, no. 4 (September 2, 1899): 29. In the area of biblical studies, "Catholic epistles" (ἐπιστολαὶ καθολικαί) are those not written by Paul (or some of his followers), nor addressed to any community in particular, but to several. There are seven, the Epistles of James (one), Peter (two), John (three), and Jude (one). "Catholic Epistles," BiblicalTraining. org, accessed June 21, 2023, https://www.biblicaltraining.org/library/catholic-epistles.
26 *El Ideal Católico*, año I, no. 8 (September 30, 1899): 60.
27 On November 27, 1897, Chapelle was appointed Archbishop of New Orleans, following the demise of Msgr. Francis August Anthony Joseph Janssens. Archbishop Chapelle devoted most of his time to his foreign duties, after being named apostolic delegate to Cuba and the Philippines in 1898 and 1899.
28 On June 12, 1899, Blenk was appointed bishop of the then Diocese of Puerto Rico by Pope Leo XIII, receiving his episcopal consecration on the following July 2 from Archbishop Chapelle, assisted by bishops Gustave Rouxel and Theophile Meerschaert. Blenk was a Marist father. "Archbishop James Hubert Herbert Blenk (1856–1917)," Find a Grave Memorial, accessed June 21, 2023, https://www.findagrave.com/memorial/62689860/james-hubert_herbert-blenk.

29 See Samuel Silva Gotay, *Catolicismo y política en Puerto Rico bajo España y Estados Unidos siglos XIX y XX* (San Juan: Editorial de la Universidad de Puerto Rico, 2005), 73, 218, 220–21, 224–25, 237, 239, and 341.
30 Salvador Brau, *Historia de Puerto Rico* (New York: D. Appleton and Company, 1917), 307; Paul G. Miller, *Historia de Puerto Rico* (Chicago: Rand McNally & Co., 1922), 307; Carmelo Rosario Natal, *Puerto Rico y la crisis de la guerra Hispanoamericana* (Hato Rey: Ramallo Brothers Printing Co., 1975), 257–70; Martínez-Fernández, *Protestantism and Political Conflict in the Nineteenth-Century Hispanic Caribbean*, 75–171; Fernando Picó, *Historia General de Puerto Rico* (San Juan: Ediciones Huracán, 2006), 239; César J. Ayala and Rafael Bernabé, *Puerto Rico in the American Century: A History since 1898* (Chapel Hill: University of North Carolina Press, 2007), 16, 126–27; Ennis B. Edmonds and Michelle A. González, *Caribbean Religious History: An Introduction* (New York and London: New York University Press, 2010), 155–61.
31 Dr. Gerardo Alberto Hernández Aponte is a Puerto Rican historian. He earned a Bachelor's degree (2001), a Master's degree (2004), and a PhD degree (2010) in the area of history from the University of Puerto Rico.
32 For a more detailed description of this contention, see Gerardo Alberto Hernández, *La Iglesia Católica en Puerto Rico ante la invasión de Estados Unidos de América: Lucha, sobrevivencia y estabilización 1898–1921* (San Juan: Decanato de Estudiantes Graduados e Investigación (DEGI), Universidad de Puerto Rico, Recinto de Rio Piedras, Academia Puertorriqueña de la historia, 2013). Also, his review of Samuel Silva Gotay's book, "El nuevo libro de Samuel Silva Gotay," *El Visitante* (May 7 to May 13, 2013): 4–5.
33 William G. Arbaugh, *Notes and Quotes from the Correspondence of William George Arbaugh*, ed. William Charles Arbaugh (Portland: personal publication, 2000), 33.
34 "First Report of the Board of Porto Rico Missions to the General Council of the Evangelical Lutheran Church in North America" (October 1903), 5–8. *El Testigo* (September 1948): 6. In the September 10, 1903, edition of the *Boletín Mercantil de Puerto Rico*, one finds a note about the beginning of the construction of the first building of the Lutheran church in Puerto Rico. See *Boletín Mercantil de Puerto Rico* (September 10, 1903): 7, Library of Congress, https://chroniclingamerica.loc.gov/lccn/sn91099739/1903-09-10/ed-1/. However, in a special bulletin celebrating the sixty-ninth anniversary of the congregation, we find the following information: In May of 1899, the church is organized as a Lutheran mission by the student for the Lutheran ministry, Gustav Sigfried Swensson. Later, in 1902, under the guidance of Rev. Charles H. Hemsoth, they started the building construction that was completed by April 1903. The first ordained minister called to the congregation was Rev. H. F. Richards (1903–5), followed by Rev. Alfred Olstrom (1905–15), Rev. Aquilino López de Aldea (1917–17), Rev. Guillermo Marrero

(1917–21), Rev. Hans Naether (1921–25), Rev. Fred W. Lindke (1925–26), Rev. Salustiano Hernández (1926–49), Rev. Herminio Díaz (1949–55), Rev. José D. Rodríguez (1955–59; 1963–66), Rev. Luis Zayas (1959–63), Rev. Edelmiro Cortés (1967–70), Rev. Rafael Marcano (1970–71), and Rev. William Nieves (1972–78). "Bulletin for the Celebration of the 69th anniversary of the Lutheran Church Divino Salvador" (1973). In a later brochure, published in 1982, more names are added: Rev. José F. Ríos (1878–81) and Rev. Carmelo Nieves Canino (1982–). "Brochure of the Iglesia Evangélica Luterana del Divino Salvador" (1982). On December 8, 1903, the newspaper *La correspondencia de Puerto Rico* mentions that the building of the Lutheran church located in front of the San Juan Roman Catholic Cathedral and next to the hotel El Convento is about to be completed. See *La correspondencia de Puerto Rico* (December 8, 1903), Library of Congress, accessed June 21, 2023, https://chroniclingamerica.loc.gov/lccn/sn91099747/1903-12-08/ed-1/. Most pastors mentioned above moved to other congregations after their service to the one in Cataño.

35 "First Report of the Board of Porto Rico Missions to the General Council of the Evangelical Lutheran Church in North America" (October 1903), 3.

36 In his book on *Documentos Históricos de la Iglesia Episcopal,* Father Jorge Juan Rivera Torres presents a series of historical documents related to this incident. The documents show that the main reason for the Episcopal Church's desire to keep the property was her intention to build Saint John's Episcopal Church and make it the "episcopal" seat for Bishop James H. van Buren. It wasn't until the episcopate of Bishop C. B. Colmore that it was proposed to build a new cathedral church of San Juan Bautista in Santurce where it stands to this day. Jorge Juan Rivera Torres, *Documentos Históricos de la Iglesia Episcopal,* vol. I (Saint Just, Puerto Rico: Taller Episcográfico de la Iglesia Episcopal Puertorriqueña, 2008), 46–47.

37 Torres, *Documentos Históricos de la Iglesia Episcopal,* vol. I, 6–7. See also Conrad Bergendoff, *The Augustana Ministerium: A Study of the Careers of the 2,504 Pastors of the Augustana Evangelical Lutheran Synod/Church 1850–1962* (Rock Island, IL: Augustana Historical Society, 1980), 1897. In a lecture given by a distinguished Puerto Rican (Matienzo Cintrón) at the Ateneo of Puerto Rico published in 1903, he mentions the presence of the Lutheran church in Puerto Rico. *La correspondencia de Puerto Rico* (September 22, 1903), image 2, Library of Congress, accessed June 21, 2023, https://chroniclingamerica.loc.gov/lccn/sn91099747/1903-09-22/ed-1/. *La correspondencia de Puerto Rico* was a Puerto Rican newspaper that took its name from *La correspondencia de España.* It was founded by Ramón B. López in San Juan on December 18, 1890. Priced at one cent, it appealed to the general public and quickly became the largest circulating daily newspaper in Puerto Rico with a print run of 5,000 copies a day. Due to its popularity, it was given the sarcastic nickname of "El periódico de las cocineras." *La correspondencia de Puerto Rico* is considered the first daily news report

on the island accessible to a wider public. "About La correspondencia de Puerto Rico (San Juan, PR) 1890–1943," Library of Congress, accessed June 21, 2023, https://chroniclingamerica.loc.gov/lccn/sn91099747/. Rosendo Matienzo Cintrón was a Puerto Rican lawyer and politician, a member of the Puerto Rican House of Representatives, and a lifelong political contrarian. He favored Puerto Rican autonomy when Puerto Rico was a Spanish colony. After the Spanish–American War, when the island was ceded to the United States, he advocated statehood for Puerto Rico. In later years, Matienzo Cintrón supported Puerto Rico's independence. It is interesting to note that, in 1905, the same newspaper noted the town of Utuado as another place in which the Lutheran church had already established a sturdy masonry building. However, given that the same newspaper article refers to the return to Puerto Rico of the Presbyterian pastor Rev. Thomas Stevenson, the journalist writing the article may have confused the Presbyterian church with the Lutheran church. *La correspondencia de Puerto Rico* (November 29, 1905), image 3, Library of Congress, accessed June 21, 2023, https://chroniclingamerica.loc.gov/lccn/sn91099747/1905-11-29/ed-1/.
38 *El Testigo* (December 1948): 5.
39 *The Lutheran* I, no. 40 (January 29, 1920): 809.
40 *The Lutheran* I, no. 40: 809.
41 The distance between San Juan and Cataño is 9.3 miles, or 15 kilometers.
42 *El Testigo* (December 1948): 5.
43 The name of this municipality comes from the Taino (original people of the archipelago) word *toa*, which means *Mamá*, and which was the original name of the La Plata River, while the word *baja* refers to the large expanses of flat land that characterize the territory of Toa Baja. The productivity of its lands and the development of the sugar industry in Toa Baja made the town one of the main suppliers of food and drivers of economic development for San Juan. As the population of the capital increased, consumption of the produce of its farms and haciendas intensified. In the early twentieth century, Toa Baja, like other municipalities, was incorporated into the municipality of Bayamón through the Law for the Consolidation of Certain Municipal Terms of 1902. Three years later, the Legislative Assembly of Puerto Rico repealed this law and reconstituted Toa Baja as an independent municipality, with the same neighborhoods that made it up in 1902. See ToaBaha.org, accessed June 21, 2023, https://www.toabaja.com/historia/.
44 *El Testigo* (December 1948): 6.
45 In its edition of June 25, 1924, the Protestant journal *El Puerto Rico Evangélico* announced the approaching construction of a Lutheran chapel and clergy housing in Palo Seco, as well as an upcoming Lutheran church building in Bayamón. *El Puerto Rico Evangélico*, año 2, no. 24 (June 25, 1914): 15.
46 *El Testigo* (December 1948): 5.

47 *El Testigo* (December 1948): 5.
48 *El Testigo* (December 1948): 6.
49 *El Testigo* (December 1948): 14. The last location for the worship services of these congregations was on the second floor of Luna Street in front of the town hall. *El Testigo* (December 1948): 14. An important reason for the Lutheran mission to restrain its work in San Juan, as well as towns and cities close to San Juan, was due in part to honor the agreement of other Protestant denominations that had decided to divide their work in different parts of the island during 1898. Another important reason was the reduced financial support they received from the mission boards in the United States.
50 *El Mundo* (December 27, 1919): 4, Library of Congress, accessed June 21, 2023, https://chroniclingamerica.loc.gov/lccn/sn86077151/1919-02-27/ed-1/.
51 Rev. Axel Peter Gabriel Anderson arrived in Puerto Rico on April 26, 1907. On April 27 the Lutheran church held a special worship service for his service in the mission. *La correspondencia de Puerto Rico*, año XVII, no. 5,915 (April 27, 1907): 3. In the edition of April 27, 1907, the *Boletín Mercantil de Puerto Rico* mentions a celebration given by the Lutheran church in San Juan to Rev. Axel Peter Gabriel from New York, on his visit to Puerto Rico. See *Boletín Mercantil de Puerto Rico* (April 27, 1907): 4, Library of Congress, https://chroniclingamerica.loc.gov/lccn/sn91099739/1907-04-27/ed-1/. The *Boletín Mercantil de Puerto Rico* first appeared on March 2, 1839, published as the *Boletín Instructivo y mercantil de Puerto Rico*, in San Juan. The Puerto Rico scholar Antonio S. Pedreira, in the voluminous *El periodismo en Puerto Rico*, underlined its importance as "a newspaper of transcendental significance in the history of newspapers in Puerto Rico." The *Boletín Mercantil* is regarded as one of the most important newspapers, second to the *Gaceta*, published in Puerto Rico during the last of the four centuries of Spanish domination on the island. It started as a biweekly publication, eventually becoming a daily paper. See https://chroniclingamerica.loc.gov/lccn/sn91099739/. In its edition of April 27, 1907, *La correspondencia de Puerto Rico* amplified this news, claiming that Rev. Axel Peter Gabriel Anderson was planning to join the mission in a special service to be held the next day at the Lutheran church. See *La correspondencia de Puerto Rico* (April 27, 1907).
52 *El Testigo* (December 1948): 5–6. After a successful surgery Miss Schoen would return to the Lutheran Mission in Puerto Rico to supervise all educational activities in the various islands, devoting special attention to the training of kindergarten teachers. *The Lutheran* I, no. 47 (March 18, 1920): 934.
53 *El Testigo* (December 1948): 6.
54 *El Testigo* (December 1948): 6.
55 *The Lutheran* I, no. 47 (March 18, 1920): 934.
56 *El Testigo*, año XXXII, no. 7 (December 1948): 5.

57 The process of identifying native leaders for the different needs of the Lutheran missions in other parts of the world varied according to the circumstances of mission sites.
58 Arbaugh, "Fred W. Lindke and the Era of Transition: Puerto Rico Lutheran History from 1918 to 1928," *El Testigo*, año XXXII, no. 8 (January 1949): 13–16.
59 This may be shown by the practical but elementary course of study provided by the North American missionaries and Mr. Marciano López de Alda (an ex-priest from Colombia, South America, who was placed as assistant to the senior missionary in San Juan and Cataño). For a more comprehensive overview of the content of the seminary curriculum, see the "Sixth Biennial Report of the Porto Rico Mission Board to the General Council of the Evangelical Lutheran Church of North America" (1913), 7, 12, in which the following courses are mentioned: History of Porto Rico, Music, Life of Christ, Life of Paul, Bible Facts and Scenes, Study of the Pericopes, History of the Christian Church, Bible Introduction, Dogmatics, Christian Evidences, and some Pastoral Theology. Additional information about this curriculum was also mentioned in the "Seventh Biennial Report of the Board of Missions for Porto Rico and Latin America of the General Council of the Evangelical Lutheran Church in North America" (1915), 12. To be sure, the curriculum of Lutheran seminaries in the United States at that time was that of a higher learning institution. At this juncture there was no talk of sending smart Puerto Ricans off to the mainland colleges. In anticipation of developing the seminary, the Lutheran church in Cataño provided lectures for students which were open to the public. On February 7, 1907, the newspaper *La democracia* mentioned the lectures on the Reformation offered by José Storer. See *La democracia* (February 7, 1907): 2, Library of Congress, accessed June 21, 2023, https://chroniclingamerica.loc.gov/lccn/sn90070270/1907-02-07/ed-1/seq-1/. *La democracia* was founded and published by the Puerto Rican poet, journalist, and politician Luis Muñoz Rivera. It was first published in Ponce in 1890. It advocated the principles of the Autonomist Party, of a liberal nature that sought greater rights with the Spanish Crown. By 1905, the newspaper was advertised as the most widely circulated newspaper in Puerto Rico and based in San Juan. At that time, the newspaper was more interested in the news that is created from the governmental spheres. See Library of Congress, accessed June 21, 2023, https://chroniclingamerica.loc.gov/lccn/sn90070270/. Swensson, "I Went to Puerto Rico," 16.
60 Swensson, "I Went to Puerto Rico," 16. In an article written by Leopoldo Cabán in *El Testigo*, the name of Alfredo Mercado is added to the list. *El Testigo*, año XXI, no. 1 (June 1937): 16. See also *El Testigo*, año XXXII, no. 8 (January 1949): 5–6; James A. McAllister, "Un Ministerio Bien Preparado," *Puerto Rico Evangélico* 2 (1914): 2–4; Santiago-Vendrell, "Give Them Christ," 4, 7–8. See also James A. McAllister, "The Presbyterian Theological Training

School," in *The Assembly Herald* 4 (1908): 207, and by the same author, "Un Ministerio Bien Preparado," *Puerto Rico Evangélico* 2 (1914): 2-4.
61 McAllister, "Un Ministerio Bien Preparado." Santiago-Vendrell, "Give Them Christ." See also McAllister, "The Presbyterian Theological Training School," and by the same author, "Un Ministerio Bien Preparado.".
62 Some of them were instrumental in facilitating the establishment of valuable relationships with North American Lutheran Church bodies for the financial support of the Lutheran mission. See *La correspondencia*, año XXX, no. 10,916 (February 28, 1922): 2. We also need to recognize the contributions of Lutheran lay people like Dr. Stimpson, who played an important role in this mission. See the newspaper *La democracia* (June 6, 1901), Library of Congress, accessed June 21, 2023, https://chroniclingamerica.loc.gov/lccn/sn90070270/1901-06-06/ed-1/.
63 Swensson, "I Went to Puerto Rico," 16.
64 Arbaugh, "Fred W. Lindke and the Era of Transition," 7. My understanding of the reasons leading to the ordination of these native candidates point to the collective contribution of the following elements: (i) the perseverance and determination of Puerto Rican candidates to request ordination; (ii) the vision and creative initiatives of church leaders (Rev. Zenan M. Corbe, Rev. B. F. Hankey, Rev. Hans Naether, and Rev. Gustav K. Huf) and, (iii) two seminarians in the Philadelphia Lutheran Seminary (Eduardo Roig and William G. Arbaugh) voicing support for this request to meet the need for additional partners in ministry for Lutheran missionary expansion in Puerto Rico. Arbaugh, 14. It is interesting to note that the prominent Protestant journal *Puerto Rico Evangélico* included an invitation to its readers to participate in this ordination celebrating that one of these ministers, Demetrio Texidor, collaborated with the journal. *Puerto Rico Evangélico* (July 9, 1926): 12. For other valuable information about this important event, see *El Testigo*, año X, no. 2 (July 1926): 1. This event was so important that other Protestant denominations in Puerto Rico also celebrated it. See *Puerto Rico Evangélico*, año XV, no. 1 (July 9, 1926): 12.
65 *Puerto Rico Evangélico*, año 1, no. 19 (April 10, 1913): 7. See also Appendix 1.
66 *Puerto Rico Evangélico*, año 1, no. 19 (April 10, 1913): 10.
67 *Puerto Rico Evangélico*, año 3, no. 24 (June 25, 1915): 7.
68 While Rev. Fred W. Lindke was not originally planning to be a missionary in Puerto Rico, he later became an important leader of the Lutheran mission. When he was pastor of Holy Trinity Lutheran Church in Bayamón, the Eighth Annual Spanish Conference of the United Lutheran Church was held in his congregation. One of the features of this two-day conference that would impress the church in the United States, was the fact that there were five sermons, in addition to five addresses upon doctrinal subjects, and six addresses upon practical and devotional subjects. *The Lutheran* I, no. 47 (March 18, 1920): 934.
69 *El Testigo* (January 1949): 4.

70 At that time the only languages available in the curriculum of Lutheran seminaries were German, the biblical languages of Hebrew and Coine Greek.
71 *El Imparcial* (May 15, 1923): 4, Library of Congress, accessed June 21, 2023, https://chroniclingamerica.loc.gov/lccn/sn88073003/1923-05-15/ed-1/.
72 *El Testigo* (January 1949): 4–5. In recognition of his valuable contributions Augustana College conferred on Pastor Ostrom the honorific degree of Doctor of Divinity. *El Testigo* (January 1949): 5.
73 Rev. Philo W. Drury (BA, MA, DD) was the executive secretary of the Puerto Rican Evangelical Union.
74 Rev. Philo W. Drury, "Las Iglesias Protestantes," in *El Libro de Puerto Rico (The Book of Porto Rico)*, ed. E. Fernández García (San Juan: El Libro Azul Publishing Co., 1923), 145–46, translation mine.
75 *El Testigo* (January 1949): 6–7. This was the first Spanish-speaking Lutheran congregation in Puerto Rico.
76 *El Testigo* (January 1949): 7, 9–10. These were established congregations and the reason to place these ordained Puerto Rican pastors was to have Puerto Ricans own the work of the Lutheran mission in Puerto Rico.
77 *El Testigo* (January 1949): 7, 9–10. Among them were Mrs. Concepción González, Miss Carmen Froylán, Miss Mariana Agostini, Miss Nieves Villarini, Miss Catalina Zambrana, Miss Berta Casos, Miss Aurora Lomeña, Miss Mariana Ojeda, Miss Carmen Matilde Rosario, Mrs. Ramona Sotomayor Lomeña, Miss Nicolasa Hernández, Miss Rosario Ojeda, Miss Rosa C. González, Miss Antonia Santana, and Miss Ana Luisa Saenz. *El Testigo* (January 1949): 12.
78 *El Testigo*, año XVII, no. 2 (March 1935): 14–15. It is interesting to note that, in 1951, a Protestant journal in Puerto Rico indicated that this congregation, along with another ministry in Spanish in this city (Iglesia Luterana Sión led by Rev. Antonio Contreras), extended its ministry to a Latinx Lutheran constituency in the city of New York. *Puerto Rico Evangélico*, año XXXIX, no. 1,089 (July 25, 1951): 13. It is important to note too that prior to the development of these Spanish-speaking ministries, leaders of the West Indies Mission Board had recognized the valuable contribution of West Indian Lutherans in enriching the Lutheran legacy in that city. In 1920, Z. M. Corbe, then executive secretary of the board, wrote an article in *The Lutheran* outlining this extraordinary contribution of Lutherans from the West Indies, including Puerto Rico. See *The Lutheran* II, no. 1 (September 30, 1920): 9.
79 *El Testigo*, año XXI, no. 1 (June 1937): 19–20.
80 Sergio Cobián was another Puerto Rican Lutheran ordained minister who became a missionary in Texas and Arizona. In a letter sent to the important Protestant journal *Puerto Rico Evangélico*, he described the infamous treatment received by African Americans, Mexicans, and Puerto Ricans workers picking cotton in these states. See *Puerto Rico Evangélico*, año XV, no. 18 (November 6, 1926): 12. Rev. Cobián had served as a Puerto Rican lay worker

THE MISSION AND ITS TRAILBLAZERS

in the Lutheran mission in 1914. He joined the US military during World War I. After his seminary studies in the Lutheran Seminary in Philadelphia, he was ordained in 1926, while serving at a Lutheran congregation in Texas. In 1931, he returned to Puerto Rico becoming the pastor of congregations in Dorado, Toa Baja, and San Juan. Finally, he was called to the Lutheran Church Santísima Trinidad in Bayamón, the place where he was born.

81 Agostini graduated from the Philadelphia Seminary on June 3, 1937, along with Elmer Herman Ganskopp. Both came to work at the Lutheran mission in Puerto Rico. Agostini became pastor of the Dorado-Higuillar-Maracayo parish. Ganskopp, who arrived in Puerto Rico on June 24 of that year, became assistant to the Rev. W. G. Arbaugh in the Puerta de Tierra parish. Full information about Agostini's life and preparation for the ministry appeared in the June 1937 edition of *El Testigo*. *El Testigo*, año XXI, no. 2 (July 1937): 12.
82 *El Testigo*, año XXII, no. 11 (April 1939): 12.
83 *El Testigo*, año XXII, no. 11 (April 1939): 4.
84 *The Lutheran* (March 18, 1920): 5.
85 *Puerto Rico Evangélico*, año 2, no. 16 (February 25, 1914): 14. See also *Puerto Rico Evangélico*, año 2, no. 23 (June 10, 1914): 14.
86 In August 12, 1920, *The Lutheran* reported that Miss Sofía Probst engaged in special training to continue her work in Puerto Rico with students in kindergarten. *The Lutheran* II, no. 15 (August 12, 1920): 256.
87 *El Mundo* (November 9, 1924): 1, 8, Library of Congress, accessed June 21, 2023, https://chroniclingamerica.loc.gov/lccn/sn86077151/1924-11-09/ed-1/. The ministry to lepers was very important for the Lutheran mission. The missionaries preached, brought gifts provided by women's organizations in the United States, and imparted entertainment. *The Lutheran* II, no. 9 (March 18, 1920): 216.
88 See *The Lutheran* II, no. 16 (September 9, 1920): 261.
89 In *The Lutheran*, September 30, 1920, an article written by Z. M. Corbe reported that Rev. Ostrom was planning a trip to Santo Domingo to establish the work of the Lutheran church, for it was said many Lutherans had been established in that country. *The Lutheran* III, no. 1 (September 30, 1920): 9.
90 *El Testigo*, año XIX, no. 12 (May 1936): 12. Donald T. Moore wrote a doctoral dissertation on a history of the progress of the evangelical mission on the island of Puerto Rico and in one of its sections he describes the work of the Lutheran mission from 1898 to 1912.
91 See, for example, *Puerto Rico Evangélico*, año 2, no. 24 (June 25, 1914): 15.
92 *The Lutheran* (March 18, 1920): 8. For a further description on the progress of the Lutheran and other evangelical missions in Puerto Rico, see Donald T. Moore, *Puerto Rico Para Cristo: A History of the Progress of the Evangelical Mission on the Island of Puerto Rico* (Cuernavaca: Centro Intercultural de Documentación, SONDEOS no. 43, 1969), 17–22.

CHAPTER 5

A Mission Coming of Age

One of Puerto Rico's important contributions to music is the *Plena*. According to several scholars, the *plena* is a Puerto Rican musical genre with a long and important tradition:

> The tradition of plena music, which is rooted historically in both the Puerto Rican and African music-cultures, encapsulates the struggles of the commoner in Puerto Rican society amid rapid, drastic sociopolitical changes, ultimately uniting the working-class against injustices and oppression. It is a mixture of the musical and cultural lineages of the native Puerto Rican people and those of Africa.[1] Plena is a musical genre that not only reminds Puerto Ricans of their culture and heritage, but also serves as a medium for catalyzing progressive social change.[2]

Among the many popular *plenas* there is one by the name *Temporal* that seems to provide a good description of the experience of Puerto Ricans under the colonial burden of the early Spanish and later North American imperial dominion, and particularly after the North American military invasion of the island at the end of the nineteenth century. The lyrics of the *plena* go like this:

> Temporal, temporal
> Allá viene el temporal
> Temporal, temporal
> Allá viene el temporal
>
> Que será de mi Borinquen
> Cuando llegue el temporal
> Que será de Puerto Rico
> Cuando llegue el temporal[3]
>
> Storm, Storm
> What a tremendous storm!
> Storm, Storm
> What a terrible storm!
>
> What will become of Puerto Rico
> When the storm passes?
> What will become of Puerto Rico
> When the storm passes?[4]

At the end of the Spanish–American War, Puerto Rico was ceded to the United States by Spain as war booty. A military government was established on the island under the command of General John A. Brook.[5] After two years, and the ratification by the United States Congress of the Foraker Law, a civil government was instituted in 1900, although the governor was still imposed by the president of the United States.[6] Puerto Rico also suffered devastation produced by the hurricanes San Ciriaco (August 8, 1899)[7] and San Ciprián (September 24, 1932). The former was unquestionably the worst natural calamity experienced in Puerto Rico up to that time. Even though Puerto Rico had experienced the misfortunes of other powerful hurricanes during the nineteenth century, San Ciriaco was exceptional, especially because it occurred immediately after the change in the archipelago's sovereignty.[8] I am using the plena *Temporal* as a popular symbolic expression of these calamities impacting the people in Puerto Rico from the turn of the nineteenth century to the present.

However, not everything experienced during this early period of Puerto Rican colonial government by the United States was adverse. In fact, at the start of the century many Puerto Ricans were eager for the United States to extend its influence in the archipelago, assuming that it would transform the Spanish colonial regime to one of democracy.[9] As we mentioned in earlier parts of this study, this was precisely the attitude of Gustav Sigfried Swensson and many of the early North American missionaries. This expectation was also shared by Lutheran Puerto Rican leaders, leading to increased development for the Lutheran mission in the archipelago.

On January 22–23, 1912, under the leadership of Rev. Alfred Ostrom, the 1st Lutheran Conference was held in San Pablo's Lutheran church. Meeting attendees decided to hold an annual conference and a bimonthly missionary meeting to continue the support and development of the mission.[10] As Puerto Rican clergy emerged, they were included in this organizational structure, yet the mission's North American missionary founders remained in control. This type of administrative supervision of the mission stayed in place until the establishment of the Caribbean Synod in 1952.

THE DEPRESSION'S LOCAL IMPACTS

In addition to the colonial nature of the Puerto Rican government, and the natural calamities suffered, the island also experienced a great economic depression from 1929 to 1940.[11] This was a time of great political changes, massive unemployment,[12] workers' strikes, the collapse of the educational system, and the demise of the sugar industry. Puerto Rico was impoverished. In 1929, Theodore Roosevelt Jr., who had been appointed governor of the island, published in the *New York Herald Tribune* the following:

We were and are a prey to diseases of many kinds. In the fiscal year ending June 30th 1929 4,442 of the people died from tuberculosis. . . . Some 35,000 in our island are now suffering from tuberculosis, some 20,000 from malaria, and some 60,000 from hookworm.[13]

This economic depression impacted Puerto Rico's society and culture. Suicides and crime increased. This crisis provoked a drop in the demand for and sale of Puerto Rican products abroad, affecting producers of goods such as tobacco, coffee, and sugar.[14]

The financial condition of all the Protestant churches during the period of the Great Depression were adversely affected. The subsidies provided by their North American boards and church bodies were severely reduced. This decline in financial resources from their respective North American partners affected the phase of church building and church improvement, as well as the financial circumstances of Puerto Rican church lay workers. Michael Saenz argues that,

The working personnel was asked to either continue working full-time with the churches at very low salaries or to obtain an extra secular job that would enable them to support their families during those years. Many pastors left the ministry to find work elsewhere.[15]

Notwithstanding the crisis of the economic depression, church attendance among Protestants in Puerto Rico did not decrease substantially during these dismal years. While the average growth in membership of the Lutheran mission from 1921 to 1928 was nineteen members each year, the average increase per year between 1929 and 1936 was twelve.[16]

Among the reasons for the continued growth of Protestantism during these periods, Saenz claims that: (i) missionaries from the United States, national pastors, and members of the congregations learned to appreciate and understand each other better; (ii) the churches and their people became evangelism-minded and everyone employed their energies to bring new people into the church; (iii) recognizing that, without warning, help from outside sources could be cut off, they began to depend on their own resources; and (iv) people developed out of their experience of hunger and spiritual searching a stronger faith, a deeper personal knowledge of God, and a greater sense of the power of prayer.[17]

Another important consideration for this growth among Protestants in Puerto Rico relates to Puerto Rican migration to the United States. While employment and better earnings in the United States were notable motivations for these early resettlements, during the Great Depression of the 1930s, migration to the United States discontinued, and in some years the flow reverted toward the island.[18] For many Puerto Ricans conditions in the United States became so bad, given the far-reaching industrial crisis, that they decided to return to their former homes.[19]

In 1937, the statistics for the Lutheran mission presented at the annual meeting of Lutheran congregations in Puerto Rico showed some growth in confirmed members (882), a new missionary from the United States (E. H. Granskopp), and another from Venezuela,[20] with sixteen students at the University of Puerto Rico[21] preparing for their seminary studies, one at a Lutheran seminary in the United States, and an increase in field contributions ($4,494.86).[22] This was also the year when *El Testigo* published the first Lutheran book in Spanish,[23] along with another Spanish version of Martin Luther's *Small Catechism* already in use in Spain.[24]

In 1940, the Lutheran mission celebrated the fortieth anniversary of its formal organization. At that time there were a total of twelve ordained pastors,[25] and the membership of congregations was greater than ever in its forty years of mission. There were a total of thirteen organized congregations, with 1,040 confirmed and 3,286 baptized members. The eighteen Sunday schools reported 101 teachers and 2,306 pupils, there were ten Luther Leagues[26] with a membership of 362, nine Women's Missionary Societies with 275 members, and five Brotherhoods with a membership of 140. Two congregations shouldered a larger share of self-support, while local contributions in sustaining this trend were superior to those at any previous time.[27] In this year, Transfiguración Lutheran Church was established in the city of Río Piedras, with Rev. Leopoldo Cabán as pastor.[28]

One of the most important highlights of the celebration was the publication of the long-awaited "Manual de Culto Cristiano," a remarkable aid for worship, with over 300 pages of worship aids and 355 hymns. This worship resource became the most comprehensive work of its kind in the Spanish language regardless of denominational sponsorship.[29] As the mission's fortieth anniversary celebrations noted, these trends were already apparent before the United States' growing involvement in World War II jump-started the country's Depression-stalled economy.

WORLD WAR II IN PUERTO RICO

In spite of these encouraging developments, at this time Puerto Ricans, in common with most parts of the world, faced the frightening threat of a second world war.[30] In preparing Lutheran congregations to face this menace, Rev. Dr. Frederick H. Knubel, then president of the United Lutheran Church in America, sent an open letter that was published in *El Testigo*. In the letter, President Knubel censured the way the advocates of nations worldwide tended to justify the conflict, calling believers for a witness of faith through a practice of love to ease the suffering of the victims, leading to the end of hostilities.[31]

In his well-documented dissertation on the economic aspects of the Protestant Church development in Puerto Rico, Saenz argues that from 1941 to 1946 some churches benefited financially from the effects of World War II, because they were forced to depend less on outside sources to carry on their work. This period was the first time that contributions from local Protestant churches exceeded the amounts sent by mission boards in the continental United States. Unfortunately, in five denominations, including the Lutheran

Church, the increases in local contributions were still insufficient to extend beyond the resources coming from their mainland mission boards. In his study, Saenz identifies the following churches as reaching this goal: the American Baptists, the Disciples of Christ, the Congregational Churches, and the Seventh-day Adventists. The following were those that, while increasing their local contributions, did not surpass the resources sent by the mission boards: the Episcopal Church, the Lutheran Church, the Methodists, the Presbyterians, and the United Brethren.[32]

In terms of church membership, between 1941 and 1946 all the island's Protestant churches reported a total increase of 5,209.[33] This buildup took place despite the fact that many sons of Protestant families registered in the military and this departure into the armed forces reduced the numbers in the churches' pews. The average increase per year in membership for this period was 1,042, as compared with 685 for the years from 1929 to 1941.[34]

Regarding national lay workers, some were recruited for military service as they were preparing for the ministry, while others volunteered for war-related positions. However, the war did not have a detrimental effect on the number of full-time workers of the different church groups.[35]

In 1941, the statistics for the Lutheran Church showed a significant increase in confirmed membership (1,041) and field contributions ($6,714.87). However, they also showed that 123 members were lost,[36] and the cumulative expenses for the mission rose to $6,165.64. Among the congregations with greater income was Divino Salvador (Cataño), one of the longer-established groups, with $1,202.92. The one with the lowest income was San Juan (Higuillar—1912), with $40.19. The total funds sent for benevolence[37] were $615.20.[38]

On June 3, 1941, Rev. Alfred Ostrom, who with his wife Betty had led the growth of the Lutheran mission work in Puerto Rico for twenty-six years, died after a long illness.[39] On June 12, one week after his funeral service in Cleveland, Ohio, a memorial service was held by Lutherans in Puerto Rico at San Pablo Lutheran Church in San Juan where he once served. At the service, Rev. Eduardo Roig, the conference president who had been a member of Rev. Ostrom's congregation during his youth, spoke on behalf of Puerto Rican Lutherans, honoring the contributions of Rev. Ostrom and his wife to the Lutheran mission in Puerto Rico, while Rev. William G. Arbaugh, board representative, provided a eulogy. In his homage to the ministry of this missionary couple, Arbaugh stated:

> Just as this beautiful St. Paul's Church, where we are gathered for this memorial service, [is] a monument that testifies of the firmness and reality of the Lutheran faith which Alfred Ostrom preached by precept and example, and a monument as well to the great love that he and his wife had for Puerto Rico and its people. So also, the Lutheran mission in Puerto Rico reveals much of the heart and mind of that same man of God, a faithful disciple, a zealous witness, a consecrated and tireless ambassador of the Kingdom.[40]

The year 1942 was a time when the Lutheran mission in Puerto Rico had to face both a world and local crisis. The ravages of World War II and distressed conditions across the world critically affected life on the archipelago. Unemployment rose; the German U-boat threat made importing an adequate supply of food more difficult; most Puerto Rican industries were crippled due to their dependance on sea transportation; commerce faced utter stagnation; sugar warehouses could not find ships for exportation; and importers' storehouses were empty of rice, flour, and potatoes. Thousands of young men entered the armed forces, yet thousands of others were standing idle and looking to the government for assistance.[41]

The effect of these conditions on the Lutheran mission was serious, but potentially hopeful. While four Puerto Rican pastors resigned their positions in local congregations, moving to other areas of employment in the secular world which were suffering from labor shortages, seven remained in service, among them only one missionary from North America (Arbaugh).[42]

In the first place, the reports [at the annual convention of the Conference] were good. President Eduardo Roig was able to record that, in spite of the shortage of ministers, the spirit and general state of the Church were good throughout the field. There are three students for the ministry. The Committee on Evangelism pointed to a gain in confirmed and communing members, the Committee on Stewardship to a gain of exactly one dollar in per capita offerings. Treasurer Guillermo E. Marrero reported the largest benevolent offering in history. The writer [Arbaugh] as representative of the Board of American Missions, revealed that three parishes had voted an increase in self-support. An augmented membership in the Sunday Schools was noted, as well as an increase in the circulation of our Conference monthly organ, "El Testigo."[43]

There was plenty to be proud of. In the April 1943 edition of *El Testigo*, Arbaugh wrote a review of the book *The Church in Puerto Rico's Dilemma* by J. Merle Davis, encouraging pastors and all missionary institutions to read it.[44] The book, the product of a study made in the island in 1941 by Davis, then head of the Social and Economic Investigations of the International Missionary Council, remained limited in its study of several areas, but made a great contribution in addressing the challenge of developing self-support for denominational congregations in Puerto Rico. For Arbaugh, who was president of the interdenominational committee that worked with the author in his investigations, the recommendations Davis offered in the book, while in need of further development given the complex character of the factors that interplayed in this process, were worth being employed to improve the plan and methods suggested, and to achieve the goal of self-support of congregations in the archipelago.[45]

The report of the 34th Annual Lutheran Missionary Conference of Puerto Rico held at Zion Church, Bayamón, on January 27–28, 1945, was notable for hopefulness and planning. According to the statistics, the previous year was again one during which much was achieved. Confirmed membership in Puerto Rican Lutheran churches increased from 1,177 in 1944, to 1,222 in 1945. Congregational offerings totaled $10,021 in 1944, and $13,132 in 1945. Benevolence offerings in 1945 were $1,371, which compared favorably with $1,114 in 1944. Pastor Arbaugh, representing the Board of American Missions, presented two new missionaries to the conference: pastors Carlos A. Torres and Richard A. Gaenslen. He also spoke at length about the afflictions facing our millions of Lutheran brothers and sisters in Germany and other lands, which led the conference to include in its 1946 budget, in addition to $500 for general United Lutheran Church in America benevolence, a further sum of $600 for Lutheran World Action.[46]

THE COMPLICATED POSTWAR WORLD

After World War II, a development policy for achieving fast industrialization of the island's economic structure was established by the government, which called it "Operation Bootstrap." This economic program had an important impact in developing new Protestant churches by raising the per capita income of Puerto Rican families. The prosperity achieved by the families, together with their commitment for stewardship, led to an increase in their local church contributions.

> Whereas before this economic program was begun per capita income was merely $121 as of 1940, and per family income was only $660 in that same period, the success of this self-help program raised the standards of living to all-time highs.[47]

This newly found prosperity in the ranks of the Protestant churches resulted in a tremendous increase in contribution to the churches on the island.[48] Yet not everything in this economic development plan was positive:

More than a half century's experience, however, indicates that Operation Bootstrap has had mixed results for Puerto Rico. There is no question that within decades the profile of its labor force changed to approximate that of the United States and other developed countries with proportionately few workers remaining in agriculture, many more in industry, and the majority in services. There is also no question that Puerto Rico's living conditions improved, though they are still far from being at a par with those in the United States. . . . But Operation Bootstrap also increased the economic dependence of Puerto Rico on the United States, undercutting [the] development of a self-sustaining economy and economic sovereignty. . . . Operation Bootstrap never accomplished one of its promised objectives: to reduce unemployment to tolerable limits. Official unemployment figures remain much higher on the island than in the United States. . . . A significant proportion of the unemployed then migrated to the United States in search of work. In 1940, before the advent of Operation Bootstrap, 96 percent of all Puerto Ricans lived on the island. . . . A significant proportion of the unemployed then migrated to the United States in search of work. . . . For the migrants though, life in the United States has proved to be problematic. Despite having on average higher incomes and less poverty than their island counterparts, their economic conditions remain among the lowest of ethnic groups in the United States, in large part owing to considerable discrimination and ethnic and racial prejudice.[49]

The Second Latin American Congress of Evangelical Youth was held August 1–4, 1946, in Havana, Cuba, at which Puerto Rican Lutheran representatives were part of the delegation meeting to explore the topic of "Christian Youth and Liberty." Among the significant recommendations made by the Commission of Religious Liberty at the event was one relating to economic considerations. This commission pronounced itself against the economic imperialism negatively affecting the Americas for being at variance with our Christian values. To that effect, a recommendation was made for an interaction among evangelical youth in the Americas for recognition of, and action against, this problem.[50] Clearly the United States of America was one of the imperialist colonial countries at the time. It is not clear whether the Puerto Rican Lutheran delegation agreed or not to this recommendation. What cannot be denied is that they did not challenge it at the Evangelical Youth Congress, but rather included it in their report that was published in the September 1946 edition of *El Testigo*, implying that it was, in their opinion, an important recommendation to share with their constituency.

An important incident which took place during 1946 was a letter written by Pastor Arbaugh on April 1, when he was secretary for Latin America of the Board of American Missions. The letter explored possible advantages and disadvantages for a proposed organization of the Lutheran Missionary Conference of Puerto Rico as a member synod of the United Lutheran Church in America, at its thirty-seventh annual convention on January 1, 1949. Among the advantages mentioned in the letter were: (i) the fact that whatever the political future of Puerto Rico, proponents of all the suggested solutions for the island's political problems (independence, statehood, dominion status, etc.) assumed that Puerto Rico would continue to have very close economic ties with the United States; (ii) Puerto Rican Lutherans saw the growth of their church as directly paralleling the diminishing of isolation and the strengthening of ties with the church in the United States; (iii) the prospect of sending delegates to the biannual ULCA conventions was particularly appealing to Puerto Rican Lutherans; and (iv) the organization of a synod might facilitate pastors in Puerto Rico participating more fully in the consideration of matters affecting the whole ULCA, such as general Lutheran causes in evangelism and stewardship, and not just the ones relating to their congregations in the archipelago.

In terms of disadvantages, the following were considered: (i) the geographical problem (the distance between Puerto Rico and the ULCA location) perhaps would be reduced, but it would not disappear; (ii) the linguistic problem (the use of Spanish instead of English), though it was not considered to be a serious one; (iii) the economic standard of living in Puerto Rico was lower than in the United States, thus making the contributions in benevolence smaller, though the recent growth in stewardship, in addition to its full membership in the ULCA, would continue to stimulate the growth in benevolence by the churches in Puerto Rico; and (iv) the condition of rural congregations (in numbers, education, and finances), some of which were so weak as to render normal congregational life impossible. The letter continues by describing the difficulties of including the Virgin Islands in the arrangement, given the obvious advantages of embracing them as part of the synod. Problems included: (i) the lack of native ministers in the Virgin Islands, with no prospects of changing the situation in the future; (ii) a resulting linguistic problem in requiring the use of both Spanish and English at synodical gatherings; and (iii) the problem of the significant difference between the field of Puerto Rico and the Virgin Islands.

The rationale for this proposal was based on the recent organization of the British Guiana mission as an autonomous synod associated with the ULCA, a territory which had fewer ministers and less economic stability than the Puerto Rican mission when comparing the 1944 statistics of the two fields. This comparison was taken further to contrast the autonomous status secured by the British Guiana Synod. The goal of Puerto Rico's Lutherans was to organize a synod as an integral part of the ULCA, rather than a sister synod, and the letter was framed as a proposal for a study to determine when such a step was to be advised.[51]

It is clear that Arbaugh shared the content of his 1946 letter with delegates at the thirty-fourth annual assembly of the Lutheran Missionary Conference of Puerto Rico. The assembly resolved to have its executive committee make a study of the possibilities of establishing a Lutheran synod in Puerto Rico. At this juncture, and when set in the context of the recognition given to the smaller, poorer, British Guiana province, the project made the transition from a pipe dream among individual ministers to a proposal shared among a wider group of Puerto Rico's Lutherans.[52]

The year 1948 saw valuable progress in most aspects of the Lutheran mission. The conference program incorporated a special celebration of the contributions of Pastor Swensson, who died at his home in Detroit, Michigan on January 13, 1948, at seventy-eight years of age. The statistics pointed to a small increase in the membership of the congregations, despite the continuous emigration of members of this mission field to the United States. There was a gain of 203 in baptized members over the previous year, as well as an increase of thirty-three confirmed members. The total financial contributions of the field were $20,240, a gain of 6 percent over the $19,077 registered in 1946. While pastors and lay delegates to the conference were pleased with the progress, they showed more interest in the upcoming celebration in 1949 of the fiftieth anniversary of the founding of the mission.[53]

As plans for the fiftieth anniversary were being developed during 1948, Pastor Arbaugh made a trip to the United States, during which he examined some of the personal documents written by Pastor Swensson during his stay in Puerto Rico and other documents written by Swensson shortly after his return to the United States at the end of his work on the island. This led to the correction of inaccuracies in previous publications of the story of the beginning of the Lutheran work in Puerto Rico. Pastor Swensson had departed from New York on October 8, 1898, and not October 5, as previously contended. His arrival in Puerto Rico was on October 13 and not October 10. The steamship that brought him to San Juan was the *Philadelphia*, rather than the *Arcadia*. The first service was held on December 4, 1898, and not in November. Swensson performed the service by himself with just an interpreter, because Rev. McKim, of the Bible Society, had not yet arrived on the island.[54] In this way, accounts of the church's first establishment in Puerto Rico had moved from recollections to records.

In an open letter sent on December 25, 1948, by Pastor Arbaugh to friends and supporters of the mission in general, he provided a detailed summary of the Lutheran mission in Puerto Rico. First, he gave a list of dates related to the fiftieth anniversary, starting from December 3, 1898, when the student Swensson met Browne, the Jamaican tailor, walking along Sol Street in San Juan while returning to his San Juan boarding house from a Spanish class. The next day, a Protestant service was held in San Juan, thus starting the United Lutheran Church mission in Puerto Rico. The narrative ends with the unfortunate experience of the Arbaughs' house being robbed by a fifteen-year-old lad while they were at church.[55] The festivities began in October with a Reformation Rally at which Arbaugh preached, but the main celebration was to be held on February 1, 1949, with an anniversary service and a final banquet. Twenty-one Lutheran visitors attended from overseas, including Pastor Herbert F. Richards, one of the two Lutheran ordained pastors sponsored by the Foreign Board of the General Council who first arrived on the island in October 1899, and his son Frank, along with Dr. Franklin Clark Fry, ULCA president.[56]

At the 37th Annual Convention of the Puerto Rico Conference, held on February 7, 1949, at Good Shepherd Lutheran Church, the statistician reported net gains in membership and stewardship: baptized members increased from 3,336 to 3,393; confirmed members increased from 1,313 to 1,375; communing members increased from 1,174 to 1,189; church offerings were up from $15,815 to $16,354; and total offerings (including Sunday schools and auxiliary societies) up from $20,240 to $20,909.[57]

The principal anniversary event took place on Sunday, February 13, at the Central High School in San Juan, with 740 persons in attendance. Ten local and seven visiting pastors participated, wearing cassocks, surplice, and red stoles. Dr. Fry's sermon made a deep impression upon those gathered. Pastor Richard also spoke, recalling the challenges encountered in the early years of the mission, and gave an eloquent missionary testimony over the progress of later years.[58]

On Wednesday, March 9, 1949, the Religion News Service[59] sent out a news release describing the commemoration of the fiftieth anniversary of Protestant mission work in Puerto Rico, with approximately four hundred Protestant leaders from the United States and Latin America arriving in San Juan to participate in a three-day celebration from March 11 to 13. Churches representing the variety of Protestant denominations on the island met at the huge Sixto Escobar Ballpark for a rally paying homage to Antonio Badillo, who in 1860 became the first Puerto Rican convert to Protestantism.[60]

In addition to the good news of the fiftieth anniversary of the Lutheran mission in Puerto Rico shared by the media at the time,[61] in its April 6, 1949 edition the *Lutheran* magazine published an article written by Joseph W. Frease on the subject of race relations. In the article, the author made a strong claim that in Puerto Rico, and especially in the Virgin Islands, the relationship among people of different races did not constitute a problem. For Frease, the source for this attitude seemed related to the influence of the Christian faith on the people's identity.[62]

> It is quite natural that where the church establishes a friendly relationship between races so that its work can go on without separations or double services, the standards of all other relationships are established on Christian principles.[63]

AT THE DAWN OF ESTABLISHING THE CARIBBEAN SYNOD

On Monday, January 30, 1950, the 38th Annual Convention of the Puerto Rican Conference was held at San Pablo Lutheran Church (Puerta de Tierra). Once again, the statistician reported modest gains in confirmed and communion members, this time alongside a significant increase in stewardship contributions. An interesting report made by a committee about the impact of radio on the mission discussed "La Voz Luterana," a program transmitted every Sunday morning from the WENA radio station in Bayamón, and the valuable impact it had on people of various sectors of the island.[64] However, the main attention of the missionary conference was on the possibility of establishing a Puerto Rican synod of the United Lutheran Church in America (ULCA), itself a follow up from Rev. Arbaugh's request after the previous synod. One of the resolutions of the assembly was to authorize the executive committee of the conference, along with the group of pastors of the mission field in Puerto Rico, to engage in conversations with the staff of the mission board and Dr. Fry, president of ULCA. These leaders would discuss the advantage of a Puerto Rican synod and the procedures to be followed if such advantage was agreed on. The executive committee was to announce its decision at the next assembly of this conference, or at an extraordinary assembly convoked by the president for this purpose.[65] An increasing number of incidents taking place in the social and political life in Puerto Rico, however, led to slower progress with this project.

On October 30, 1950, an insurrection of the Nationalist Party took place in Puerto Rico, continuing into the early days of November.[66] The Nationalist Party had been founded in 1922 as a political organization with the main objective of the reinstatement of the Republic of Puerto Rico. This had been an objective of the liberating deed of 1868, known as El Grito de Lares, but it was not until 1930, when Pedro Albizu Campos was elected its president, that this liberating movement reached its highest national point. Under Albizu's leadership, the party became a frontline of political struggle and a national liberation movement.[67]

Meanwhile, even events taking place after World War II at an international level could not play a significant role in addressing the Puerto Rican colonial condition. From the time of its founding on October 24, 1945, the United Nations gave colonial territories around the world hope that the new institution would proclaim the end of colonization. Despite the liberating rhetoric of the US government after winning the war, the government showed no sign that it would even consider giving Puerto Rico freedom. As a substitute, it instituted several improvements to disguise Puerto Rico's colonial condition to the United Nations. For this reason, President Harry S. Truman selected for the first time a Puerto Rican to be governor of the territory: Jesús T. Piñeiro Jiménez (1946).[68] In 1949, Luis Muñoz

Marín became the first governor elected by the people. Muñoz argued that, with his election, Puerto Rico had practically ceased to be a colony. As governor, he worked with the federal government on Law 600, allowing Puerto Ricans to draft a "constitution," to be presented to the US Congress and the president for final approval. The plan was to disguise the colony as a "commonwealth," promoting the idea to the United Nations and the world that Puerto Rico had resolved its colonial "status."

Nationalists had other ideas. Early in the morning of October 27, 1950, the nationalist commander Rafael Burgos Fuentes, who was part of the group that escorted Albizu, was arrested along with a group of his companions. In the process, firearms were seized. The media announced that the police had uncovered a nationalist "conspiracy" and "plot." Albizu Campos's home was raided by the police and the leader received information that the government would initiate several searches and arrests against his followers. To avoid losing the weapons they had accumulated over the course of two years, and to prevent his followers being taken prisoner without fighting, Albizu Campos decided to start the Insurrection,[69] although it had been planned for more adequate social conditions. The Insurrection, which aimed at the transformation of the colonial condition of Puerto Rico to that of an independent country, was launched in the early morning of October 30, when the police went to Peñuelas to raid a residence where a group of nationalists was located, and the insurgents received them with gunfire. Nationalists subsequently carried out attacks in San Juan, where a group of five attacked the executive mansion with the intention of kidnapping Muñoz Marín, proclaiming a republic and appealing to the United Nations. They also attacked the police barracks of Hato Rey, Jayuya, Arecibo, Naranjito, and Utuado, where four nationalists were executed by the National Guard. The official reaction escalated, and the next day planes attacked the town.

In the aftermath of the rising's suppression, two nationalists attacked President Truman's temporary residence in Washington with the intention of drawing the world's attention to what was happening in Puerto Rico. The nationalist Griselio Torresola was killed in the attack, and his partner Oscar Collazo was wounded and arrested. Approximately 140 insurgents participated in the uprising, most of them members of the Nationalist Party, and among these three women: Blanca Canales, in the capture of the town of Jayuya where she proclaimed the republic, and Carmín Pérez and Doris Torresola, who fought alongside Albizu Campos from the National Board. Even though Governor Luis Muñoz Marín called the events "riots," he still summoned the National Guard, with their tanks and aviation, and militarized the police. The FBI, even though they wanted to preserve the impression that they were only investigators and not persecutors, participated in the operations to suppress the Insurrection. The poorly armed nationalists could not stand against the military power of the state forces, and most of the fighters were arrested. On November 10, when José Negrón, who held out in the mountains of Naranjito, was arrested, the actual insurrection came to an end, though its cause was publicized across Puerto Rico and the Puerto Rican diaspora.

The revolt left in its wake a forty-eight wounded: twenty-three policemen, six members of the National Guard, nine nationalists, and ten civilians. It also left in its aftermath a balance of twenty-nine dead: seven policemen, one national guard, sixteen nationalists, and five civilians. Muñoz Marín's government took advantage of the situation to initiate a wave of raids and illegal mass arrests against nationalists, relatives of nationalists, ex-nationalists, communist leaders, labor leaders, and members of the Puerto Rican Independence Party who had nothing to do with the Insurrection. This was done to intimidate the opposition so that they could not campaign against the registration of people voting for the Popular Party in the elections that would take place between November 4 and 5. The news of the uprising swept the world, but the United Nations chose not to intervene on the island. To discourage solidarity with the Insurrection, the federal and colonial governments initiated a public relations and propaganda campaign with the intention of making the revolutionary process invisible.

Unsurprisingly, there was no information about this event in *El Testigo*. However, Arbaugh wrote a letter on November 1, 1950, describing Albizu as "the great nationalist rabble rouser," and his followers as fanatics who would be proud to die for Albizu and his cause. The pastor also stated:

> They know there is no chance of overturning the government but that is not their major concern. They probably hope that if only they can provoke the United States, the president . . . and the Congress will give P.R. independence in disgust.[70]

As a Lutheran Puerto Rican myself, I have a hard time figuring out why *El Testigo* decided to abstain from commenting on such an important event taking place on the island. It seems like decisions made by Congress and the presidency of the United States in establishing a military government in Puerto Rico and imposing governors on the island, along with the first military draft for young Puerto Rican men to serve in World War I, were of great importance, and they did indeed find a place in *El Testigo* to support these measures. But the fact that the United Nations refrained from challenging the United States for establishing a neocolonial government in Puerto Rico, after proclaiming the need to end colonization worldwide, seems to be a contradiction in terms that should have been noted by any truly impartial informational medium on the island for further examination. In terms of the comments made by Arbaugh in his letter mentioned above, I believe that, along with many people in the United States, he suffered from some type of selective amnesia that led them forget about the revolution that led to their independence from Great Britain, giving birth to their nation back in 1776.

In any case, at the 39th Annual Assembly of the Lutheran Missionary Conference at Transfiguración Lutheran Church in Río Piedras on January 29, 1951, and in spite of acknowledging the challenges involved in the organization of a synod, the pastors and lay delegates at the assembly, including the fraternal delegates from the Virgin Islands,[71] considered that the time had arrived to organize the Caribbean Synod.[72] In its edition of September 19, 1951, *The Lutheran* published an article on these plans written by Merle G. Franke, a pastor who had served in the Virgin Islands before returning to the Midwest, where he had become a senior administrator in the Lutheran Church.[73] Franke provided a brief historical sketch of Lutheranism in Puerto Rico (since January 1, 1900) and the Virgin Islands (since 1666), organized respectively as conferences, along with the news that "after several years of discussion, these two conferences are ready to organize as the Caribbean Evangelical Lutheran Synod."[74]

In an effort to facilitate the organization of such a synod, the assembly resolved: (i) to make a Spanish translation of the model constitution for the organization of a synod; (ii) to invite the Virgin Islands Conference to name a committee of three pastors and three lay people to meet with a similar committee from the Puerto Rican conference in St. Thomas before October 30, 1951, to prepare the constitution for the synod; (iii) for this committee to choose between the names, "The Caribbean Synod of the U.L.C," or "The West Indies Synod of the U.L.C.";[75] (iv) that copies of the suggested constitution in Spanish and English be distributed to the congregations of both conferences; (v) that pastors explain to their congregations the plans for the organization of the synod with the privileges and obligations they implied;[76] (vi) that the suggested constitution be submitted for its approval to both conferences at their meeting in 1952; (vii) that the constitution being approved be submitted to the Executive Board of the United Lutheran Church in America; and (viii) that secretary Pastor Arbaugh become part of the joint committee to prepare the constitution.[77]

In the February 1952 edition of *El Testigo* we find the report of the president of the fortieth assembly of the Lutheran Missionary Conference of Puerto Rico. Pastor Eduardo Roig informed readers that, after completing its task, the constitution committee was suggesting a constitution for the Caribbean Synod which had the support of executive board of the Lutheran Church in North America and it was to be sent to the congregations of the conference for their approval before May of the current year. The committee was also recommending an extraordinary meeting of the assembly in May for the constitution of the Caribbean Synod.[78]

On Saturday, March 8, 1952, a first extraordinary assembly of the Lutheran Missionary Conference of Puerto Rico took place at Divino Salvador Lutheran church in Cataño, to read and study the proposed constitution for the Caribbean Synod. The editorial board of *El Testigo* reported the unanimous support for the constitution by the congregations.[79] In May 1952, in the section "English Notes," *El Testigo* published an explanation written by Pastor Franke of the meaning and significance of the organization of the Caribbean Lutheran Synod for Lutherans in the West Indies.[80]

At the assembly for the constitution of the Caribbean Synod from May 29–31, 1952, reports were presented by the committees established for the organization of the synod from both mission conferences. These reported that the idea of organizing a synod in the Caribbean could be traced back to 1919, when Pastor Zenan M. Corbe, then executive secretary of the Board of Missions for the West Indies, had suggested it to Pastor Ostrom. In 1927, pastors Roig, Fred W. Lindke, and Jans C. Pedersen had submitted a constitutional project for the Puerto Rican Conference to the Board of American Missions, but that proposed constitutional project was not approved by the new Board of American Missions because it was presented during the years of economic depression.[81] Instead, they had to wait until 1949 for this constitutional project to receive the support of all parties.[82]

All nineteen congregations at the event submitted their request to become part of the synod, and all were unanimously approved.[83] Pastor Arbaugh then introduced four candidates for the ordained ministry.[84] Dr. Fry and Dr. Gerberding, representing the United Lutheran Church in America and the Board of American Missions of the ULCA respectively, brought greetings and their support for the organization of the new synod.[85]

In June 1952, *El Testigo* published a special edition providing the details of the organization of the Caribbean Synod of the ULCA. The synod was constituted by nineteen congregations and thirteen pastors. From Puerto Rico the following congregations were represented by delegates: First Church, Bethel, San Pedro, Divino Salvador, Sión, Getsemaní, San Juan, Redentor, Betania, Transfiguración, Nuestro Salvador, Buen Pastor, San Pablo, and Santísima Trinidad. From the Virgin Islands, the following congregations were represented by delegates: the parishes of Christiansted, Frederiksted, Kingshill, St. Thomas, and St. John. The ordained pastors represented were: Eduardo Roig, William G. Arbaugh, Evaristo Falcó, Guillermo E. Marrero, Sergio Cobián, Cesar A. Cotto, Miguel Sevilla, Herminio Díaz, Carlos A. Torres, Curtis E. Derrick, Merle G. Franke, Clarence G. Schnorr, and Francisco Molina.[86] The assembly took place at San Pablo Lutheran Church in Puerta de Tierra, and Rev. Roig was installed as president of the synod.[87] The assembly completed its work on the afternoon of May 31, 1952.[88] In a letter sent by William C. Arbaugh to his friends on December 25, 1952, expressing his delight for the creation of the Caribbean Synod, we read:

> In our church work the headline events were the formation of The Caribbean Synod May 30 at St. Paul's Church, San Juan, and the Synod's admission to the ULCA Oct. 9 at Seattle. Two unforgettable experiences! Together they constitute a vivid climax in the development of this mission field and in our lives.[89]

Rev. Roig, assessing the successful organization of the Caribbean Synod, looked with optimism toward the future challenges of this church structure:

> I am confident of the Christian Lutherans of Puerto Rico and the Virgin Islands. We have placed our faith and hope in God.

The rest is in our own hands. Let us come together in laboring for the expansion of the Evangelical Lutheran Caribbean Synod, for the glory of God.[90]

Presently, the Caribbean Synod is one of the sixty-five synods constituting the Evangelical Lutheran Church in America (a further development of the United Lutheran Church in America since 1988), with Rev. Idalia Negrón as its bishop.[91]

CONCLUDING REMARKS

This chapter has provided a summary of the events that led to the organization of the Caribbean Synod of the Evangelical Lutheran Church in America (ELCA). After a brief review of the social, economic, and political conditions of Puerto Rico after the Spanish–American War, it described the impact of the Great Depression of the 1920s in Puerto Rico, as well as the social and economic restraints in the archipelago caused by the advent of World War II. The chapter then outlined the effects of this economic crisis on the Lutheran mission and other Protestant denominations, along with the effects of the economic programs developed after the war to improve social and economic conditions in Puerto Rico. It described the preliminary efforts formulated in planning for the organization of the synod, and, lastly, the celebration on May 29–31, 1952, of the organization of the Caribbean Synod, with Rev. Eduardo Roig elected as its president.

The journey to reach the establishment of the synod was certainly hard and full of challenges. However, the benefits of reaching this goal proved worthwhile for the constituents of the synod and its North American Lutheran supporters. Today we can look back to receive from our forerunners, in their hardships and achievements, the inspiration to continue to move forward with the mission and ministry of this Lutheran synod in the Caribbean.

NOTES

1. Vega H. Drouet, "Some Musical Forms of African Descendants in Puerto Rico: Bomba, Plena, and Rosario Frances," in *New Grove Dictionary of Music and Musicians* vol. 20, ed. Stanley Sadie (London: Macmillan, 2001), 585–86.
2. "Plena: A Music of the Puerto Rican People," The Classic Journal, accessed June 22, 2023, https://theclassicjournal.uga.edu/index.php/2017/04/10/plena-a-music-of-the-puerto-rican-people/. For a more extensive description of Puerto Rican music, see "Puerto Rican Music and Its History," EnciclopediaPR, September 4, 2014, https://enciclopediapr.org/content/musica-puertorriquena-historia/. This type of music can be added to what James C. Scott calls "everyday forms of peasant resistance, or the weapons of the weak." James C. Scott, *Weapons of the Weak: Everyday Forms of Peasant Resistance* (New Haven, CT, and London: Yale University Press, 1985), xv–xviii. To explore the type of resistance vehicle of the *Plena* see Temporal, Puerto Rican Resistance Education Guide, published by Columbia College (Chicago), accessed July 12, 2023, https://www.mocp.org/resources/education-guide-english/.
3. For the full lyrics of the *plena* see https://www.musixmatch.com/lyrics/Tony-Croatto/Temporal.
4. See Museum of Contemporary Photography, "Temporal: Puerto Rican Resistance Education Guide," accessed June 22, 2023, https://www.mocp.org/wp-content/uploads/2021/09/temporal_education_guide_english-v9-readers-spreads.pdf.
5. For an extensive description of this event and its consequences in Puerto Rico, see "Guerra Hispanoamericana en Puerto Rico," "Spanish–American War in Puerto Rico," EnciclopediaPR, April 21, 2021, https://enciclopediapr.org/content/guerra-hispanoamericana-en-puerto-rico/; Ángel Rivero, *Crónica de la guerra Hispanoamericana en Puerto Rico* (Río Piedras: Editorial Edil, 1998); Carmelo Rosario Natal, *Puerto Rico y la crisis de la guerra hispanoamericana (1895–1898)* (Hato Rey: Ramallo Brothers Printing Co., 1975); and this author's review of Ángel Rivero's aforementioned book for the course Hist. 6005 Historiografía Puertorriqueña at the Interamerican University (May 13, 2011).
6. See "Brief History of the Government of Puerto Rico," EnciclopediaPR, September 11, 2014, https://enciclopediapr.org/content/breve-historia-del-gobierno-de-puerto-rico/. The first military governor of Puerto Rico was John Rutter Brooke (October 18–December 6, 1898). After the Foraker Law and the establishment of the civil government, the governor was Charles Allen Helbert (May 1, 1900–September 15, 1901). "Timeline of American Governors (1898–1946)," EnciclopediaPR, September 11, 2014, https://enciclopediapr.org/content/cronologia-de-gobernadores-estadounidenses-1898-1946/.

7 "On August 8, 1899, Puerto Rico experienced one of the most destructive hurricanes in history. It rained for 28 days straight, and the winds reached speeds of 100 miles per hour. The loss of life and property damage were immense. Approximately 3,400 people died in the floods and thousands were left without shelter, food, or work. The most devastating effect of *San Ciriaco* was the destruction of the farmlands, especially in the mountains where the coffee plantations were located. *San Ciriaco* aggravated the social and economic situation in Puerto Rico at the time and has serious repercussions in the years that followed." "Hurricane San Ciriaco – The World of 1898: The Spanish–American War," Hispanic Division, Library of Congress, accessed June 22, 2023, https://www.loc.gov/rr/hispanic/1898/sanciriaco.html.

8 "The U.S. military government's response to the hurricane of San Ciriaco reflected the prejudices of its administrators and their perception of the economic needs and social realities on the island. . . . The hurricane of San Ciriaco presented an excellent opportunity for the United States to demonstrate its efficiency and supposed benevolence in a time of crisis. It did this within the ideological constraints of its leaders and its representatives on the island, whose opinions about class and race were often shared by the Puerto Rican upper class. . . . Slowly, however, Puerto Ricans began to question the charitable nature of the aid and to realize the social and political program behind its organization. The final question is, from 1899 to 1901, at a crucial historical moment when the political destiny of the island was being determined, whether the material and psychological effects of San Ciriaco were so great, the destruction so widespread, and the alternatives so limited that they weakened not only the island's economy but also the resolve of those in both Washington and Puerto Rico to consider the option of independence." Stuart B. Schwartz, "The Hurricane of San Ciriaco: Disaster, Politics, and Society in Puerto Rico, 1899–1901," *Hispanic American Historical Review* 72, no. 3 (1992): 303–34.

9 An interesting and conflictive experience of this sentiment was led by what was then called "las partidas auxiliaries a los invasores" (the auxiliary bands for the invaders), later called "las partidas de los tiznados" (the blackened bands) given that they blackened their faces with ashes during the nightly raids to avoid recognition. These were bands of armed Puerto Rican volunteers coming from the mountains of the island, recruited by the United States military to suppress the Spanish military and political resistance. José Maldonado, the famous "Aguila Blanca" (White Eagle), who was among the leaders of these factions, was later persecuted by the United States military for leading a resistance against the United States military invasion of the island. See Fernando Picó, *1898: La Guerra después de la guerra* (San Juan: Ediciones Huracán, 1987), 41–160. This book was translated to English by Sylvia Korwek and Psique Arana Guzmán, *Puerto Rico 1898: The War after the War* (Princeton, NJ: Markus Wiener Publishers, 2004).

10 *El Testigo*, año XXI, no. 10 (March 1912): 5–6.

11 See "La Gran Depresión en Puerto Rico," accessed June 22, 2023, http://www.mrsruthie.net/wp-content/uploads/2015/10/La-Gran-Depresi%C3%B3n-en-Puerto-Rico-15.pdf.
12 A total of 65 percent of the Puerto Rican working class were unemployed.
13 Denis Bechara, "The Development of Puerto Rico," The Foundation for Economic Education, October 1, 1982, https://fee.org/articles/the-development-of-puerto-rico/.
14 "La gran depresión y sus efectos en Puerto Rico," MonographsPlus.com, accessed June 22, 2023, https://www.monografias.com/docs/La-Gran-Depresion-Y-Sus-Efectos-En-PKYRM3PZBZ.
15 Saenz, *Economic Aspects of Church Development in Puerto Rico*, 54.
16 Saenz, 54–57. Among other Protestant congregations the growth for this period was more significant. The increase for American Baptists from 1920 to 1930 was from 2,303 to 4,057, for the Disciples of Christ from 734 to 1,635, and for the Episcopal Church from 436 to 2,710. Saenz, 47. For the period from 1930 to 1940, the increase for American Baptists was from 4,057 to 4,920, for the Disciples of Christ was from 1,635 to 3,475, and for the Episcopal Church from 2,710 to 2,882. Saenz, 40.
17 Saenz, 57–58.
18 "Puerto Rican Migration Before World War II," Lehman.edu, accessed June 22, 2023, https://tinyurl.com/ms2rh4wn.
19 "Puerto Rican Migration Before World War II."
20 Evaristo Falcó Esteves, a former priest and canon at the cathedral of Barquisimeto.
21 The Lutheran Church required their candidates for ordination to have a Bachelor's degree to begin seminary studies. Candidates in Puerto Rico had to complete a Bachelor's degree to enter a Lutheran seminary.
22 Saenz, *Economic Aspects of Church Development in Puerto Rico*, 13–16.
23 The book was *El Camino*, a Spanish translation of Dr. Charles M. Jacobs, *The Way*. *El Testigo*, año XXI, no. 1 (June 1937): 19.
24 *El Testigo*, año XXI, no. 1 (June 1937): 19–20. The first Spanish translation of Martin Luther's *Small Catechism* brought to Puerto Rico was in 1901. This was a donation from a friend of the Lutheran mission (1,000 copies) of a Spanish translation that was already in use in Spain. *El Testigo*, año XXI, no. 1 (June 1937): 19–20. In 1902, before leaving Puerto Rico, Gustav Sigfried Swensson translated into Spanish and published his own version of Luther's *Small Catechism*. *El Testigo*, año XXI, no. 1 (June 1937): 15. In April 1908, Rev. Ostrom published his revised Spanish translation of Luther's *Small Catechism* along with his translation of the *Augsburg Confessions*. *El Testigo*, año XXI, no. 1 (June 1937): 17. These developments were noted at the time. In the June 1940 edition of *El Testigo* there was an article by Ana L. Sáenz de Morales providing an assessment of the Christian Education provided by the Lutheran Church in Puerto Rico. *El Testigo*, año XXIII, no. 8 (June 1940): 8–9.

25 Among these ordained pastors, ten were Puerto Ricans (Francisco Agostini, Leopoldo Cabán, Sergio Cabán, Alfredo Ortiz, Evaristo Falcó, Francisco Molina, Salustiano Hernández, Eduardo Roig, Guillermo Marrero, and Juan Zambrana (retired)), along with two North American missionaries (William G. Arbaugh and John Pettit). *El Testigo*, año XXIII, no. 11 (April 1940): 13.
26 This was a church youth organization.
27 The two congregations were the Iglesia Luterana Sión (Bayamón) and the Iglesia Luterana Divino Salvador (Cataño). While both congregations continued to receive financial support from the American Mission Board, the first added to its self-support the amount of $180 from 1940 to 1941 and from 1942 on, the amount of $300 a year. The latter increased the amount of $180 on a yearly basis. *El Testigo*, año XXIII, no. 11 (April 1940): 17.
28 It is interesting to note that the development of Lutheran congregations continued to follow the trend established during the early years of the Lutheran mission, that is, they were developed in towns and cities in the metropolitan area, or close to San Juan. It was only during the 1960s that a Lutheran mission was developed in the city of Ponce (in the south of the island) and later in the city of Mayaguez (in the southwest of the island). Unfortunately, those two mission developments were later discontinued. Other Protestant groups diverged from their initial commitment in 1898 to stay in a specific geographical part of the island, moving to other cities and rural areas, including San Juan.
29 William G. Arbaugh, "Zeal Renewed at Forty," *The Lutheran* XXIII, no. 17 (January 22, 1941): 9. The "Manual de Culto Cristiano" incorporated translations from the *Common Service Book* and *Hymnal* produced earlier by the United Lutheran Publication House in Philadelphia, hymns created by Lutheran congregations in South America, and other Protestant denominations in Puerto Rico. The latter "Manual de Culto Cristiano" was originally published by Publicaciones El Escudo, Chicago, Illinois, 1941. *The Lutheran* XXIII, no. 17 (January 22, 1941): 9.
30 It is noteworthy to mention that in July 1936 Benjamín Ayala, a young member of Santísima Trinidad Lutheran Church in Bayamón (Puerto Rico), published an article in *El Testigo* providing his impressions on the war. In the article he argued that the war "has been, is, and will be an enemy against humanity." For Ayala, war is based in mistrust among nations, it enriches the manufacturers of weapons, and destroys in minutes that which has taken years to build. While the efforts employed to avoid partial or full war by nations have so far failed, our God's calling is to continue to work toward peace and reconciliation among nations. Benjamín Ayala, "Impresiones sobre la guerra," *El Testigo*, año XIX, no. 14 (July 1936): 11. However, in 1951, *El Testigo* published an article by its editorial board on the topic of the Christian and the war. In the article, it mentions that Benjamín Ayala, at that time a noncommissioned officer serving in the 65th Regiment of the US

Army in Korea, was decorated for his heroism displayed in the battlefield. "El Cristiano y la Guerra," *El Testigo* (April 1951): 8.
31 "Caminos cristianos en tiempo de guerra," *El Testigo* (December 1939): 4–5.
32 Saenz, *Economic Aspects of Church Development in Puerto Rico*, 62.
33 The growth went from 26,149 in 1941 to 31,358 in 1946. Saenz, 63.
34 Saenz, 63.
35 Saenz, 63.
36 In the mission's early years, new members came from a variety of age groups, not just younger adults. As the Lutheran mission continued to grow, people from a variety of age groups persisted to incorporate themselves in the religious community.
37 This amount was sent abroad to the West Indies Board of the United Lutheran Church to support missions in other parts of the world.
38 *El Testigo*, año XXV, no. 10 (March 1942): 7–9. The average sent for benevolence by North American districts was 35 percent of their annual budget.
39 A service that marked the death of one of the last of the founding handful of Lutheran North American missionaries. Similar services took place at this juncture in the other Protestant churches on the island.
40 William G. Arbaugh, "Faithful unto Death," *El Testigo*, año XXV, no. 2 (July 1941): 11.
41 *El Testigo*, año XXV, no. 2 (July 1941): 12.
42 *El Testigo*, año XXV, no. 2 (July 1941): 12. On December 25, 1942, William G. Arbaugh send a Christmas greeting to his family and friends in the United States describing in graphic detail the difficult year experienced in missionary work in Puerto Rico. See Arbaugh *Notes and Quotes*, 5–13.
43 *El Testigo*, año XXIII, no. 8 (March 1942): 12. For a brief summary of the president's report see *El Testigo*, año XXIII, no. 8 (March 1942): 4. Another important highlight of the conference was the special presentation made by Dr. Fritz W. Fromm, an Austrian Lutheran professor of science at San German's Polytechnic Institute (presently the San German campus of the Interamerican University), who brought information about the historical origins and present status of the Lutheran church in his country of origin, and a plea for the Lutheran mission in Puerto Rico to provide aid to the church in Austria once the war was over. *El Testigo*, año XXIII, no. 8 (March 1942): 1, 13.
44 J. Merle Davis, *The Church in Puerto Rico's Dilemma* (New York: International Missionary Council, 1942).
45 William G. Arbaugh, "Revista de libros," *El Testigo*, año XXVI, no. 11 (April 1943): 9–10. While Davis arrives at the conclusion that congregations can indeed reach self-support in the archipelago of Puerto Rico, providing examples of successful experiments in this area (51–56), his recommendations require the support of pastors, missionaries, training in church finance, the elimination of assumptions and prejudgments as to the inability of congregational members to support their church, supplementary training

for North American missionaries and Puerto Rican pastors, and a host of development in other areas to achieve this goal. Davis, *The Church in Puerto Rico's Dilemma*, 71–77. See also Carmelo Santos Álvarez and Carlos F. Cardoza Orlandi, *Llamados a construir el Reino: Teología y estrategia misionera de los Discípulos de Cristo 1899–1999* (Bayamón: Iglesia Cristiana Discípulos de Cristo, 2000), 59–61.

46 *El Testigo*, año XXIX, no. 10 (March 1946): 20.
47 See Saenz, *Economic Aspects of Church Development in Puerto Rico*, 65. Also "Operation Bootstrap," Encyclopedia.com, accessed June 22, 2023, https://www.encyclopedia.com/social-sciences/applied-and-social-sciences-magazines/operation-bootstrap; *A Summary of Facts and Figures* (New York: Commonwealth of Puerto Rico, Migrant Division, Department of Labor, January 1959), 3–13.
48 Saenz, *Economic Aspects of Church Development in Puerto Rico*, 65–71.
49 "Operation Bootstrap."
50 Nora Dorothy Arbaugh and Herminio Díaz, "Impresiones del Segundo Congreso Latinoamericano de Juventudes Evangélicas," *El Testigo*, año XXX, no. 4 (September 1946): 8. The work with young people was important for the ministry and mission of Protestants in the island. See, for example, the celebrative note that a prominent Protestant journal, *Puerto Rico Evangélico*, shared for the Lutheran work with young people in 1914. *Puerto Rico Evangélico*, año 2, no. 19 (April 10, 1914): 14.
51 See "Possible Advantages and Disadvantages in the Proposed Reorganization of the Lutheran Missionary Conference of Puerto Rico as a Member Synod of the United Lutheran Church in America," a letter written on April 1, 1946, by William G. Arbaugh, secretary for Latin America of the Board of American Missions. This letter was published in the book *A Caribbean Mission: The Correspondence of William George Arbaugh*, ed. William Charles Arbaugh (Victoria, BC: Erbach Books, 2006), 53–54.
52 *El Testigo*, año XXIX, no. 10 (March 1946): 7. In May 1946, the letter was made available in *El Testigo*. See *El Testigo*, año XXIX, no. 12 (May 1946): 19–20.
53 *El Testigo*, año XXXI, no. 10 (March 1948): 12. Other resolutions approved by the conference were: (i) to send $50.00 to each of the three Puerto Rican seminary students in the United States; and (ii) to establish January 1, 1899, as the official date for the celebration of the beginning of the Lutheran mission in Puerto Rico. *El Testigo*, año XXXI, no. 10 (March 1948): 4. It is noteworthy to record that, at this time, the Puerto Rican Lutheran Missionary Conference had a total of ten ordained pastors for fifteen congregations. Two of these pastors were originally from North America (R. Gaenslen and E. S. Oleson) the other eight were Puerto Rican (Sergio Cobián, Cesar Cotto, Salustiano Hernández, Carlos A. Torres, Francisco Molina, Edwardo Roig, Evaristo Falcó, and Guillermo E. Marrero). Two of the Puerto Rican pastors listed (Guillermo E. Marrero and Salustiano

Hernández) were part of the first generation of pastors at the Lutheran mission still in service, that had also been brought up for their leadership role by the congregations of the mission.
54 *El Testigo*, año XXXII, no. 2 (July 1948): 16.
55 Arbaugh, *Notes and Quotes*, 31.
56 William G. Arbaugh, Letter of December 25, 1948.
57 *El Testigo*, año XXXIII, no. 9 (February 1950): 3–7.
58 *El Testigo*, año XXXIII, no. 9 (February 1950): 3–7. In the February 1950 edition of *El Testigo*, Pastor William G. Arbaugh, then historian at the conference, gave a month-by-month account of the activities of 1949.
59 Religion News Service is an independent, nonprofit, and award-winning source of global news on religion, spirituality, and ethics. Founded in 1934, RNS, which is not affiliated with any religious tradition, seeks to inform readers with objective reporting and insightful commentary and is relied upon as a responsible source by secular and faith-based news organizations around the world. See "Who We Are," Religion News Foundation, accessed June 22, 2023, https://www.religionnewsfoundation.org/who-we-are/.
60 Religion News Service, Wednesday, March 9, 1949.
61 On April 6, 1949, the *Lutheran* magazine published a brief yet important article describing the Lutheran mission in Puerto Rico from its beginning in 1898 up to the celebration of the fiftieth anniversary in the island. *The Lutheran* (April 6, 1949): 14–16.
62 The author had been present at the celebration of the fiftieth anniversary of the Lutheran mission in Puerto Rico, representing the Luther League of America. *The Lutheran* (April 6, 1949): 19–21. It is interesting to note that even today in the United States, race continues to be an issue of conflict and division of Christian congregations. In an article published by Tony Hunt on January 21, 2005, he claims, "I suspect that many persons of all races in the churches forty years ago would have hoped and expected that the church of the early 21st Century would be a church where racism no longer exists, and perhaps that the churches would be color-blind. But we know that this is not the case." Tony Hunt, "The Church and Race Relations— Then and Now," Leading Ideas, Lewis Center for Church Leadership, January 21, 2005, https://www.churchleadership.com/leading-ideas/the-church-and-race-relations-then-and-now-1968-2008/.
63 *The Lutheran* (April 6, 1949): 21.
64 It is interesting to note that this radio program became so important that even the ecumenical journal *Puerto Rico Evangélico* mentioned it as a valuable radio program for Puerto Rican Protestants in its issue of 1951. See *Puerto Rico Evangélico*, año XXXIX, no. 1,089 (July 25, 1951): 13, and año XXXX, no. 1,090 (August 10, 1951): 14. Later on, in 1951, the Lutheran Church initiated the publication of two magazines. One, *Luz Cotidiana*, became a monthly devotional. The other, *Orientación*, published quarterly, became a resource for the formation for ministry. Both publications were

edited by Rev. Leopoldo Cabán. *Puerto Rico Evangélico*, año 40, no. 1,101 (January 25, 1952): 4. By 1951, Dr. Ángel Mattos began the Coro Luterano de Bayamón at the Iglesia Luterana Sión (Bayamón), that became one of the most celebrated choirs in Puerto Rico. *Puerto Rico Evangélico*, año 40, no. 1,103 (February 25, 1952): 1, 16.

65 *El Testigo*, año XXXIII, no. 9 (February 1950): 3–7. The president of the conference, Pastor Edwardo Roig, mentioned his support for this action in his address to the delegates.

66 The following information on this topic was taken from "Nationalist Insurrection of 1950," EnciclopediaPR, April 29, 2021, https://enciclopediapr.org/content/insurreccion-nacionalista-1950/.

67 "Nationalist Insurrection of 1950."

68 "Nationalist Insurrection of 1950."

69 Given that Spain's decision to surrender Puerto Rico at the end of the Spanish–American War as a booty of war to the United States was not considered a legal transaction, because at the time Spain had granted Puerto Rico some governmental autonomy to govern itself, the Nationalist Party had gone to the courts to challenge this political arrangement and considered publicly its right to established Puerto Rican independence, even at the cost of an armed insurgency against the United States to meet this goal.

70 Arbaugh, November 1, 1950, in *A Caribbean Mission*, 32. See also Arbaugh, November 1, 1950, in *Notes and Quotes*, 36–38. I was not able to find any denominational newspaper/magazine, including the Roman Catholic Church, discussing these events.

71 Throughout the years, relations between Virgin Islanders and Puerto Ricans became close. An article in the newspaper *El Imparcial* describes the marriage of a distinguish Puerto Rican, Monserrate Estrada, to Fredericka Clementina Peterson from a high-class family in St. Thomas, at a Lutheran church in St. Thomas. See *El Imparcial* (February 23, 1923): 4, Library of Congress, https://tinyurl.com/33r44p44.

72 It is important to note that the leadership of the Lutheran Church in the United States encouraged the Lutheran constituency in Puerto Rico to move forward with their interest in establishing a Caribbean synod of the United Lutheran Church in America.

73 Pastor Merle George Franke, 1924–2020, was born in Arthur, North Dakota on October 6, 1924, to Max and Louise Franke. His first six years in ministry were spent in the US Virgin Islands serving Holy Trinity Lutheran in Frederiksted, St. Croix, and Frederick Lutheran in Charlotte Amalie, St. Thomas. He was instrumental in the formation of the Caribbean Synod of the Lutheran Church. After leaving the Virgin Islands, he organized several congregations in Minnesota before serving as the secretary of English Missions with the Lutheran Church's Board of American Missions in Chicago, overseeing new congregations throughout the United States. He died on January 28, 2020.

74 *The Lutheran* 39, no. 20 (September 19, 1951): 12.
75 In 1945, Rev. William G. Arbaugh made a trip to Cuba to explore possibilities of developing a Lutheran mission. Later, in 1968, Rev. Victor Rodríguez, while holding the position of president of the Caribbean Synod, went to Cuba and Santo Domingo hoping to incorporate these countries to the synod. Unfortunately, these efforts failed and eventually the synod became constituted only by Puerto Rico and the Virgin Islands. See *El Testigo* (June 1945): 5.
76 To encourage and facilitate this task, the editorial board of *El Testigo* published the privileges and obligations of the New York Synod's constitution which had been amended on June 20, 1935. *El Testigo*, año XXXIV, no. 9 (February 1951): 8.
77 *El Testigo*, año XXXIV, no. 9 (February 1951): 3–4. For the favorable report made to the assembly by Pastor Edwardo Roig, president of the Missionary Conference of the Lutheran Mission of Puerto Rico, and Pastor William G. Arbaugh, secretary of the Board of American Missions, see *El Testigo*, año XXXIV, no. 9 (February 1951): 6–7. There is also an article written in *The Lutheran* by Pastor William G. Arbaugh describing the proceedings of the annual convention of the Virgin Islands Missionary Conference addressing this topic. *The Lutheran* (May 2, 1951): 31–32.
78 *El Testigo*, año XXXV, no. 9 (February 1952): 6.
79 *El Testigo*, año XXXV, no. 10 (March 1952): 3, 6. In its edition of April 9, 1952, *The Lutheran* published an article written by Pastor William George Arbaugh regarding the adoption of the Associate Free State of Puerto Rico. In the next chapter I will explore the relationship of this political entity with the organization of the Caribbean Synod. See William George Arbaugh, "Puerto Rico Adopts Constitution: Island's Voters Give Overwhelming Approval to Document Which Assures Them Independence in Their Internal Affairs," in *The Lutheran* 34, no. 28 (April 9, 1952): 2021.
80 *El Testigo*, año XXXV, no. 12 (May 1952): 11–12. See also two valuable articles on the history leading to the constitution of the Caribbean Synod in *El Testigo*, año XXXV, no. 12 (May 1952): 4–6, 9, 11. This event was promoted in the *Puerto Rico Evangélico*. See *Puerto Rico Evangélico*, año 40, no. 1,106 (April 10, 1952): 16. It was also mentioned in the newspaper *El Mundo*, see *El Mundo*, año XXXIII, no. 14726 (February 20, 1952): 17.
81 Another important concern raised later by Rev. Eduardo Roig, when he was president of the Puerto Rican Lutheran Mission Conference in 1950, was that being a synod of the United Lutheran Church in America required synodical congregations to provide a financial quota for benevolence, which at an earlier time (1927) was practically impossible for the Puerto Rican Lutheran Conference to raise. However, by 1950, President Roig acknowledged that at that later time (1950) the ULCA would be mindful of the financial conditions of the Caribbean Synod and would not be expecting that which would be impossible for the synod to provide. "Informe del

presidente a la Trigesimoctava Asamblea Anual de la Conferencia Misionera Luterana de Puerto Rico," *El Testigo* (February 1950): 7.
82 "Minutas de la Asamblea Constituyente del Sínodo Evangélico Luterano del Caribe de la Iglesia Luterana Unida en América mayo 29-31, 1952," 5-11.
83 Five congregations were from the Virgin Islands and the rest (thirteen) from Puerto Rico. "Minutas de la Asamblea Constituyente del Sínodo Evangélico Luterano del Caribe de la Iglesia Luterana Unida en América mayo 29-31, 1952," 12-13.
84 Víctor Astacio, Ramón Vázquez, and Víctor Rodríguez from the Puerto Rican Conference (the latter the uncle of the author of this dissertation research), and Claude Peterson from the Virgin Islands Conference. "Minutas de la Asamblea Constituyente del Sínodo Evangélico Luterano del Caribe de la Iglesia Luterana Unida en América mayo 29-31, 1952," 13.
85 "Minutas de la Asamblea Constituyente del Sínodo Evangélico Luterano del Caribe de la Iglesia Luterana Unida en América mayo 29-31, 1952," 13.
86 *El Testigo*, año 40, no. 1,111 (June 1952): 8. At that time there were five preaching points, 6,114 baptized members, 2,747 confirmed members, five kindergartens, with 181 pupils, with a value of all church properties reaching $55,9000, and a total of $8,963 for benevolence. *The Caribbean Call* (October 1952): 8.
87 Rev. Eduardo Roig Vélez was born on 1903 in the barrio Percha in San Sebastián del Pepino. His parents were Don Ramón B. Roig and Doña María Vélez. His first years of studies were undertaken in his town of origin, later graduating at a high school in Arecibo. His family moved to Cataño, where they were introduced to the Lutheran Church. He graduated from Wartburg College (Iowa) in 1923 and completed his studies at the Lutheran Seminary in Philadelphia in 1926. He was ordained for the ministry of Word and Sacrament by the Synod of New York and New England in 1926 at the city of Rochester. He married Doña Rosario Esteves and was installed as pastor of San Pablo Lutheran Church in Puerta de Tierra. In July 1932, he was assigned to begin the work of Buen Pastor Lutheran Church in Monteflores, Santurce. He became director of the journal *El Testigo* (1926-32) and president of the Missionary Conference (1933-52), at which time he was raised to become president of the Caribbean Lutheran Synod. He held this position until 1962. In 1959 he was granted the honorary title of Doctor of Divinity by Thiel College in Pennsylvania. *Bulletin for the Fiftieth Anniversary of the Ministry of Rev. Eduardo Roig Vélez Iglesia Luterana El Buen Pastor* (September 1, 1968): 2-3.
88 *El Testigo*, año XXXVI, no. 1 (June 1952): 1-15. *The Caribbean Call*, the English news bulletin of the Caribbean Evangelical Lutheran Synod of the ULCA also has a valuable edition describing the organization of the Lutheran Caribbean Synod. See *The Caribbean Call* 1, no. 1 (October 1952): 1-8. The ecumenical journal *Puerto Rico Evangélico* also published

information about the event, see *Puerto Rico Evangélico*, año 40, no. 1111 (June 25, 1952): 13. In the United States, *The Lutheran* magazine rendered an English version of the event written by Rev. Merle G. Franke. The article provided full details of this important event. See Merle G. Franke, "Caribbean Synod Is Born," *The Lutheran* 34, no. 40 (July 2, 1952): 31–33.

89 Arbaugh, *Notes and Quotes*, 88.
90 Editorial desk of *El Testigo*, año XXXVI, no. 1 (June 1952): 9, 15.
91 According to John H. P. Reumann, a common trait of most Lutheran bodies in the United States (excluding the Lutheran Church Missouri Synod), is their experience of merger at various of times. The Evangelical Lutheran Church in America was formed in 1988, from a merger of three Lutheran bodies: the Lutheran Church in America, the American Lutheran Church, and the Association of Evangelical Lutheran Churches. At that time the Caribbean Synod was one of the synods of the Lutheran Church in America. For a thorough review of this development in North American Lutheranism see, John H. P. Reumann, *Ministries Examined: Laity, Clergy, Women, and Bishops in a Time of Change* (Minneapolis: Augsburg Publishing House, 1987), 199–219.

CHAPTER 6

The Leadership of Women in the Mission

Given the valuable role played by women in the early development and continuing work of the Lutheran Church in Puerto Rico, this chapter will endeavor to provide some of the accounts that express these contributions. In this area, the wives of North American clergy missionaries deserve a special mention. Given their various skills, they played a vital role in broadening the work of their spouses.[1] Those with previous missionary experience and the ability to speak Spanish became useful translators, and those with a teaching degree provided leadership in developing kindergartens for the education of Puerto Rican children.[2] Others contributed to the administration of Sunday and Vacation Bible schools or fundraising.

The role of spouses in supporting the work of Lutheran and Protestant clergy can be traced back to the sixteenth century. Historian Roland H. Bainton notes that women "played a prominent role in the Catholic and Protestant reform movements in the early years of the 16th century."[3] The role of Katherine von Bora is especially prominent because she married Martin Luther on June 13, 1525.[4] In addition to tending to Luther's health,[5] Katherine tended the Augustinian cloister given to the couple by the Elector of Saxony, which had forty rooms on the first floor, with cells above, and at times was fully occupied.[6] "Katie herself herded, milked, and slaughtered the cattle, made butter and cheese, brewed, planted, and reaped."[7] She was a lively conversationalist. "Luther said she could teach an Englishman German better than he ever could." She welcomed instruction and asked demanding questions. Simultaneously, she did not shy away from criticizing her husband.[8] In fact, Alicia E. Walter's book on *Catarina Lutero: Monja Liberada* (here I am using the text in Spanish. The original title in English is *Katharine Luther: Liberated Nun*) argues that Katherine's theological interest and knowledge developed to such an extent that she participated actively in table talks with students and notable theologians. Even Luther recognized her intellectual sharpness, commending her healthy opinions, her comprehensive understanding, and her ability in persuasion. At a time when a woman was consigned to domestic labors and childbearing, Katherine attained the distinction of playing a major role in her husband's labor as a reformer.[9] In summing up the qualities of Katherine as the spouse of Luther, Bainton claims:

> She emerges as a woman of character and courage, sensible, non-sentimental, hard-headed, tender, determined, and usually right. She discussed with her husband the issues of the Reformation and supported him in his polemical endeavors.... She presided over the first well-known Protestant parsonage and did much to give the tone to German domestic life—authoritarian, paternalistic, with no nonsense, and at the same time tenderly affectionate and marked by utter devotion.[10]

Several of the qualities embodied by Katherine von Bora continued to represent goals for minister's wives in the centuries that followed. In her foreword to Alice Taylor's mid-twentieth-century book *How to Be a Minister's Wife and Love It*, Helen Smith Shoemaker asserted that:

> Mrs. Taylor represents in her own person, the type of minister's wife we should all be—one who not only tactfully and wholeheartedly supports her husband in his ministry without

usurping in any way his function, but one who also complements him by daring to stir up the gifts that are in her.[11]

The creative and valuable role of women for the mission and ministry of the church in mainline Protestant denominations expanded notably in North America, however, when, in 1853, Antoinette Brown became the first woman to be ordained by the Congregational Church. The American Lutheran Church and the Lutheran Church in America followed suit in 1970.[12]

Another important vehicle for women's leadership venture in the Lutheran mission was the work of La Sociedad Misionera de Damas Luteranas de Puerto Rico (the missionary society of Lutheran women of Puerto Rico). This society had a long history in the United States Lutheran Church. It was started by spouses of pastors, to pray and collect offerings to respond to the needs of society, expanding God's reign on earth. A goal of the society was to establish a group in every Lutheran congregation. In Puerto Rico, the congregational women's society was established in January 1921, meeting annually to assess and renew its work in the island.[13]

As mentioned in chapter 6, shortly after Swensson and then two ordained Lutheran pastors arrived in Puerto Rico, Miss Annette Wahlstedt joined them.[14] Miss Wahlstedt had been a member of Immanuel (Swedish) Lutheran Church in Chicago, but had previously been a missionary in Africa. She visited Puerto Rico during 1900 with an ailing family member, and there she met Rev. H. F. Richards. She shared with him her willingness to assist him in his labors and, given her previous experience in mission work, that same year the Lutheran General Council's Board of Foreign Missions appointed her as teacher and visitor for the field under Rev. Richards' supervision.[15] She became an active missionary and a cherished teacher in the city of Cataño. Miss Wahlstedt started her vigorous work in the mission in the fall of 1900. She became a teacher, visitor, and general helper. Most of her time was dedicated to visiting prospective members and searching for nonreligious candidates to be given catechetical instruction and prepared for confirmation. At the Spanish-speaking Iglesia Luterana San Pablo in San Juan and Divino Salvador in Cataño she began successful classes in English and sewing.[16] However, a trying incident occurred during the summer of 1902. Miss Wahlstedt went into a Roman Catholic church in Cataño to see inside, and in a conversation held with the sacristan, she shared her perspectives on the topic of images, focusing on an image of the Virgin of Carmen. She argued about the futility of praying to inanimate objects such as a doll. The sacristan became angry at such an insult to the Virgin, and this anger spread within the Catholic community. The Roman Catholic bishop was made aware of the reproach and made public his displeasure. The matter was resolved after Swensson published an article in a newspaper providing the Lutheran perspective on the event, and after a short time the controversy was forgotten.[17] In November 1905, Miss Wahlstedt returned home due to her declining health.[18] However, other episodes of this kind had previously taken place, fostering strong Catholic antagonism. During the winter months of 1901–2, the Sunday school in Cataño reached an attendance of 197, and:

> A house centrally located on a principal street was then bought. This aroused strong Catholic opposition. A priest was sent there. Women were sent about to frighten and urge the parents not to send their children to us. During the summer months the school declined very much. In the fall, the priest having died and the active opposition having subsided, the school revived.[19]

These incidents were evidence of the struggle of Protestant groups in developing their mission on the island of Puerto Rico during the turn of the twentieth century. Fortunately, this bitterness between Protestants and Roman Catholic groups eventually changed. While this shift of mental attitude took years to develop, presently a great number of socially oriented projects in Puerto Rico and other parts of the world are jointly sponsored by Roman Catholic and Protestant organizations.

In his report for the biennium, September 1901–3, to the Board of Porto Rico Missions of the General Council of the Evangelical Lutheran Church in North America, Rev. H. F. Richards registered the urgency for more helpers to meet the needs of the Puerto Rican mission.

> Our mission has reached a point where more helpers are urgently needed if we are to make the most of our opportunity.... Our total membership has increased in the last two years from 34 to 88, and there are 11 more who have applied for membership.[20]

At that time, the board had failed in securing additional missionaries or helpers, but persisted in their commitment to continue searching, hoping to find someone suitable for the next year. In October 1904, Miss Clara Hazelgreen joined the missionaries from the United States in Puerto Rico,[21] but her brief service on the island ended on April 23, 1907, when she returned to the United States.[22] However, during her tenure and with the skillful leadership of Rev. Alfred Ostrom, the Lutheran mission was established in the closer communities of San Juan,[23] and the first Puerto Rican male workers were recruited.[24]

PUERTO RICAN WOMEN JOIN IN MINISTRY

In June 1906, Gabriela Cuervo, the first Puerto Rican Lutheran missionary, arrived on the island after two years of study at the Lutheran Deaconess Missionary School in Milwaukee, Wisconsin, and began her labors in the areas of San Juan, Cataño, and Bayamón.[25] She worked for approximately seven years in the Lutheran mission. For the first three years prior to her studies in Milwaukee she received no compensation, but on her return to Puerto Rico in 1906 she became a missionary financially supported by the Ladies Home and Foreign Mission Society of the Augustana Synod. Her missionary work consisted of visiting prospective members at their homes and sharing with them biblical stories. She cared for the poor and assisted the families of the deceased. She contributed to the evangelism of the church and its instructional programs through its various organizations. She worked with youth, the elderly, and women, and on other church-related activities. On April 26, 1913, she married Charles H. Marks, an Episcopalian gentleman from England residing in Puerto Rico, while continuing her faithful and assiduous labor for the Lutheran mission.[26]

Miss Cuervo had been confirmed on April 15, 1900, at the first Puerto Rican catechumens' class by pastors Richards and Hankey, the first United States Lutheran ordained missionary pastors in Puerto Rico. She was the only one of four young women confirmed at that time (founders of la Iglesia San Pablo) remaining faithful to her church. Mrs. Felícita Rosario de Deza, who had earlier been impressed by the "Protestants that sing and name God," introduced Miss Cuervo to the Lutheran Church. Doña[27] Gabriela was the only one that personally knew and worked with the early missionaries from the United States, as well as with the first Puerto Rican church workers. She became a widow during World War I and was left with two children, Ana Mercedes and George.[28]

Cuervo Marks's contribution to the Lutheran mission in Puerto Rico was greatly appreciated by many of her coworkers and the Ladies Home and Foreign Mission Society. In a report of the latter women's organization of July 13, 1931, it was registered that shortly before her death Miss Annette Wahlstedt requested that the society assist Mrs. Gabriela Cuervo Marks by supporting her daughter's education. While this request was not followed, the Augustana Synod's Women Society considered allowing Mrs. Cuervo Marks and her two children to live at a home the society had acquired in Puerto Rico. On September 12, 1939, and by an early recommendation made by Rev. William Arbaugh to the Augustana Synod's Women Society,[29] the said women's organization sold the house to Mrs. Cuervo Marks for the amount of $300.

The role played by Mrs. Cuervo Marks and other women in the mission and ministry of the church was, from the beginning, very significant. The conviction, resilience, and initiative of these native pioneers served to establish creative models of lay and ordained ministry throughout these one hundred years of Lutheranism in Puerto Rico.

There is a song in the new Spanish hymnal produced by the Evangelical Lutheran Church in America (ELCA) for its Spanish-speaking constituency in the United States and Puerto Rico that brings to my mind some important dimensions of the contribution of these women.[30] Its title, "God's Calling Now Is for a New Experience" (*Dios hoy nos llama a un momento nuevo*), suggests the type of vision and commitment expressed by these women as they accepted their call for ministry. The hymn is a celebration of the foresight and stimulating witness of these faithful leaders, compelling us to join them today in moving forward the transformative power of the gospel.

> God's calling now is for a new experience,
> to walk along with God's people.
> It's time to transform that which has no future,
> our separation and loneliness
> will render barren our efforts.
>
> So, come,
> join us and let's be together with others,
> you are very important.
> Therefore come,
> join us in our circle of togetherness,
> your presence is very significant, so come.
>
> It's useless to believe that things are easy
> we are encircled by death-producing forces
> which bring us pain, sadness, and desolation,
> that's why we need to strengthen our union.

The power source that brings life today
empowers us with its graciousness
inviting us to join efforts in sharing God's love with
others.[31]

In September 1906, Miss May Mellander arrived in Puerto Rico as a missionary from the United States, to take charge of the Lutheran parochial school established in the town of Cataño.[32] Miss Mellander was born in Kane, Pennsylvania, in 1877, and was the daughter of Rev. J. Mellander, pastor of the Bethlehem Church in Saint Charles, Illinois. Her missionary work on the island lasted more than ten years until her departure on May 23, 1917. While in Puerto Rico, she also taught courses at the seminary established in Cataño for the formation of native lay workers. After her return to the United States, Miss Mellander traveled for a few years as a speaker for the Woman's Missionary Society. She also worked as a teacher in the town of Laton, near Kingsburg, California, with Mexican children; in the final eight years of her life she served under the auspices of the California Conference of the Woman's Missionary Society, ministering to the physical and spiritual needs of migrant seasonal crop workers. On December 31, 1936, Miss Mellander died and she was buried at Saint Charles, Illinois, after services at Bethlehem Lutheran Church.[33]

From 1909 until 1923 a number of women from both the United States and Puerto Rico continued to join the work of the Lutheran mission, mostly in the area of education: Leonor Shaw and María E. González (1909); Dolores Q. de Martínez (1910); Matilde Llanes, Carmen Froilán, Genoveva Fernández, and Demetria Sánchez (1912); Mariana Agostini (1913); Emma Schmid, Sofía Probst, and Concepción González (1914); Dolores Rosado, Aurora Lomeña, Mariana Ojeda, Nanca Schoen, Catalina Zambrana, Mariana Ojeda, Aurora Lomeña, and Carmen Froylán (1917); Carmen Matilde Rosario (1919); Nicolasa Hernández González (1920); Rosario Ojeda (1921); Rosa C. González and Antonia Santana (1923); and Berta Casos (1924).[34]

In 1925, Miss Frieda M. Hoh and Miss Florence Hines arrived in Puerto Rico. The latter came from the Virgin Islands, where she had been laboring as a missionary, but she returned to the United States the following year. Miss Hoh was born in Wheeling, West Virginia. She graduated from the Lankenau School for Girls in Philadelphia, and from Lankenau Hospital School of Nursing in the same city. She also studied at the University of Pennsylvania.[35] Having a nursing degree, she began her missionary work in Puerto Rico in health-related endeavors.[36] Given the high child mortality rate and the reality that epidemics of all kinds took a large number of lives, with no free clinics, health education, or sanitation in the poorer sectors of the island, she started a clinic in her home. With the help of the women's missionary societies and personal friends in the United States, she opened the first milk station in the island.

> Mothers were taught how to make formulas for babies, how to bathe and dress them, how to isolate them in cases of contagion. She taught hygiene in the public schools as an extra-curricular course and told stories in homes and in daily vacation Bible schools.[37]

Later she employed her musical talents to develop congregational choirs and improve the worship liturgy. She participated in translating the *Common Service Book* in Spanish. As a member of the Committee on Religious Education, she also helped in the translation of courses for children, programs for the women of the church, and creating literature for vacation Bible schools. Miss Hoh passed away on February 25, 1962, at the home of her brother, the Rev. Ernest Hoh.[38]

A PROMINENT LEGACY

In 1960, the *Lutheran Women* journal published an article by Mrs. Ofelia Falcó, spouse of Rev. Evaristo Falcó, describing the work of

Lutheran women in Puerto Rico and the Virgin Islands. At four years old, Mrs. Falcó started attending the kindergarten established by the San Pablo Lutheran Church in San Juan, Puerto Rico. Eventually, her seven brothers and sisters, her mother, grandmother, and aunt became Lutherans as well. She served her church through all its organizations and in due course became involved with the Women's Society at all levels of its programs. In the summer of 1951, a group of women from Puerto Rico and the Virgin Islands met and organized the Synodical Society of the Caribbean, with Mrs. Falcó elected as its first president. By 1960, she became an executive board member of the United Lutheran Church Women.[39] As in the case of previous women mentioned above, the work of Mrs. Falcó marked an important contribution of women in developing the Lutheran Church in Puerto Rico, as well as their valuable involvements beyond the borders of the Caribbean.

Another important but more recent example of the leadership of Lutheran Puerto Rican women is that of Doña Juana de Sardén. During the early 1950s, my father accepted the call as pastor of El Divino Salvador Lutheran Church in the city of Cataño. The church's lay worker at the time was Doña Juana, as we fondly called her. Doña Juana was an awesome and terrific leader. She was everywhere doing everything. On Sundays she led the Sunday school program and later sat in one of the pews at the end of the sanctuary, where she took attendance for the worship service. During the week she visited those absent from the service and kept my father and the rest of the congregational leaders informed of the physical, spiritual, and emotional needs of the community. She never failed to attend a worship service or any of the church's activities. She served people in the church and the community at large. She was their friend, confidante, and advocate. She lived a humble life with her spouse and six children in an apartment in the *caserío*, a location equivalent to the projects in big cities like New York or Chicago.

I've been told that once she requested funds from the church to pay for health insurance. At that time the costs for health insurance ran at about 60 dollars a month. For a while, the church refused her petition.

THE LEADERSHIP OF WOMEN IN THE MISSION

Despite this incident, she continued her work with enthusiasm and faithfulness. I've always wondered the reason for the church leader's refusal of her request. My familiarity with the history of the North American Protestant expansion in Puerto Rico leads me to suggest that, rather than focusing on the individual intentions of these church leaders, we might be better served by exploring this matter in the broader framework of the economic, political, and ideological context of this Protestant expansion to Puerto Rico.

The scope and pace of change has shifted over the last half century. On February 27, 1983, after the Lutheran Church began ordaining women for the ministry of Word and Sacrament, Rafaela Hayde Morales Rosa, previously an elementary school teacher, became the first Puerto Rican woman to be ordained in the Caribbean Synod of the Lutheran Church in America. Later that year, on March 1, Rev. Morales Rosa, a graduate of Interamerican University in Puerto Rico, who completed her theological and ministerial formation at the Lutheran Seminary in Philadelphia (Pennsylvania), became pastor at St. Matthew Lutheran Church in Jersey City (New Jersey).

Last, but hardly least, members of the Caribbean Synod have recently celebrated the leadership of women by electing them as their bishops. On October 28, 2001, Rev. Margarita Martínez, a Puerto Rican born in New York but raised in Puerto Rico, became the first woman to be invested as bishop of the Caribbean Synod of the Evangelical Lutheran Church in America. With a strong academic background,[40] a professional career in government,[41] and previous pastoral experience in two congregations,[42] Martínez was elected with 90 percent of the votes of the synod, which is presently constituted by thirty-four congregations. Tragically, on March 12, 2007, Bishop Martínez died of cancer. In a eulogy celebrating her passing, Rev. Mark Hanson, then presiding bishop of the Evangelical Lutheran Church in America, stated:

> Bishop Margarita Martinez challenged us to confront the barriers we erect to divide us from one another and to cross those barriers for the sake of reconciliation. In her leadership

of the Caribbean Synod she gave us a vision of a more inclusive and multicultural church. In ecumenical relationships she modeled the gifts of women in ministry and leadership. She was a strong mentor and spiritual friend to countless young people and newly ordained pastors. Deeply centered in the community of the church gathered around the means of grace, she exuded joy as she presided and preached.[43]

In a later expression of the synod's celebration of the leadership of women, on June 16, 2018, the Caribbean Synod elected Rev. Idalia Negrón Caamaño for a six-year term as bishop of the synod. Bishop Negrón earned a bachelor's degree at the University of Puerto Rico in Río Piedras, and a Master's in Divinity from the Lutheran School of Theology at Chicago. At the time of writing she continues her service as bishop of the Caribbean Synod.

NOTES

1 In the report of October 1903 by D. H. Geissinger, president of the Porto Rico Mission of the General Council of the Evangelical Lutheran Church in North America, he mentions that, "Mrs. Richard (wife of Rev. Herbert F. Richards), being familiar with the Spanish language and having had previous experience in missionary work among Spanish-speaking people, has been of invaluable assistance to her husband." "First Report of the Board of Porto Rico Missions to the General Council of the Evangelical Lutheran Church in North America" (October, 1903), 4.
2 See the interesting evaluation made by Mrs. Ana L. Sáenz de Morales in 1940 of the educational efforts made by the Lutheran Church during its first forty years of religious education. Ana L. Sáenz de Morales, "Panorama de Educación Cristiana de la Iglesia Luterana en Puerto Rico," *El Testigo* (June 1940): 8–9.
3 Roland H. Bainton, *Women of the Reformation: In Germany and Italy* (Minneapolis: Augsburg Publishing House, 1971), 9. Bainton also provided scholarly research about the women of the Reformation's role in France, England, and from Spain to Scandinavia. His research shows, not only that the spouses of other reformers in different European countries played similar roles as Katherina Luther, but also the significant role played by women during the sixteenth century in moving forward the Reformation

in Europe. See Bainton, *Women of the Reformation: In Germany and Italy* and Bainton, *Women of the Reformation: From Spain to Scandinavia* (Minneapolis: Augsburg Publishing House, 1977).

4 Bainton, *Women of the Reformation: In Germany and Italy*, 27. Unfortunately, the information we have about the contributions of Katherine as the spouse of Martin Luther comes from Luther himself. Bainton, *Women of the Reformation: In Germany and Italy*, 27.

5 "Her son, later a distinguished physician, praised her as half a doctor." Bainton, *Women of the Reformation: In Germany and Italy*, 29.

6 Bainton, 30.

7 Bainton, 32.

8 Bainton, 37.

9 Alicia E. Walter, *Catarina Lutero: Monja liberada* (Mexico: El Faro SA, 1984), 74–75.

10 Walter, *Catarina Lutero*, 42.

11 Helen Smith Shoemaker, "Forward," in Alice Taylor, *How to Be a Minister's Wife and Love It* (Grand Rapids, MI: Zondervan Publishing House, 1968), 7. As we mentioned earlier, this was the role that the wives of the North American Lutheran missionaries played during their service in the Puerto Rican mission field.

12 "The last of the mainline Protestant denominations (the Episcopal Church) did not approve ordination of women until 1976.... The Southern Baptist Convention and the Presbyterian Church, U.S., took the step in 1964; the Methodist Church and the United Presbyterian Church U.S.A., voted to ordain in 1956." Judith L. Weidman, ed., Women Ministers: How Women Are Redefining Traditional Roles (San Francisco: Harper & Row, 1985), 2. For a more detailed information about the ordination of women in the Evangelical Lutheran Church in America and its predecessor bodies, see "50 Years On: A Half Century of Ordaining Lutheran Women," StOlaf.edu, accessed June 22, 2023, https://pages.stolaf.edu/lutheranwomensordination/, documenting the decision in 1970, the effects within the churches, and the experiences of women.

13 See Clara E. de Arbaugh, "La Obra de las damas luteranas: ¿Qué significa la sociedad misionera de damas? *El Testigo* (June 1951): 11–12. Also "Primicias puertorriqueñas," *El Testigo* (April 1939): 14. In 1951, Rosario Ojeda wrote an article highlighting the achievement of Doña Genoveva Morales de Cotto, spouse of Rev. Cesar Cotto who, being granted a scholarship from the government of Puerto Rico, completed a Master's degree at Columbia University (New York) in School Supervision and Administration. Rosario Ojeda, "Se recibe de maestra," *El Testigo* (July 1951): 11.

14 Swensson arrived in 1898, Pastor H. F. Richards and B. F. Hankey in 1899. Miss Annette Wahlstedt arrived in 1900. Miss Wahlstedt was the first missionary to be supported by the Woman's Missionary Society of the Augustana Lutheran Church. *Mission Tidings* (Monthly journal of the

Women's Missionary Society of the Augustana Lutheran Church) XLVII, no. 1 (June 1952): 13.
15 "1901 Report of the Lutheran General Council's Foreign Missions," 31.
16 "First Report of the Porto Rico Mission," 4.
17 *El Testigo* (September 1948): 4. The incident was made public in *El Heraldo Español*, año VIII, no. 173 (July 30, 1902): 2. It was also mentioned in *El Ideal Católico*, año IV, no. 156 (August 2, 1902): 366. For an interesting Roman Catholic response to building images of the saints, see *El Ideal Católico*, año II, no. 10 (October 20, 1900): 111.
18 *El Testigo* (June 1937): 15.
19 "First Report of the Porto Rico Mission," 7.
20 "First Report of the Porto Rico Mission," 8.
21 *El Testigo* (September 1948): 7, 14.
22 *El Testigo* (September 1948): 5.
23 Prior to 1905 only three congregations had been established (two in San Juan and one in Cataño), but from 1905 up to 1918 six more congregations were launched (two in Bayamón, one in Monacillo, one in Palo Seco, one in Toa Baja, and one in Dorado). *El Testigo* (December 1948): 14.
24 *El Testigo* (December 1948): 5.
25 *El Testigo* (December 1948): 15. Also "Doña Gabriela Cuervos Vda. De Marks," *El Testigo*, año XIX, no. 12 (April 1936): 2.
26 *El Testigo* (April 1936): 2.
27 An endearing name for respected and distinguished women.
28 *El Testigo* (April 1936): 2.
29 The letter was sent by Rev. Arbaugh to Mrs. J. W. Lanstrom, secretary of the Women's Missionary Society of the Augustana Synod, on November 2, 1933.
30 *Libro de liturgia y cántico* (Minneapolis: Fortress Press, 1998).
31 Translation mine.
32 On April of that year, Rev. A. P. G. Anderson and his sister Naomi had arrived in Puerto Rico as United States missionaries. Miss Naomi Anderson returned to the United States in March 1909. *El Testigo* (June 1937): 16.
33 Carl H. Sandgren, *My Church: A Yearbook of the Lutheran Augustana Synod of North America Vol. XXIV* (Rock Island, IL: Augustana Book Concern, 1938), 140–41.
34 *El Testigo* (January 1949): 12.
35 *Lutheran Women* 3 no. 6 (June 1962): 22.
36 It is interesting to note that, originally, Miss Hoh went to Puerto Rico to care for a missionary's wife expecting her first baby, pondering that this trip would constitute just a brief venture. But loving Puerto Rico from the first day, when asked by the missionaries to stay as a missionary nurse, she returned briefly to the United States and, in September 1926, returned to the island as a regular missionary. *Lutheran Women* 2, no. 6 (June 1961): 22.

37 *Lutheran Women* 2, no. 6 (June 1961): 22.
38 *Lutheran Women* 2, no. 6 (June 1961): 22.
39 Ofelia Falcó, "Lutheran Women in the Caribbean," *Lutheran Women* 1, no. 1 (March 1960): 6–7.
40 Bishop Martínez earned a bachelor's degree from the Universidad Mundial in Puerto Rico and a Master's degree in Business Administration from the same university. She also received her Master of Divinity degree at the Lutheran Theological Seminary in Philadelphia. Sandra Ivelisse Villarreal, "Puerto Rican Woman Invested as Bishop in Lutheran Church," *El Nuevo Día* (October 28, 2001): 4.
41 "Martínez left a career in government to follow her religious vocation . . . was the director of the Human Resources Office of the Municipality of Carolina from 1979 to 1983, and worked at the Planning Board." Villarreal, "Puerto Rican Woman Invested as Bishop in Lutheran Church," 4.
42 Martínez served at Bethel Lutheran Church in Dorado and the San Marcos Lutheran Church in Guaynabo. At the time of her election as bishop, she was a mission developer in Cayey. All congregations are in Puerto Rico.
43 "Margarita Martinez, Bishop of ELCA Caribbean Synod, Dies," ELCA.org, March 12, 2007, https://www.elca.org/News-and-Events/5872.

CHAPTER 7

Findings

In his book *Terrazo* Abelardo Díaz Alfaro,[1] one of the best Puerto Rican storytellers, tells the following story about Peyo Mercé, a fictional Puerto Rican school teacher with approximately twenty years' experience, schooling children in a poor rural sector of Puerto Rico by the name of Cuchilla. The small school where Peyo taught was a building with two meeting rooms. In one of them Peyo taught his classes. In the other, Johnny Rosas, a recently graduated teacher who had arrived after a period spent in the United States, and who had been sent by Rogelio Escalera, their supervisor, endeavored to acquaint Peyo with newly developed pedagogical techniques. The supervisor had told Johnny that the main reason he had been sent to Cuchilla was to improve Peyo's pedagogical skills as they were about forty years behind the times, in order to modernize his teaching, but most of all, to teach English, a lot of English.

The day Peyo saw Johnny arrive to Cuchilla, instead of resentment he felt pity and said to himself, "Life will be tracing him furrows as the plow to the land." One day, Johnny told Peyo that the rural sector was in need of renewal: "We need to teach a lot of English and reproduce North American patterns." Without getting too heavy-handed, Peyo dropped the following words, "To be sure, we need to learn English for it is good and we need it but, 'bendito' (how silly), we can't even pronounce Spanish well, and being hungry leads our children to be demeaned. The fox told the snails once that, in order to run, you need to learn to walk first." But Johnny could not understand what Peyo told him.

Given that Christmas was approaching, Johnny told Peyo, "This year Santa Claus will make his debut in La Cuchilla, because the celebration of the three kings is already old-fashioned." Peyo scratched his head and responded dispassionately, "Since I am just a 'jíbaro' (country person) and have not traveled at all, I bear the three kings in my soul." In preparation for the "Gala Premier" of Santa Claus at Cuchilla, Johnny showed his students some pictures of Santa Claus sliding on a sled pulled by reindeer, and asked his students, "Who is this character?" The mischievous Benito raised his hand and said, "Mistel, that is the figure of 'Año Viejo' (the Old Year) in red." Johnny Rosas was surprised by the ignorance of his students, and at the same time became enraged by the carelessness of Peyo Mercé.

Christmas night arrived, and students came with their parents. For his class, Peyo prepared a typical Puerto Rican party with Christmas carols accompanied by native instruments, alluding to the three kings. At the end, he shared with those attending some island sweets. After the party, Peyo directed his students to move to "mister" Rosas's room for a surprise. He had also invited the supervisor "mister" Rogelio Escalera. In the middle of the room was a small artificial Christmas tree. The room was decorated with green leaves and a sign covered in snow bearing the words *Merry Christmas*. Those attending were dumbfounded, for they had not seen anything like that, yet "mister" Rogelio Escalera seemed very satisfied. Some students climbed an improvised platform creating a crossword with the name of Santa Claus, and others began singing "Jingle Bells." The parents looked at each other stunned.

The supervisor spoke to the audience, congratulating them for such a great party, and for having such an active and progressive teacher as "mister" Rosas. Then he required from the participants the most profound silence, for he would soon present a strange and mysterious character. Immediately, a small choir began to sing, "Santa Claus is coming to town..." Suddenly, the red and white figure of Santa Claus carrying a big sack arose from the door's threshold, saying in a cavernous voice, "Here is Santa, Merry Christmas to you all." A scream of terror shuddered around the room. Everyone looked for an escape. Some tossed themselves out through the windows, and children stuck themselves to the skirts of their mothers, who ran in disarray. "Mister" Rosas ran behind them to explain that it was him who had dressed himself in such a strange form, but that brought an increase in the people's screams, and the panic became more acute. An old lady making the sign of the cross, summoned in a sacred name, "It is the very demon speaking in American!"

In the distance, you could hear the shouting of the people who had already dispersed, and "mister" Escalera, seeing that Peyo had remained indifferent and disconnected, blamed him for having such savagery take place in the twentieth century. Peyo, undeterred, responded, "'Mister' Escalera, I can't be blamed for not having this saint in the collection of Puerto Rican saints."[2]

In this story, a classic in Puerto Rican literature, the author describes in a modest and humorous literary form the challenges for Puerto Rican identity imposed by the violent process of "Americanization" of the Puerto Rican territory by the United States after 1898. While I mentioned earlier in this study that the US military had an important role in the "Americanization" of the Puerto Rican people's identity, as Díaz Alfaro suggests in his story, there were many other powerful forces involved in this process of "Americanization" that continue their elusive yet strong impact into the present. Following a common mode of resistance described by James C. Scott in his studies on forms of peasant resistance and the weapons of the weak, Díaz Alfaro presents a humorous yet ironic story of how Puerto Ricans (both) supported and resisted the Americanization of Puerto Rican culture. This is a struggle that continues to be carried out by Puerto Ricans on the island as well as in their diasporic experience in the United

States.[3] As I investigated various segments of the Lutheran mission in Puerto Rico in this research, I was also made aware that this same struggle became an important element in the emergence and development of this missionary experience.

RECKONING WITH THE THEOLOGICAL FOUNDATIONS OF LUTHERAN MISSIONS

Since the focus of this study is the Lutheran mission in Puerto Rico, I consider it important to provide the theological background that guided the missionary endeavor of Lutheranism during this period. To be sure, given our previous examination of the sixteenth-century European colonization of the Caribbean, Lutheranism was not the only religious expression of Protestantism brought by European Protestant *conquistadores*. However, I have briefly described the German colony established in 1528 in Venezuela that some historians have claimed was led by Lutherans. In addition, I also mentioned that, as early as January 7, 1519, the Roman Catholic bishop in Puerto Rico, Manuel Alonso, who had also been named Inquisitor to the Indies, attended the case of maestre Juan, probably the first case of Lutheranism prosecuted in the Indies.

To describe this Lutheran theological background, I want to highlight that the distinguished German missiologist Gustav Adolf Warneck (1834–1910), still considered the father of the theory of missions, makes a short reference to the history of the Protestant missions in Puerto Rico in his book *Outline of a History of Protestant Missions: From the Reformation to the Present Time* (1901). Ninety years later, the Puerto Rican missiologist Carlos Cardoza Orlandi emphasized the importance of this book for the study of the history of missions due to its analysis of the Protestant and missiological perspective. Warneck divides his book into two parts. In the first, he presents the understanding of Protestant missions during and after the European Reformation. In the second, the author describes the different territories where Protestant missionary labor took place. In the chapter where he portrays the missionary work in the Americas, we find the brief mention of Puerto Rico:[4]

> Porto Rico, whose population of 950,000 including 363,000 coloured people, is likewise nominally Catholic, has during its subjection to Spanish rule scarcely been touched by evangelical missions, but now, like Cuba, has become the object of evangelization by eight American societies (2500 communicants).[5]

For Cardoza Orlandi, the thought-provoking point about the quote is that the author places Puerto Rico among the Antilles. Therefore, in any analysis of the missionary work, the presence of the Black population will stand out. On the other hand, while Warneck mentions the change in government in Cuba, making a pejorative reference to Spanish rule and insinuating a positive change under the United States, he fails to make any mention of the colonial political reality in Puerto Rico that was like that of Cuba during this epoch. What is clear is that, given the change in government, the Protestant North American missions were the ones in charge of the evangelization.[6]

In addition to the above comments on the perceptive early insights of Warneck into the history of Protestant missions, I want to add some other elements to the legacy of the "father of the theory of missions." In a 1987 article written for an international journal of missions, Valdir R. Steuernagel contends that among Warneck's many contributions to the theory of missions stands the fact that he provided an essential biblical foundation for understanding Christian mission. Citing numerous biblical references, Warneck showed that the missionary venture is God's work, reaffirmed by Jesus's ministry, for human salvation. Another of Warneck's important contributions was the claim that we are called both individually and collectively as Jesus's body in the world to be part of God's mission. For Warneck, this is the principal task of the church. Last, but not least, Warneck emphasized the need to develop an adequate vision of history and the social reality, to provide an effective witness of the missionary activity of the church.[7]

For Warneck, there are three important epochs in the history of Christian missions: (i) the apostolic and postapostolic period (mission among the Greeks and Romans); (ii) the medieval and postmedieval period (mission to the German and Anglo-Saxon world); and (iii) the period that began in the nineteenth century (to every corner of the world). It was during these times when the power of God's Spirit renewed the missionary work of the church. Warneck, who died in 1910, viewed the development of science and human knowledge that took place during the nineteenth and twentieth centuries as signaling the promise of the church's missionary activity in all parts of the world.[8]

Although Warneck's contributions were provocative, Steuernagel reminds us that the father of mission theory was so much influenced by the progress developed by the wealthy industrial nations of his time that he failed to become aware of the tragic consequences of the imperialistic and colonial actions of the powerful nations over the poor countries of the world. Despite this omission, Steuernagel contends that Warneck's contributions are still important for our understanding of the mission and ministry of the church. To be sure, among these various contributions was his ability to demonstrate that, in most cases, the missionary activity of the church had been the product of the dreams and yearnings of the oppressed sectors of society, which had to confront the sociopolitical and religious powers of their time in their efforts to carry out their witness of faith.[9]

In his biography of Gustav Warneck, Hans Karsdorf notes that due to possessing an insatiable yearning for knowledge and learning, and by sheer self-determination and the reluctant consent of his parents, Warneck succeeded entering the *gymnasium* (grammar school) of the Francke Foundation in Halle. From there he graduated with honors and entered theological studies at Halle University, where at a later date (1896) he occupied the first chair of mission studies in Germany, a position he held for twelve years.[10]

This constructive experience with Halle's educational tradition became an important element in the formation of pastors who participated in the Puerto Rican mission field. Two pastors in the early stages of the Lutheran mission on the island, Gustav Sigfried Swensson and Alfred Ostrom, were both trained at the Augustana Theological Seminary. B. F. Hankey and H. B. Richards, the first two Lutheran ordained pastors who continued the mission in Puerto Rico after Swensson, received their theological formation at the Lutheran Seminary in Philadelphia. Both seminaries had a strong connection with the conservative, pietistic, and missionary tradition of Lutheranism.[11] The latter traces the history of its theological center to the efforts of Henry Melchior Muhlenberg,[12] along with the rejection by the Ministerium of Pennsylvania[13] of Samuel Simon Schmucker and his followers' "American Lutheranism."[14] The former was a product of the Augustana Church missionary heritage which, given its early conservative pietistic character typical of the Swedish Lutheran church tradition,[15] had also rejected the liberalism of the "New Lutheranism" which Samuel Simon Schmucker and his friends called "American Lutheranism."[16] In other words, two common perspectives between the establishment of both seminaries were a commitment to the Lutheran pietistic tradition and a conservative Lutheran theological position.[17]

Regarding their course of studies, in 1891, when Dr. Olof Olsson became president of the Augustana Seminary, a new curriculum was established dividing the whole course of instruction into fourteen separate and self-regulating areas of study. Students were required to complete all introductory courses before taking more advanced studies. "The divisions were: First year Hebrew; first year New Testament Greek; Theological Encyclopedia; Biblical Introduction; Swedish and English Exegesis; Church History; Biblical Theology and Ethics; Second year Hebrew; Second year New Testament Greek; Apologetics, Symbolics, and Confessions; Dogmatics and History of Dogma; Catechetics, Evangelistics, and Diaconics; Homiletics and Practical Exercises; Pastoral Theology, Liturgics, and Church government (Catalogue, 1891–1892). Each week classes were programmed to meet from two to four hours. Students had a limited number of elective courses to take, according to their productiveness and competence. Students were allowed to present themselves for a final examination of any course, whether through class attendance or independent study. To graduate from the Seminary each student was compelled to invest one full year at the Seminary and a successful final examination in all four divisions of the Theological program (Bible, Systematic Theology, History, and Practical Theology). A certificate of such graduation from the Seminary was required for ordination."[18]

Both seminaries required entering candidates to have graduated from church-related colleges, although at times a small number of students were admitted without a college degree. At the Lutheran Seminary in Philadelphia, the demand for German-speaking ministers led to a curriculum taught in English and German, but eventually all courses were imparted in the English language. The curriculum envisaged classes covering the areas of biblical exegesis, systematic theology, historical, and practical theology with reference to a three-year course of studies.[19] By 1889, the following courses were added to the program of study: Introduction, Hermeneutics, and Exegesis of the New Testament, along with a course on a homiletical treatment of the appointed lessons of the church year by Professor Adolph Spaeth; Dogmatics, Apologetics, Introduction to the Study of Theology, Symbolics, and the History of Doctrine, by Professor Henry Eyster Jacobs; Homiletics, and Pastoral Theology by Professor Jacob Fry; Church History, Hebrew, and Old Testament by Professor George Frederick Spieker.[20]

However, despite this conservative strand in the training of the earliest North American Lutheran missionaries in Puerto Rico, this study has shown that, when confronted by native leaders studying at the seminary developed by these missionaries in Cataño, the missionaries, along with a Lutheran Synod in the United States, eventually endorsed the students' ordination in the Lutheran Church. Our analysis of this event in an earlier part of this study also draws examples from James C. Scott's analysis of forms of peasant resistance and the weapons of the weak.

ACHIEVEMENTS—AND CHALLENGES—FOR THE INDIGENOUS PUERTO RICAN CHURCH

In an earlier section of this study, I shared a story related to the time of the emergence of Puerto Rican men and women, eager to play a leadership role in further developing the Lutheran mission and ministry on the island. On February 1, 2001, I had the privilege of preaching at the concluding service of the second anniversary celebration of the Evaristo Falcó Esteves lecture series in Puerto Rico at San Marcos Lutheran Church. This service also served for the installation of Ms. Carmen Rabell as executive director of El Centro Luterano de formación teológica y Pastoral José D. Rodríguez (Lutheran Center for Theological Formation José D. Rodríguez). The center, which the Lutheran School of Theology at Chicago (LSTC) contributed toward establishing and which it continues to support, plays a significant role in the theological education of lay candidates for the variety of ministries in the church, in the continuing education of pastors, and in witnessing to the relevance of the Lutheran legacy in the Caribbean and Latin America. I took this opportunity to reflect on the role of Indigenous leaders and the challenges they faced in developing the Lutheran mission in Puerto Rico.

The biblical text for the sermon focused on the Gospel of Luke 4:21–30. This reading provides a description of the beginning of Jesus's ministry in Nazareth at a time when he reveals the nature and extent of his mission, thus suffering the rejection of those offended by the radical inclusiveness of the gospel. What captured my attention in the reading of this text was its description of the radical inclusive nature of the power of the gospel. Not only is this incident paradigmatic of Jesus's life and ministry, but it is also a reminder that God's grace is never subject to the limitations and boundaries of any nation, church, group, or race. Those who would exclude others thereby exclude themselves. Human beings may be instruments of God's grace for others, but we are never free to set limits on who may receive that grace. Throughout history, the gospel has always been more radically inclusive than any group, denomination, or church.

We are called to break the patterns of prejudice, racism, and injustice that set people apart, to struggle for a witness that may show the radical inclusiveness in the power of the gospel.[21]

Francisco Molina, a native Puerto Rican pastor and writer, captured the popular celebration of and support for the struggle of those native leaders who pioneered the Lutheran mission in Puerto Rico in a delightful and compelling poem. The poem tells the story of three young men whose candid and faithful yearnings led them to pursue a lifelong quest as witnesses. As they moved forward in their mission, they confronted a sorceress who tried to dissuade them from their journey. "Don't you know," she said, "the negative consequences of your quest? Give it up, it's not worth it." They replied, "We are willing to pay the price. It's our choice and we want to carry on." Again, she tried to discourage them, saying, "Don't you know that when the going gets rough, you'll be disregarded and abandoned by those who now support you?" They answered, "Our convictions will not tremble, for we know well what we are up to." "Fools!" She riposted, "Yours is an ungrateful and unfortunate quest. You still have time to turn back. Give it up, it's not worth it." But the three young men stood their ground. "It's too late to turn around," they said. "Our call is from up high and we are moving on forward." The author ends the poem with the following remarks: "They were three courageous young and good men. One has already given account of his stewardship. We hope to have the other two with us for a long time. We pray God to have a greater number like them among us."[22]

One of the most intriguing chapters in the history of the North American Protestant expansion in Puerto Rico deals with the challenge posed by emerging Puerto Rican leaders. For most North American missionaries, the idea of integrating these leaders in the missionary project consisted first of all of assisting in congregational tasks, or perhaps responding to the social needs of the people in the island.[23] The main role of Indigenous leaders was to provide support for North American missionaries to carry out their pastoral ministry. An incident in the history of the Lutheran mission in Puerto Rico places this Protestant missionary experience in a wider perspective, if we are willing to discern it in light of the reading of Luke's Gospel mentioned above.

To be sure, we need to acknowledge the great contribution of North American Protestant missionaries for the proclamation and expansion of the gospel in Puerto Rico. At the same time, we need to point out that this expression of the gospel was strongly influenced by the prejudice in the dominant culture of their country of origin against our people in the mission field. Gustav Swensson, to whom the establishment of Lutheranism in Puerto Rico has been attributed by many, once mentioned in a published article that "I saw the Puerto Ricans as a people in misery, ignorance, superstition and fatal errors . . ."[24] As we learned from the reading of Luke, Jesus's proclamation of the gospel cannot be restricted to a specific nation, culture, race, gender, or sexual preference. We are called to witness to God's gracious initiative to all peoples. For this reason, we need to resist the temptation to limit not just our understanding of the recipients of this gift, but also our perceptions of those that become the most effective vehicles of this gracious divine initiative among us.

William G. Arbaugh commented that eventually, nearly thirty years after Swensson's initiative to begin a Lutheran mission in Puerto Rico, the native lay preachers studying at the seminary in Cataño were able to successfully complete the requirements established for ordination:

> In the presence of a large congregation at San Pablo Lutheran Church in San Juan, Demetrio Texidor, Guillermo E. Marrero and Salustiano Hernández were Ordained to the ministry of the gospel on Sunday July 10th, 1926.[25]

After a slow start, however, the installation of Carmen Rabell as executive director of El Centro Luterano de Formación Teológica y Pastoral José D. Rodríguez at the Caribbean Synod on February 1, 2001, and Francisco Molina's poem celebrate the continuous and collective effort of people from Europe, North, Central and South America, Puerto Rico, and many other countries in their faithful contribution of their leadership and gifts to the call of expanding the borders of God's reign in the context of the Lutheran mission in Puerto Rico.

The installation of Rabell as executive director also constitutes another valuable expression of the leadership of native Lutheran women in Puerto Rico that I have explored in the previous chapter. As mentioned earlier, our first Puerto Rican Lutheran missionary was Gabriela Cuervos. What caught my attention while becoming acquainted with her story was that for the first three years of her work with the church in Puerto Rico she received no salary. To be sure, she was not alone in this predicament. Many of the Protestant missionaries from the United States had a similar experience. It is common knowledge that Swensson just had a five-dollar bill and some small change when he arrived in Puerto Rico back in October 1898. Yet he had been promised assistance that later supported the work on the island. His income as an English-language teacher in Puerto Rico also served to support him and his work until the arrival of the financial assistance sent by Lutheran bodies on the mainland. The situation of native Puerto Rican workers was different. They did not have those minimal additional resources to depend on. While I never had a conversation with Gabriela Cuervos, I do recall the contribution of many other women who followed in her ministry. Doña Juana de Sardén, whose story I recounted in chapter 6, offered one such powerful testimony.

Recent studies show that while the extension of North American Protestantism in the Caribbean accompanied the military and commercial expansion of the United States in the region, it also contributed to the ideological goal to *civilize* this non-Protestant world. An imperialistic theology based on the writings of Josiah Strong was intentionally developed to connect the twofold intention of the puritan, Protestant providential vision to civilize and proclaim the gospel in these lands.[26] Lutheran missionaries shared this common vision. An additional consequence of this religious ideological influence was the disposition of Puerto Rican leaders to internalize this foreign and onerous disposition. These and other related elements provide a better understanding of the decision of these church leaders in rejecting the legitimacy of Doña Juana's request mentioned in the previous chapter.

Not too long ago I faced a similar experience when, during my studies for the doctoral degree at the Lutheran School of Theology at Chicago (LSTC), I solicited from representatives of the local synod the opportunity of serving as interim pastor in one of the local Latinx congregations. While this incident took place way before the organization of the Evangelical Lutheran Church in America, of which I am a registered retired ordained pastor, their response to my request continues to disturb me. While they affirmed and supported my petition, they warned me that, given the condition of poverty of many Latinx in the *barrio*, I should expect lower pay for my work in the parish. This was probably the common predicament of those choosing to minister with other communities of lower income.

There is a story in Mark's Gospel that helps me reflect on this issue. It's the story of the widow's gift (12:41–44). I am convinced that any ecclesial body committed to expanding its mission among ethnic communities whose social and economic history has been characterized by exploitation and racism will need to engage in a thoughtful reflection of economic models more in tune with the gospel than with the fundamental premises of a market or money-making economy. The story in the Gospel of Mark serves as a resource for Jesus to share with his followers an important teaching. Jesus's understanding of the widow's conduct subverts the whole notion of traditional religious economy. In contrast to the sterility of the dominant religious and social conventions that tend to give so much priority to matters of money, the poor widow demonstrates her strength and true faith in God. With God, all things are possible. God's loving mercy grants us that which we don't even dare imagine. The future belongs to God who has dwelled amongst us, making available an enduring and unparalleled power. We are called to live by faith in God's power and promise. I am convinced this was the source of the vision and witness of Gabriela Cuervos, Doña Juana, and the host of Puerto Rican women who followed in their footsteps.

In conclusion, among the valuable contributions of Puerto Rican Lutheran leaders, both in the archipelago and abroad, was their willingness to confront social and political issues with their understanding of the gospel. This effort was evident in resisting the war efforts during the two world wars fought during the twentieth century and by defying the forced "Americanization" of the island. Those serving in the diaspora of the United States in Arizona or Texas publicly spoke out against the onerous treatment which those of African descent, Mexicans, or Puerto Rican *jibaros*, experienced in the rural areas for their service as cotton pickers, or in urban areas such as New York or Chicago,[27] by participating in activities claiming the dignity of their culture and social achievements.

NOTES

1 Abelardo Milton Díaz Alfaro (b. Caguas, 1919, d. San Juan, 1999) was a "writer and educator remembered especially for his stories and costumbrista [traditional] prints, in which he masterfully portrayed the idiosyncrasy of the Puerto Rican people.... His experience as a social worker in rural areas helped him to relate to the peasants, who in the long run would be the fundamental figures of his work." See "Biography of Abelardo Díaz Alfaro," biografiasyvidas.com, accessed June 22, 2023, https://www.biografiasyvidas.com/biografia/d/diaz_alfaro.htm. See also "Abelardo Díaz Alfaro," EnciclopediaPR, June 22, 2021, https://enciclopediapr.org/content/abelardo-diaz-alfaro/, where you also discover that he was the son of a Protestant pastor whom he helped in the newsroom magazine of *Puerto Rico Evangélico*.

2 Abelardo Díaz Alfaro, *Terrazo* (San Juan: Editorial Plaza Mayor, 2009), 80–84, translations mine.

3 Two important examples of these efforts are *The Story of the Young Lords Society* (1969–71) in the United States, see Michael Abramson, *Palante: Voices and Photographs of the Young Lords, 1969–1971* (Chicago: Haymarket Books, 1971). See also Lester McGrath, *Quo Vadis, Vieques: Ética social,*

política y ecumenismo (Río Piedras: Fundación Puerto Rico Evangélico, 2000).

4 Carlos F. Cardoza Orlandi, "Protestantismo en Puerto Rico: Un encuentro entre misioneros y nacionales," in *Llamados a construir el Reino*, 50–51.

5 Warneck, *Outline of a History of Protestant Missions*, 200.

6 Cardoza Orlandi, "Protestantismo en Puerto Rico," 51. In this chapter, the author also provides a very important historiography of the Protestant mission in Puerto Rico, Cardoza Orlandi, 49–83.

7 Valdir R. Steuernagel, "El despertar misionero del Tercer Mundo," *Mission* 6 (June 1987): 7–17.

8 Warneck, *Outline of a History of Protestant Missions*, 3–7, 74–85.

9 Steuernagel, "El despertar misionero del Tercer Mundo," 15. For another valuable description of Warneck's missionary theory, see *Augustana Theological Seminary Foreign Missions Seminar: Studies in Mission Theories*, ed. Ross H. Larson and Arnold G. Levin (Rock Island, IL: Augustana Theological Seminary, 1957), 12–15.

10 Hans Karsdorf provides a notable biography of this German pastor and eminent missiologist. He was born on March 6, 1834, to Gustav Traugott Leberecht Warneck, and his wife Johanne Sophie, both of Naumburgnear, Halle (East Germany) on the Saale River. His parents were extremely poor, and in addition Gustav was a delicate boy suffering from a serious lung illness. As the oldest son of a master craftsman in needle making, and in keeping with tradition, Warneck entered his father's workshop counting heaps of needles, thereby helping to eke out a living for a rapidly growing family. Hans Karsdorf, "The Legacy of Gustav Warneck" *International Bulletin of Missionary Research* (July 1980): 102, https://www.scribd.com/doc/123497360/Legacy-of-Gustav-Warneck?secret_password=1y9oi8unr4oumofmce4r#. See also William Richey Hogg, "The Rise of Protestant Missionary Concern 1517–1914," in *The Theology of the Christian Mission*, ed. Gerald H. Anderson (New York, Toronto, and London: MacGraw-Hill, 1961), 95–111.

11 For a valuable examination of this theological legacy and its impact in the mission field, see Eric W. Gritsch, *A History of Lutheranism* (Minneapolis: Fortress Press, 2002), 141–78.

12 Muhlenberg became one of the best graduates of the Halle Foundation, and later the "church father" of Lutheranism in the United States.

13 The Pennsylvania Ministerium was founded in Philadelphia in 1748 when six pastors and lay representatives of ten Lutheran congregations, with the encouragement of Rev. Henry Melchior Muhlenberg, formally organized the "Ministerium of North America." In 1792 it changed its name to the Ministerium of Pennsylvania. See https://www.cuchicago.edu/academics/centers-of-excellence/center-for-church-music/hymnal-collection-index/pennsylvania-ministerium/.

14 Gritsch, *A History of Lutheranism*, 171-78. Also Theodore G. Tappert, *History of the Philadelphia Seminary* (Philadelphia: The Lutheran Theological Seminary at Philadelphia, 1964), 1-32. For an insightful exploration of this seminary's original and continuing developing theological perspective for 125 years, see *Philadelphia Vision: Mt. Airy Tradition: Essays for the 125th Anniversary of the Lutheran Theological Seminary at Philadelphia* (Philadelphia: Lutheran Theological Seminary in Philadelphia, 1991).

15 See G. Everett Arden, *A History of the Augustana Lutheran Church* (Rock Island, IL: Augustana Press, 1963), 115-33.

16 See G. Everett Arden, *The School of The Prophets: The Background and History of Augustana Theological Seminary 1860-1960* (Rock Island, IL: Augustana Theological Seminary, 1960), 34-86. Here it is important to clarify that the establishment of the Lutheran Seminary in Philadelphia was also the result of the rejection by the Ministerium of Pennsylvania, along with members of the Augustana church, of Schmucker and his followers' "American Lutheranism."

17 According to Eric W. Gritsch, the growth of Lutheranism in the United States was afflicted by constant controversy associated with ethnic and doctrinal differences. Regularly, there were ambitious yet unworkable proposals to bring Protestants together as a group against Roman Catholics. Schmucker's proposal to adjust the Augsburg Confessions to "American Lutheranism," was one of them. Yet, as for Gritsch, he did much more, "he rejected the biblical and ecumenical view of baptism especially cherished by Luther, as rebirth by water through the Holy Spirit (Titus 3:5). He also rejected the confessional Lutheran assertion of Christ's real presence in the Lord's supper; his view was closer to the Calvinists, indeed, the Zwinglian view." Gritsch, *A History of Lutheranism*, 191.

18 Arden, *The School of The Prophets*, 206-7.

19 Theodore G. Tappert, *History of the Lutheran Theological Seminary at Philadelphia 1864-1964* (Philadelphia: Lutheran Theological Seminary, 1964), 40, 44.

20 Tappert, *History of the Lutheran Theological Seminary at Philadelphia*, 71-73.

21 *The New Interpreter's Commentary on the Bible: A Commentary in Twelve Volumes*, vol. IX (Nashville: Abingdon Press, 1995), 106.

22 My paraphrased translation. Francisco Molina, "Hace muchos años: Para Sergio Cobián y Guillermo E. Marrero," in *Ciudad allende el alba* (Dorado: Sínodo Luterano del Caribe, 1999), 106-8.

23 For this purpose, the early Puerto Rican leaders served as readers of the Bible in the worship services, lay congregational workers, and preachers, etc.

24 Swensson, "I Went to Puerto Rico," *El Testigo* (October 1948): 16.

25 Arbaugh, "Alfredo Ostrom y la era de expansión," in *El Testigo* (December 1948): 7.

26 Silva Gotay, *Catolicismo y política en Puerto Rico*, 53–101. To explore more profoundly the relationship between colonialism and mission in the past and present, see the article written by Joerg Rieger, "Theology and Mission between Neocolonialism and Postcolonialism," *Mission Studies* 21 (2004): 201–27.

27 See Darrel Enck-Wanzer, ed., *The Young Lords: A Reader* (New York: New York University Press, 2010); Johanna Fernández, *The Young Lords: A Radical History* (Chapel Hill: University of North Carolina Press, 2020).

Conclusion

As we arrive at the end of this study, the question that comes up is the one that always crops up after the completion of a task, or at the end of a long journey. What have we accomplished; what has been our contribution as we depart, for the well-being of others? On October 25, 2012, I took part in the funeral service of my father at Santísima Trinidad Lutheran Church in Bayamón, Puerto Rico. At that time, I was rector (president) of the University Institute ISEDET in Buenos Aires, Argentina. I had just returned from Wittenberg, Germany, where I was asked to present a lecture on "Lutheran Education and Social Transformation" at a Lutheran World Federation gathering which took place from October 18–23. On my arrival in Buenos Aires the morning of October 24, I received a telephone call at home from Rev. Dr. Rafael Malpica-Padilla.[1] He began with a word of greeting for me and my wife Kathryn, but fast forwarded to the dreaded news, "Your father has died. I made arrangements for you and Kathryn to fly to Puerto Rico today, so you can participate in the funeral service scheduled for tomorrow."

At the funeral service attended by friends and family, I was asked to say a few words. During my walk toward the podium, I began to think about conversations I'd had with my father about ministry, and the role of the pastor. "My dear family and friends," I began, "as we gather to celebrate the life of my father, I want to share with you some words of wisdom that I will always remember from our past hours of conversation. He said to me that the best contribution a pastor can make for a congregation is that when he or she leaves, that community of faith has been so well nurtured to carry on, that the contributions of the pastor are not anymore needed." My hope is that my work in the investigation of the emergence and development of the Lutheran mission in Puerto Rico into the Caribbean Synod of the United Lutheran Church in America may provide similar nurture for those interested in the topic.

At the beginning of my study, I aimed to provide a reading from a Caribbeanist and postcolonial[2] historiographical perspective of the mission and expansion of Lutheranism in Puerto Rico from 1898 up to the development of the Caribbean Synod in 1952.[3] My efforts in accomplishing this task incorporated the collective expressions of stories, poems, homiletical reflections, visual images, hymns, references to primary sources in places such as the institutional archives of the Evangelical Lutheran Church in America (ELCA) and its predecessors in the United States, original documents of the Lutheran mission in the archives of the Caribbean Synod, letters, articles in journals and newspapers of the period, theological reflection, summaries of sermons, and other documents in furnishing the testimony of the protagonists of this story. An important effort in this task was to provide a brief but valuable description of the Spanish–American War, along with an early North American view of Puerto Ricans in the archipelago through the letters of George Glenn King, a volunteer North American soldier in the war. The goal was to render a language and understanding of these events closer to the experience of the people of Puerto Rico. They are the ones who can best judge the success of my labor.

I do want to conclude with the following reflections. First, this study constitutes just a preliminary analysis of the topic, and requires further and more probing examination. I consider my contribution to this task not that of an expert, but rather one that is characteristic of a devoted student with a great deal of enthusiasm and curiosity to continue to pursue it. I hope to have stimulated enough interest to encourage others to join in this venture. I am committed to continue exploring this topic, hoping that an increasing number of colleagues will further pursue this area of research.

Second, I am confident that this reading has taught us something significant about the missionary experience of Lutheranism on the archipelago. One of the most important learnings is to avoid a naïve or romantic approach in reading this story, or, for that matter, history as a whole. Clearly traditional efforts to stress the heroism of the North American missionaries at the cost of demeaning the dignity and contribution of Puerto Rican leaders are based on the limitations and prejudice of those telling the story. To be sure, an uncritical description of the role of native Puerto Rican leaders is equally problematic. A more faithful account will describe the ambiguities, failures, and promise of all the characters. In this regard, it seems to me that the presence and initiation of Lutheranism in Puerto Rico is the product of complex processes and a greater number of people than usually assumed. While North American missionaries and church institutions were certainly an important element in this development, people from the West Indies such as John Christopher Owen Browne, the Jamaican tailor who initiated the encounter with Swensson, other people from the various Caribbean islands, religious leaders of other countries who became Lutheran ordained pastors once in Puerto Rico, and Puerto Rican trailblazers were other key elements in the development of this missionary enterprise.

In assessing the continuing significance of the Christian mission in North America since the sixteenth century the Rt. Rev. Steven Charleston, a citizen of the Choctaw Nation and at one time president and dean of the Episcopal Divinity School in Cambridge, Massachusetts, points to the experience of transformation produced by the gospel as the legitimate faithful exchange among peoples of different cultures as they encounter each other.[4] This transformative power of the gospel was then, and continues to be today, the most important component of the church's mission. Granted this framework of interpretation, all the characters in the story play, in their unique way, a significant role in witnessing to the power of the gospel to move forward in their witness—and at times in spite of it—the Lutheran mission in Puerto Rico.

Vítor Westhelle argued that the most valuable contribution of Protestantism in Latin America lies in witnessing to what Luther understood as *teologia crucis*. According to Westhelle, Luther chose the use of the expression "theologian of the cross," instead of "theology of the cross," to emphasize the practical nature of this notion and avoid confusing it with a doctrinal locus. The reformer's intention was not to articulate the conceptualization of another theological topic, but to point to a theological praxis, that is, a unique form of theological and historical reflection that emerges from, and is fundamentally expressed through, a liberating practice:

> What unites the Reformation and the liberation movements in Latin America and the Caribbean is the eschatological vision, an understanding of revelation, an apocalyptic one that recognizes the end and possesses it as its own, as well as an appropriate place for the beginning. This eschatological space that, for the powers represents only the limit, is for those who inhabit it, those who are on the margins, the environment where they experience condemnation, but where liberation is a true possibility. . . . United by the experience of "liminality," of being on the edge, both the Reformation and the emancipatory movements in Latin America and the Caribbean are committed to a fundamental management that guides all their theological effort. This can be expressed in Luther's famous definition: *Crux sola est nostra theologia*.[5]

It is in this sense that the challenges and hardships experienced by those participating in the Lutheran mission in Puerto Rico, as well as their vision and enthusiasm to continue their witness driven by the transformative power of the gospel, are examples of Luther's understanding of the praxis of the theologians of the cross. The stories I chose to investigate for my research focused primarily on

CONCLUSION

the contribution of Puerto Rican leaders in this witness of faith. Those interested in exploring the experience of other characters will provide additional components for this history.

In this regard, one distinctive character of the Lutheran mission in Puerto Rico was to move away from the traditional experience of Lutheran missionaries in foreign missions accompanying Lutheran colonists in their efforts to develop their ethnic culture, language, and traditions overseas. The Lutheran mission in Puerto Rico used the vernacular Spanish language in Puerto Rico early on, and had North American missionaries learn Spanish to carry on the mission in the archipelago. While the First English Evangelical Church of San Juan was established in January 1, 1900, San Pablo Lutheran Church, a Spanish-speaking congregation, was established three months later on April 15, 1900. Given the lack of funds from Lutheran Church bodies in the United States, along with a very limited number of North American missionaries willing to work in Puerto Rico, the early Lutheran missionaries had to incorporate and train native Puerto Rican leaders to help them move forward in their missionary efforts.

A second important character of the Lutheran mission in Puerto Rico was the contribution of foreign and native religious leaders who, leaving behind their ideological and racist prejudices, were able to move forward together in developing opportunities for the emergence of a church body that struggled for the well-being of people in the margins of society. This was the case in the confrontation between Swensson and Browne.

Another important element of this early expression of Lutheranism in the archipelago was the valuable role that Puerto Rican women played in moving forward the work of the mission. History shows that not only were they among the first to engage in this enterprise and lead the social and educational dimension of the Lutheran work among Puerto Rican society, but their leadership role is manifested today by having Rev. Idalia Negrón as the bishop of the Caribbean Synod.

A further important quality of this missionary venture was the initiative of foreign Lutheran leaders such as Eduardo Heylinger, who moved to Puerto Rico from the Virgin Islands and was willing to participate in social revolts like the Grito de Lares (1868) to support the revolution of Puerto Rican leaders against the Spanish colonial empire, even to the point of being imprisoned for his participation in this insurrection.

An additional characteristic of the Lutheran mission in Puerto Rico was its cooperation with other Protestant denominations in expanding the presence and impact of Protestantism in the island. This ecumenical commitment was instrumental to addressing some important projects of social concern for the well-being of Puerto Rican society.[6] It was also a vehicle to support the Protestant work in Spain.[7] The fact is that this Protestant ecumenical approach has continued and increased into the present day. One important sign of this intentional ecumenical strategy in the mission field is that currently the Seminario Evangélico de Puerto Rico (The Evangelical Seminary of Puerto Rico), the main Protestant center for the theological formation of pastors for Protestant churches on the island, incorporates in its board of directors, faculty, students, and programs of studies[8] representatives of the Caribbean Synod, as well as Latinx Lutheran scholars in the United States.

An added valuable development in the area of theological reflection is the increasing cooperation and dialogue of Lutherans with the Roman Catholic Church and other worldwide religions, both internationally and on the island of Puerto Rico. On October 16, 2016, at Lund, Sweden, there was a call by Pope Francis and Bishop Munib Junan, president of the Lutheran World Federation, for the celebration of the five-hundred-year anniversary of the sixteenth-century European Protestant Reformation.[9] Earlier, in 2004, an ecumenical and interreligious coalition was established in Puerto Rico to promote peace and social well-being in the archipelago.[10]

Finally, following the lead of other Protestant denominations in Puerto Rico, Lutherans contributed to the education of Puerto Ricans, developing private elementary schools along with creative programs for the education of the population,[11] and attending to the needs of those with leprosy both in San Juan and St. Croix.

CONCLUSION

These, and other stories mentioned in this study, highlight the struggles of Lutheran leaders in Puerto Rico against imperialists' colonial burdens, whether from Spanish or North American countries. In so doing, these efforts show that not every Lutheran in Puerto Rico was in favor of its "Americanization."[12] Others struggled to maintain their Puerto Rican culture and identity. One recent example of this expression of resistance is the leadership role that bishops of the Caribbean Synod have played in the efforts to get the US Navy out of Vieques.[13]

To conclude, I also want to share that I am still truly intrigued by the motives that continue to lead the Caribbean Synod to describe its organizational character similarly to the one established in 1952. While an investigation of the reasons for this occurrence goes beyond the limits of this research and needs to be the subject of a different study, I want to make the following reflections. First, the reason for my interest lies in the fact that other Christian denominational ventures in Puerto Rico, such as the Baptists, Disciples of Christ, Presbyterians, Methodists, and many others, while sharing a somewhat similar experience to that of the Lutheran mission at the beginning of their missional experience on the island, later on developed into Puerto Rican national churches. Second, ironically, the experiences of members of the Lutheran Caribbean Synod followed a similar path to that of the politics of the island since 1952. I wonder whether, due to the following facts—(i) that the constituency of the Caribbean Synod is numerically smaller than many of these other Protestant denominations; (ii) that for a long period of time those seeking ordination in the Caribbean Synod were required to study at a Lutheran seminary in the United States; and (iii) that the complex process of the Americanization of Puerto Rico has been more thoroughly experienced by Lutherans than by members of other denominations—the synod will need more time to develop into a national church.[14] It also may be that the congregational/episcopal type of organization of the Caribbean Synod may be too rigid to make changes easy to achieve. The fact is that, in recent years, the Caribbean Synod has experienced the emergence of a significant number of its members requesting the development of a Lutheran national church, but these efforts have failed to yield results. In any case, this topic will need further study. For now, I hope that this volume will contribute to renewing and further improving the contributions of Lutheranism, not just in Puerto Rico or the Caribbean, but as it continues to become a reformation movement of the church catholic in all parts of the world.

NOTES

1 Since our trip to Argentina was as missionaries sponsored by the global unit of the Evangelical Lutheran Church in America, and during that time my sister Raquel was the regional director of the unit for Mexico, the Caribbean, and Latin America, to avoid future controversies Rafael Malpica Padilla, executive director of the unit, was made my supervisor.

2 Postcolonial theory in historiography is an effort to explore historical events beyond traditional dominant approaches in order to find what was missing in these narratives. To achieve this goal postcolonial theory engages in an interdisciplinary methodology extending to areas beyond the long-established discipline of history to fill these gaps. Postcolonial historiography is part of what the renowned historian Peter Burke claimed in his study *New Perspective on Historical Writing* as another way of writing history.

3 As mentioned earlier, the two most important studies about Protestantism in Puerto Rico (Rodríguez, Silva-Gotay) used imperialist historiographies (Marxist, and the Annales School, or the history of the mentalities respectively).

4 Steven Charleston, "The Good, the Bad and the New: The Native American Missionary Experience," *Dialog* 40, no. 2 (Summer 2001): 99–104.

5 Translation mine. Vítor Westhelle, *Voces de protesta en América latina* (Mexico: Lutheran School of Theology at Chicago, 2000), 111. See also Vítor Westhelle, *The Scandalous God: The Use and Abuse of the Cross* (Minneapolis: Fortress Press, 2006).

6 See, for example, the Lutheran cooperation with other Protestant denominations in the island such as Congresos misioneros, "El Congreso misionero Cierra sus debates," *La Correspondencia*, año XXV, no. 9,325 (March 25, 1926): 7. And more recently, the ecumenical movement in Vieques to expel the US Navy from the island. See, Rev. Wilfredo Estrada Adorno, *Pastores o políticos con sotanas? Pastoral de la guardarraya en Vieques* (Trujillo Alto, Puerto Rico: Editorial Guardarrayas, 2003).

7 See "El viaje de propaganda por la isla, del representante de los evangélicos españoles," *El Imparcial*, año VI, no. 128 (June 1, 1923): 8.
8 At the end of the 1990s, the Seminario Evangélico de Puerto Rico incorporated in its programs of studies, courses, lectures, and special educational seminars, developed by El Centro Luterano de Formación Teológica José David Rodríguez.
9 See Foro Encuentro Interreligioso, "La iglesia católica y la iglesia luterana," December 5, 2016, https://foroencuentrointerreligioso.blogspot.com/2016/12/la-iglesia-catolica-y-la-iglesia.html.
10 Zury, "La religión Puerto Rico," April 18, 2012, https://zury-wolf-class.blogspot.com/2012/04/la-religion-puerto-rico.html. See also https://www.elnuevodia.com/noticias/locales/notas/religiosos-hacen-llamado-al-gobierno-para-reflexionar-en-semana-santa/ (accessed July 12, 2023).
11 See *La correspondencia*, año XVIII, no. 6, 170 (January 7, 1908): 1.
12 Although there were indeed some who felt so strongly about this trend for the "Americanization" of the island that on some occasions it led to special religious celebrations of some North American presidents. See *El Mundo* (August 9, 1923): 6, Library of Congress, https://tinyurl.com/yja7n29x.
13 For valuable information about this topic, see Lester McGrath-Andino, *Quo Vadis, Vieques: Ética social, política y ecumenismo* (San Juan: special publication by Seminario Evangélico de Puerto Rico, 2000); Wilfredo Estrada Adorno, *¿Pastores o políticos con sotanas? Pastoral de la guardarraya en Vieques* (Trujillo Alto: Editorial Guardarraya, 2003). See also "Church Leaders Rally against Navy Base," *The Christian Century* (March 8, 2000): 268–69; Paul Jeffrey and Chris Herlinger, "Despite Arrests Church Leaders Vow to Continue Vieques Protest," ChristianityToday.com, May 10, 2000, https://www.christianitytoday.com/ct/2000/mayweb-only/35.0a.html.
14 Another reason may be that the larger number of constituents of the Caribbean Synod might favor the present political status of the Estado Libre Asociado de Puerto Rico (the Free-Associated State of Puerto Rico).

Afterword

This book is an important contribution to the history of the Lutheran Church in Puerto Rico, the Caribbean, and Latin America. Its author—José David Rodríguez—has evidently studied and researched carefully and diligently the story of Lutheranism in the Caribbean archipelago.

His academic perspective is clear and radical: a postcolonial and decolonial perspective. As a Puerto Rican, Rodríguez originates from a Caribbean Island that has been aptly described by a foremost juridical scholar as "the oldest colony of the world."[1] During several decades, Rodríguez has developed a critical theological analysis of that colonial history. His writings might be considered a prophetic theological perspective, another crucial form of liberation theology.

This book begins by analyzing the political and religious history of Puerto Rico, a Caribbean island colonized by Spain, then conquered militarily by the United States. Under the rule of Spain, the Roman Catholic Church prevailed; when the United States prevailed, the Protestant denominations began to arrive on the island. Coloniality has traditionally designed a religious perspective.

And then, Rodríguez has carefully researched and analyzed the diverse ways the North American Lutheran Church decided to participate in a process of academic and religious education of the Puerto Ricans, and of members of other Caribbean islands that were also conquered and ruled by the United States. I am impressed by the amount of information provided in this excellent book.

AFTERWORD

This volume is a fine analysis of the history of the Lutheran Church in the Caribbean and Latin America. I enjoyed reading it and recommend its careful analysis!

Luis N. Rivera-Pagán
Henry Winters Luce Professor of Ecumenics Emeritus
Princeton Theological Seminary
February 7, 2023

NOTE

1 José Trías Monge, *Puerto Rico: The Trials of the Oldest Colony in the World* (New Haven, CT: Yale University Press, 1997).

Bibliography

Aagaard, Johannes. "Missionary Theology." In *The Lutheran Church Past and Present*, ed. Vilmos Vajta, 00. Minneapolis: Augsburg Press, 1977, 206–27.

Abramson, Michael. *Palante: Voices and Photographs of the Young Lords, 1969–1971*. Chicago: Haymarket Books, 1971.

Altmann, Walter. *Lutero e libertação*. São Leopoldo: Editora Sinodal, 2016.

Álvarez, Carmelo Santos, and Carlos F. Cardoza Orlandi. *Llamados a construir su Reino: Teología y estrategia misionera de los discípulos de Cristo 1899–1999*. Bayamón: Iglesia Cristiana Discípulos de Cristo, 2000.

Anderson, Gerald H., ed. *The Theology of the Christian Mission*. New York, Toronto, and London: McGraw-Hill, 1961.

Appleby, Joyce, Lyn Hunt, and Margaret Jacob. *Telling the Truth about History*. New York: W. W. Norton, 1995.

Arbaugh, William G. "Alfredo Ostrom y la era de expansión: Historia de la misión luterana en Puerto Rico desde 1905 hasta 1918." *El Testigo*, año XXXII, no. 7 (December 1948): 5–6, 14.

———. "Because He Looked Like a Man of God." *El Testigo*, año XXXI, no. 11 (April 1948): 16.

———. *A Caribbean Mission: The Correspondence of William George Arbaugh*. Edited by William Charles Arbaugh. Victoria, BC: Erbach Books, 2006.

———. "Fred W. Lindke and the Era of Transition: Puerto Rico Lutheran History from 1918 to 1928." *El Testigo*, año XXXII, no. 8 (January 1949): 13–16.

———. "Gustav Sigfried Swensson and the Puerto Rico Lutheran Mission." (This essay was written on March 22, 1948, and mimeographed for distribution at Frederick Lutheran Church, St. Croix, Virgin Islands during the 1960s).

———. "November 1, 1950." In *A Caribbean Mission*, 32.

———. *Notes and Quotes from the Correspondence of William George Arbaugh*. Edited by William Charles Arbaugh. Portland: personal publication, 2000.

———. "Principios de la iglesia luterana en Puerto Rico." *El Testigo*, año XIX, no. 12 (February and March 1924): 1, 4.

———. "Revista de libros." *El Testigo*, año XXVI, no. 11 (April 1943): 9–10.

———. "Witnessing through Twenty Years." *El Testigo*, año XXI, no. 2 (July 1937): 17.

Arbaugh, Nora D., and Herminio Díaz. "Impresiones del Segundo Congreso Latinoamericano de Juventudes Evangélicas." *El Testigo*, año XXX, no. 4 (September 1946): 8.

Arden, G. Everett. *A History of the Augustana Lutheran Church*. Rock Island, IL: Augustana Press, 1963.

———. *The School of the Prophets: The Background and History of Augustana Theological Seminary 1860–1960*. Rock Island, IL: Augustana Theological Seminary, 1960.

Ashcroft, Bill, Gareth Griffiths, and Helen Tiffin. *The Post-Colonial Studies Reader*. London and New York: Routledge, 1995.

———. *Key Concepts in Post-Colonial Studies*. London and New York: Routledge, 1998.

Bachmann, E. Theodore, and Mercia Brenne Bachmann. *Lutheran Churches in the World: A Handbook*. Minneapolis: Augsburg, published in cooperation with the Lutheran World Federation, 1989.

Bainton, Roland. *The Martin Luther Christmas Book*. Philadelphia: The Westminster Press, 1948.

———. *Women of the Reformation: In Germany and Italy*. Minneapolis: Augsburg Publishing House, 1971.

———. *Women of the Reformation: From Spain to Scandinavia.* Minneapolis: Augsburg Publishing House, 1977.

Baralt, M. *Historia de Venezuela.* París: Desclée de Brower, 1939.

Bastian, Jean-Pierre. *Historia del Protestantismo en América Latina.* Mexico: Casa Unida de Publicaciones, 1986.

———. "Colonial Protestantism, 1492–1808." In *The Church in Latin America 1492–1992*, ed. Enrique Dussel. New York: Orbis Books, 1992, 314–17.

Benito, José A. "Alonso Manso, Primer Obispo de América, De Salamanca a Puerto Rico. 500 años de su llegada." Jabenito.blog.com, November 11, 2012.

Beozzo, J. O., ed. *Escravidao Negra e História da Igreja na América Latina e no Caribe.* Petrópolis: Vozes, 1987.

Blank, Roberto. *Teología y Misión en America Latina.* St. Louis: Concordia Publishing House, 1996.

Boletín Mercantil de Puerto Rico (September 10, 1903): 7.

———. (April 27, 1907): 4.

Brochure of the Iglesia Evangélica Luterana del Divino Salvador. 1982.

Budd, Richard M. *Serving Two Masters: The Development of American Military Chaplaincy, 1860–1920.* Lincoln and London: University of Nebraska Press, 2000.

Bulletin for the Fiftieth Anniversary of the Ministry of Rev. Eduardo Roig Vélez Iglesia Luterana El Buen Pastor. September 1, 1968, 2–3.

Bulletin for the Celebration of the 69th Anniversary of the Lutheran Church Divino Salvador. 1973.

Burke, Peter. *New Perspectives on Historical Writing*, 2nd ed. University Park: The Pennsylvania State University Press, 2001.

Cabrera, Miguel A. "On Language, Culture, and Social Action." *History and Theory* 40, no. 4 (December 2001): 82–100.

Cancel, Mario R. "Historiografía puertorriqueña hoy: una meditación y una crítica." In *Historias Marginales: Otros rostros de Jano.* Mayagüez: Centro de Publicaciones Académicas UPR-RUM Facultad de Artes y Ciencias, 2007, 17–56.

BIBLIOGRAPHY

Cardoza Orlandi, Carlos F. *Mission: An Essential Guide.* Nashville: Abingdon Press, 2002.

Caribbean Call 1, no. 1 (October 1952): 1-8.

Carr, David. "Place and Time: On the Interplay of Historical Points of View." *History and Theory* 40, no 4 (December 2001): 153-67.

Carr, Edward H. *What Is History?*, 2nd ed. London: The Macmillan Press, 1986.

Centro Journal XXVI, no. I (Spring 2014): 148-71.

Chamberlain, Mary. "Elsa Goveia: History and Nation" *History Workshop Journal* 58 (November 3, 2015): 167-68.

Charleston, Steven. "The Good, the Bad and the New: The Native American Missionary Experience." *Dialog* 40, no. 2 (Summer 2001): 99-104.

"A Chronology of Protestant Beginnings: Puerto Rico/Una cronología de los comienzos de la obra Protestante en Puerto Rico 1598-2011." Compiled by Drs. Daryl L. Platt, Clifton L. Holland. and Dorothy Bullón. https://www.ranchocolibri.net/prolades/historical/pri-chron.pdf.

"Church Leaders Rally against US Navy Base." *The Christian Century* (March 8, 2000): 268-69.

Corbe, Zenan M. *In the Land of Unending Summer.* Philadelphia: Prepared by the Board of American Missions and the Women's Missionary Society of the United Lutheran Church in America, October 1930.

La correspondencia de Puerto Rico. (September 22, 1903).

———. año XV, no. 5,347 (September 29, 1905): 3.

———. año XVIII, no. 6,170 (January 7, 1908): 1

———. (December 8, 1903).

———. (April 27, 1907).

———. año XXX, no. 10,916 (February 28, 1922): 2.

———. año XXV, no. 9,325 (March 25, 1926): 7.

Crespo Vargas, Pablo L. *La Inquisición española y las supersticiones en el Caribe hispano, siglo XVI.* Lajas: Editorial Akelarre, 2013.

Critchlow, G. W. "The Virgin Isles' First Missionary Effort." *The Lutheran* (May 8, 1919).

Davis, J. Merle. *The Church in Puerto Rico's Dilemma*. New York: International Missionary Council, 1942.

Deiros, Pablo A. *Historia del Cristianismo en América Latina*. Florida and Buenos Aires: Fraternidad Teológica Latinoamericana, 1992.

La Democracia. (June 6, 1901): 4.

———. (February 7, 1907): 2.

Díaz Alfaro, Abelardo. *Terrazo*. San Juan: Editorial Plaza Mayor, 2009.

Donoghue, Eddie. *Negro Slavery: Slave Society and Slave Life in the Danish West Indies*. Bloomington and Milton Keynes: AuthorHouse, 2007.

"Doña Gabriela Cuervos Vda. De Marks." *El Testigo*, año XIX, no. 11 (April 1936): 2.

Drouet, Vega H. "Some Musical Forms of African Descendants in Puerto Rico: Bomba, Plena, and Rosario Frances." In *New Grove Dictionary of Music and Musicians*, ed. Stanley Sadie, vol. 20, 585–86. London: Macmillan, 2001.

Dubois, Laurent, and John D. Garrigus. *Slave Revolution in the Caribbean 1789–1804: A Brief History with Documents*. Boston and New York: Bedford/St. Martins, 2006.

Editors of the *Encyclopaedia Britannica*. "Evangelical Lutheran Church in America." Britannica.com, accessed June 23, 2023, https://www.britannica.com/topic/Evangelical-Lutheran-Church-in-America.

Edmonds, Ennis B., and Michelle A. Gonzalez. *Caribbean Religious History: An Introduction*. New York and London: New York University Press, 2010.

Elton, G. R. *The Practice of History*, 2nd ed. Oxford: Blackwell, 2002.

Enck-Wanzer, Darrel, ed. *The Young Lords: A Reader*. New York and London: New York University Press, 2010.

Estados Font, María E. *La presencia militar de Estados Unidos en Puerto Rico: 1898–1918*. Río Piedras: Editorial Universitaria, Universidad de Puerto Rico, 1986.

Estrada Adorno, Wilfredo. *¿Pastores o políticos con sotanas? Pastoral de la guardarraya en Vieques.* Trujillo Alto: Editorial Guardarrayas, 2003.

Evans, Richard J. *In Defense of History.* New York: W. W. Norton, 2000.

Fernández, Johanna. *The Young Lord: A Radical History.* Chapel Hill: The University of North Carolina Press, 2020.

"First Report of the Board of Porto Rico Missions to the General Council of the Evangelical Lutheran Church in North America." October 1903.

Fox, Lewis R. "The Lutheran Church in Puerto Rico." *El Testigo* (May 1936): 11.

Franqui-Rivera, Harry. *Soldiers of the Nation: Military Service and Modern Puerto Rico, 1898–1952.* Lincoln and London: University of Nebraska Press, 2018.

Friede, Juan. *Los Welser en la conquista de Venezuela.* Caracas and Madrid: The commemorative edition of the IV centenary of the death of Bartolomé Welser, leader of the German company from Augsburg, 1961.

García-Rivera, Alex. *St. Martín de Porres: The "Little Stories" and the Semiotics of Culture.* New York: Orbis Books, 1995.

Gilderhus, Mark T. *History and Historians: A Historiographical Introduction*, 7th ed. Upper Saddle River, NJ: Prentice Hall, 2010.

Goveia, Elsa V. *A Study on the Historiography of the British West Indies to the End of the Nineteenth Century.* Mexico: Instituto Panamericano de Geografía e Historia, 1956.

Granquist, Mark. *Lutherans in America: A New History.* Minneapolis: Fortress Press, 2015.

Gritsch, Eric W. *A History of Lutheranism.* Minneapolis: Fortress Press, 2002.

Guha, Ranajit, and Gayatri Chakravorty Spivak. *Selected Subaltern Studies.* New York and Oxford: Oxford University Press, 1988.

Gutiérrez, Ángel L. *Evangélicos en Puerto Rico en la época Española.* Guaynabo: Editorial Chari, 1997.

Haefeli, Evan. *Accidental Pluralism: America and the Religious Politics of English Expansion, 1497–1662*. Chicago and London: University of Chicago Press, 2021.
Hall, Neville A. T. *Slave Society in the Danish West Indies*. Mona: University of the West Indies Press, 1992.
Harrington, Mark W. "Porto Rico and the Portorricans." *Catholic World* 70, no. 416 (November 1899): 164.
Hei Yip, Man. *Interrogating the Language of "Self" and "Other" in the History of Modern Christian Mission: Contestation, Subversion, and Re-Imagination*. Eugene, OR: Pickwick, 2020.
El Heraldo Español. año VIII, no. 173 (July 30, 1902): 2.
Herzel, Catherine B. *She Made Many Rich: Sister Emma Francis of the Virgin Island*. Frederiksted: CRIC Productions, 1990.
Higman, B. W. "The Development of Historical Disciplines in the Caribbean." In *General History of the Caribbean: Vol. VI, Methodology and Historiography of the Caribbean*, ed. B. W. Higman, 3–18. London and Oxford: UNESCO Publishing/Macmillan Education, 1999.
Hunt, Tony. "The Church and Race Relations—Then and Now." Leading Ideas, Lewis Center for Church Leadership, January 21, 2009, https://www.churchleadership.com/leading-ideas/the-church-and-race-relations-then-and-now-1968-2008/.
Hunte, Keith. "Protestantism and Slavery in the British Caribbean." In *Christianity in the Caribbean: Essays on Church History*, ed. Armando Lampe, 86–125. Barbados, Jamaica, Trinidad and Tobago: University of the West Indies Press, 2001.
El Ideal Católico. año I, no. 1 (August 15, 1899): 1–2.
———. año I, no. 3 (August 26, 1899): 17–19.
———. año I, no. 4 (September 2, 1899): 29.
———. año I, no. 8 (September 30, 1899): 60.
———. año I, no. 9 (October 6, 1899): 68.
———. año I, no.16 (November 25, 1899): 125.
———. año II, no. 8 (October 6, 1900): 77.
———. año II, no. 10 (October 20, 1900): 106 and 111.

———. año II, no. 11 (October 27, 1900): 120.
———. año IV, no. 156 (August 2, 1902): 366.
Iggers, Georg G., and Q. Edward Wang, with contributions from Supira Mukherjee. *A Global History of Modern Historiography*. Edinburgh: Pearson Education, 2008.
El Imparcial. año V, no. 220 (September 21, 1922): 7.
———. año V, no. 213 (February 23, 1922): 4.
———. año VI, no. 127 (May 15, 1923): 5.
———. año VI, no. 128 (June 1, 1923): 8.
Iran, Isfahan. "A Critical Examination of Postmodernism Based on Religious and Moral Values Education." *International Education Studies* 8, no. 9: 98–106.
Ivison, Duncan. "Postcolonialism." Britannica.com, May 20, 2023, https://www.britannica.com/topic/postcolonialism.
Jenkins, Keith. *On What Is History*. London and New York: Routledge, 1995.
Jensen, Lars. "Postcolonial Denmark: Beyond the Rot of Colonialism." *Postcolonial Studies* 18, no. 4 (2015): 440–52.
Karsdorf, Hans. "The Legacy of Gustav Warneck." *International Bulletin of Missionary Research* (July 1980): 102. https://www.scribd.com/doc/123497360/Legacy-of-Gustav-Warneck?secret_password=1y9oi8unr4oumofmce4r#.
Kennedy, Dane. *Decolonization: A Very Short Introduction*. Oxford: Oxford University Press, 2016.
Lake, Edgar O. "The Role of the Artist in the Liberation Struggle." The Leonard Tim Hector Annual Memorial Lecture, Anglican Cultural Center, St. John's, Antigua, West Indies, November 7, 2005.
Lampe, Armando. "Christianity and Slavery in the Dutch Caribbean." In *Christianity in the Caribbean: Essays on Church History*, ed. Armando Lampe, 126–53. Barbados, Jamaica, Trinidad and Tobago: University of the West Indies Press, 2001.
Lawson, Kenneth E. *With Courage and Confidence: The US Army Chaplaincy and the Puerto Rico Campaign of 1898*. Ft. Buchanan, PR: Installation Chaplain's Office, 2008.

Libro de liturgia y cantico. Minneapolis: Fortress Press, 1998.

Lord, Albert B. *The Singer of Tales.* Cambridge, MA: Harvard University Press, 1964.

Luther, Martin. "The Christian in Society II." In *Luther's Works*, vol. 45, ed. Walther I. Brandt, gen. ed. Helmut T. Lehman. 55 vols. Philadelphia: Muhlenberg Press, 1962, 70–71.

———. "The Gospel for the Festival of the Epiphany, Matthew 2:1–12 (1527)." In *Luther's Works*, vol. 52, ed. Jaroslav Pelican and Helmut T. Lehman, 159–286. 55 vols. Philadelphia: Fortress Press, 1955.

The Lutheran (Official Organ of the United Lutheran Church in America). IV, no. 8 (November 9, 1899): 5.

———. IV, no. 9 (November 30, 1899): 3.

———. IV, no. 19 (February 8, 1900): 6.

———. I, no. 40 (January 29, 1920): 809.

———. I, no. 47 (March 18, 1920): 934.

———. II, no. 15 (August 12, 1920): 256.

———. II, no. 19 (September 9, 1920): 286.

———. III, no. 1 (September 30, 1920): 9, 320.

———. XXIII, no. 17 (January 22, 1941).

———. 32, no. 28 (April 6, 1949): 14–16.

———. 33, no. 28 (May 2, 1951): 31–32.

———. 34, no. 27 (April 2, 1952): 12–16.

———. 34, no. 28 (April 9, 1952): 20–21.

———. 34, no. 40 (July 2, 1952): 31–33.

Lutheran Women. 2, no. 6 (June 1961).

———. 3, no. 6 (June 1962).

Mayer, Alicia. *Lutero en el Paraíso: La Nueva España en el espejo del reformador alemán.* Mexico: Fondo de Cultura Económica, 2008.

Mayor, Federico. "Preface." In *General History of the Caribbean*, vol. VI: *Methodology and Historiography of the Caribbean*, ed. B. W. Higman. London and Oxford: UNESCO Publishing/Macmillan Education, 1999.

Majumdar, Rochona. *Writing Postcolonial History.* London: Bloomsbury Academic, 2010.

Martínez-Fernández, Luis. "'Don't Die Here': The Death and Burial of Protestants in the Hispanic Caribbean, 1840-1885." *The Americas* XLVIV, no. I (July 1992): 23-47.

———. *Protestantism and Political Conflict in the Nineteenth-Century Hispanic Caribbean*. New Brunswick, NJ: Rutgers University Press, 2002.

Marx, Karl. *Critique of Hegel's Philosophy of Right*. Edited by Joseph O'Malley. Cambridge: Cambridge University Press, 1970.

McAllister, James. "The Presbyterian Theological Training School." *The Assembly Herald* 4 (1908): 207.

McAllister, James A. "Un Ministerio Bien Preparado." *Puerto Rico Evangélico* 2 (1914): 2-4.

McGrath-Andino, Lester. *¿Quo Vadis, Vieques? Ética social, política y ecumenismo*. San Juan: special publication by Seminario Evangélico de Puerto Rico, 2000.

"Memorial Program: Fortieth Anniversary of the First Lutheran Congregation Organized in Puerto Rico." English Supplement to *El Testigo*, January 1940.

Mission Tidings (monthly journal of the Women's Missionary Society of the Augustana Lutheran Church). XLVII, no. 1 (June 1952): 13, 16.

"Minutas de la Asamblea Constituyente del Sínodo Evangélico Luterano del Caribe de la Iglesia Luterana Unida en América mayo 29-31, 1952," 5-11.

Molina, Francisco. "Hace muchos años: Para Sergio Cobián y Guillermo E. Marrero." In *Ciudad allende el alba*, 106-8. Dorado: Sínodo Luterano del Caribe, 1999.

Moore, Brian L., B. W. Higman, Carl Campbell, and Patrick Bryan. *Slavery, Freedom and Gender: The Dynamics of Caribbean Society*. Barbados, Jamaica, Trinidad and Tobago: University of the West Indies Press, 2003.

Moore, Donald T. *Puerto Rico Para Cristo: A History of the Progress of the Evangelical Mission on the Island of Puerto Rico*. Cuernavaca: Centro Intercultural de Documentación, SONDEOS no. 43, 1969, 17-22.

El Mundo. (December 27, 1919): 4.
———. (April 28, 1922): 6.
———. (August 9, 1923): 6.
———. (November 9, 1924): 1, 6.
———. (February 20, 1952): 17.
Murga Sanz, Vicente, and Alvaro Huerga. *Episcopologio de Puerto Rico.* Ponce: Universidad Católica de Puerto Rico, 1987.
Naffier, Vernon H. *Historical Sketch of Lutheranism in the Caribbean.* Unknown Binding, January 1, 1987.
Neve, Juergen L. *A Brief History of the Lutheran Church in America.* Burlington, VT: The German Literary Board, 1916/2020.
El Nuevo Día. (October 28, 2001): 4.
Ostrom, Alfredo. "Principios de la Iglesia Luterana en Puerto Rico." *El Testigo*, año VII, 9 and 10.
Pantojas García, Emilio. *La Iglesia Protestante y la americanización de Puerto Rico.* Río Piedras: privately printed, 1972.
Peñaranda, Nicolette. "The Oldest ELCA Church Resides in the US Virgin Islands." *The Living Lutheran* (January/February 2023).
Pereyra, Carlos. "Historia, ¿para qué?" In *Historia, ¿para qué?* Mexico/España: Siglo Veintiuno Editores, 1998, 11–31.
Philadelphia Vision: Mt. Airy Tradition: Essays for the 125th Anniversary of the Lutheran Theological Seminary at Philadelphia. Philadelphia: Lutheran Theological Seminary in Philadelphia, 1991.
Picó, Fernando. *1898: La Guerra después de la Guerra.* San Juan: Ediciones Huracán, 2004.
———. "Historiography of Puerto Rico." In *General History of the Caribbean*, vol. VI: *Methodology and Historiography of the Caribbean*, ed. B. W. Higman. London and Oxford: UNESCO Publishing/Macmillan Education, 1999, 417–49.
Pomada, Alicia. "Puerto Rico, School Language Policies." In *Encyclopedia of Bilingual Education*, weebly.com, accessed June 23, 2023, http://aliciapousada.weebly.com/uploads/1/0/0/2/10020146/puerto_rico_school_language_policies___encyclopedia_of_bilingual_education.pdf.

BIBLIOGRAPHY

"Possible Advantages and Disadvantages in the Proposed Reorganization of the Lutheran Missionary Conference of Puerto Rico as a Member Synod of the United Lutheran Church in America." A letter written on April 1, 1946, by William G. Arbaugh, Secretary for Latin America of the Board of American Missions.

Puerto Rico Evangélico. año 1, no. 19 (April 10, 1913): 7, 10.

———. año 2, no. 16 (February 25, 1914): 14.

———. año 2, no. 19 (April 10, 1914): 14.

———. año 2, no. 23 (June 10, 1914): 14.

———. año 2, no. 24 (June 25, 1914): 15.

———. año 3 no. 24 (June 25, 1915): 7.

———. año XV. no. 1 (July 9, 1926): 12.

———. año XV, no. 14 (October 9, 1926): 11–12.

———. año XV, no. 18 (November 6, 1926): 12.

———. año XXXIX, no. 1,089 (July 25, 1951): 13.

———. año XXXX, no. 1,090 (August 10, 1951): 14.

———. año 40, no. 1,101(January 25, 1952): 4.

———. año 40, no. 1,103 (February 25, 1952): 1, 16.

———. año 40, no. 1,106 (April 10, 1952): 16.

———. año 40, no. 1111 (June 25, 1952): 13.

———. año 41, no. 1112 (July 14, 1952): 10.

Ranjan, Ritwik. "Postcoloniality and the Two Sides of Historicity." *History and Theory* 56, no. 1 (March 2017): 38–53.

Report of the Board of Foreign Missions to the General Council of the Evangelical Lutheran Church in North America, 1899.

Report of the Board of Foreign Mission to the General Council of the Evangelical Lutheran Church in North America, 1901.

Reumann, John H. P. *Ministries Examined: Laity, Clergy, Women, and Bishops in a Time of Change*. Minneapolis: Augsburg Publishing, 1987.

Rieger, Joerg. "Theology and Mission Between Neocolonialism and Postcolonialism." *Mission Studies* 21 (2004): 201–27.

Rivera Pagán, Luis N. *Historia de la conquista de América: Evangelización y violencia*. Barcelona: CLIE, 2021.

———. *A Violent Evangelism: The Political and Religious Conquest of the Americas.* Louisville, KY: Westminster/John Knox Press, 1992.

Rivera Torres, Jorge Juan. *Documentos Históricos de la Iglesia Episcopal*, vol. I. Saint Just, PR: Taller Episcográfico de la Iglesia Episcopal Puertorriqueña, 2008.

Rivero, Ángel. *Crónica de la guerra Hispanoamericana en Puerto Rico.* Río Piedras: Editorial Edil, 1998.

Robinson-Hammerstein, Helga. "The Lutheran Reformation and Its Music." In *The Transmission of Ideas in the Lutheran Reformation*, ed. Helga Robinson-Hammerstein, 141–71. Dublin: Irish Academic Press, 1989.

Rodríguez, Daniel R. *La primera evangelización norteamericana en Puerto Rico 1898–1930.* Mexico: Ediciones Borinquén, 1986.

Rodríguez, Ileana, ed. *The Latin American Subaltern Studies Reader.* Durham, NC, and London: Duke University Press, 2001.

Rodríguez Hernández, José David. "North American Historians of the British West Indies." Research Paper presented to the class on Historiography at the University of the West Indies, October 2016.

———. Review of Ángel Rivero, *Crónica de la Guerra Hispano Americana*, for the course Hist. 6005 Historiografía Puertorriqueña at the Interamerican University (May 13, 2011).

Rooy, Sidney. *Misión y encuentro de culturas.* Florida and Buenos Aires: Editorial Kairós, 2001.

Saenz, Michael. "Economic Aspects of Church Development in Puerto Rico: A Study of the Financial Policies and Procedures of the Major Protestant Church Groups in Puerto Rico from 1898 to 1957." A dissertation in economics to the Faculty of the Graduate School of Arts and Sciences of the University of Pennsylvania, 1961.

Sáenz de Morales, Ana. "Panorama de Educación Cristiana de la Iglesia Luterana en Puerto Rico." *El Testigo* (June 1940): 8–9.

Sandgren, Carl H. *My Church: A Yearbook of the Lutheran Augustana Synod of North America Vol. XXIV.* Rock Island, IL: Augustana Book Concern, 1938.

Santiago-Vendrell, Ángel. "Give Them Christ: Native Agency in the Evangelization of Puerto Rico, 1900 to 1917." *Religions* 12, no. 3 (2021): 196. https://doi.org/10.3390/rel12030196.

Scherer, James A. *Gospel, Church, & Kingdom: Comparative Studies in World Mission Theology.* Minneapolis: Augsburg Publishing House, 1987.

———. *Justinian Welz: Essays by and Early Prophet of Mission.* Grand Rapids, MI: William B. Eerdmans, 1969.

———. "The Relation of Mission and Unity in Lutheranism: A Study in Lutheran Ecumenics." A dissertation submitted in partial fulfillment of the requirements for the degree of Doctor of Theology at Union Theological Seminary in the city of New York, 1968.

Schmidt, Alvin J. *Hallmarks of Lutheran Identity.* St. Louis: Concordia Publishing House, 2017.

Scott, James C. *Domination and the Arts of Resistance: Hidden Transcripts.* New Haven, CT, and London: Yale University Press, 1990.

———. *Weapons of the Weak: Everyday Forms of Peasant Resistance.* New Haven, CT, and London: Yale University Press, 1985.

"Seventh Biennial Report of the Board of Missions for Porto Rico and Latin America of the General Council of the Evangelical Lutheran Church in North America." 1915, 12.

Sheen, Fulton. *Christmas Inspirations.* New York: Maco Publications, 1966.

Shepherd, Verene, and Hilary McD. Beckles, eds. *Caribbean Slavery in the Atlantic World.* Kingston, Jamaica: Ian Randle Publishers, 2000.

Silva Gotay, Samuel. *Catolicismo y política en Puerto Rico: Bajo España y Estados Unidos Siglos XIX y XX.* San Juan: Editorial de la Universidad de Puerto Rico, 2005.

———. *Protestantismo y política en Puerto Rico 1898–1930: Hacia una historia del protestantismo evangélico en Puerto Rico.* San Juan: Editorial de la Universidad de Puerto Rico, 1997.

Singmaster Lewars, Elsie. *The Story of Lutheran Missions*. Columbia: Survey Publishing Co., 1917.

Smith, Linda T. *Decolonizing Methodologies: Research and Indigenous People*, 2nd ed. Dunedin: Otago University Press, 2012.

Steuernagel, Valdir R. "El despertar misionero del Tercer Mundo." *Mission* 6 (June 1987): 7–17.

Stover, Earl F. *Up from Handymen: The United States Army Chaplaincy 1865–1920*, vol. III. Washington, DC: Office of the Chief of Chaplains Department of the Army, 1977.

Strong, Josiah. *Our Country: Its Possible Future and Its Present Crisis*. New York: The Baker & Taylor Co., 1891.

Swensson, Gustav S. "I Went to Puerto Rico." *El Testigo* (October 1948): 16.

Tappert, Theodore G. *History of the Philadelphia Seminary*. Philadelphia: The Lutheran Theological Seminary at Philadelphia, 1964.

Telelboim, Voloida. *El amanecer del capitalismo y la conquista de América*. Havana: Casa de las Américas, 1979.

El Testigo (The Witness). año I, no. 1 (June 1917).

———. año XIX, no. 12 (February and March 1924): 1, 4.

———. año XVII, no. 2 (March 1935): 14–15.

———. año XIX, no. 11 (April 1936).

———. año XIX, no. 12 (May 1936): 11–12.

———. año XXI, no. 1 (June 1937): 11–12.

———. año XXI, no. 2 (July 1937): 17.

———. año XXI, no. 10 (March 1938): 13–16.

———. año XXII, no. 11 (April 1939): 3.

———. año XXIII, no. 7 (December 1939): 11–12.

———. año XXIII, no. 8 (January 1940): 8–9.

———. año XXV, no. 2 (July 1941): 11.

———. año XXIII, no. 8 (March 1942): 7–9.

———. año XXIX, no. 10 (March 1946): 20.

———. año XXIX, no. 12 (May 1946): 19–20.

———. año XXXI, no. 10 (March 1948): 12.

———. año XXXI, no. 11 (April 1948): 16.

———. año XXXII, no. 2 (July 1948): 16.
———. año XXXII, no. 3 (August 1948): 15–16.
———. año XXXII, no. 4 (September 1948): 4–7, 14.
———. año XXXII, no. 5 (October 1948): 16.
———. año XXXII, no. 7 (December 1948): 5–6, 14.
———. año XXXII, no. 7 (December 1948): 15–16.
———. año XXXII, no. 8 (January 1949): 4–7, 9–10, 12.
———. año XXXII, no. 8 (January 1949): 13–16.
———. año XXXIII, no. 9 (February 1950): 3–7.
———. año XXXIV, no. 9 (February 1951): 8.
———. año XXXV, no. 9 (February 1952): 6.
———. año XXXV, no. 10 (March 1952): 3, 6.
———. año XXXV, no. 12 (May 1952): 11–12.
———. año XXXVI, no. 1 (June 1952): 1–15.
Thompson, Alvin O. *Flight to Freedom: African Runaways and Maroons in the Americas*. Kingston, Jamaica: University of the West Indies, 2006.
Vethanayagamony, Peter. *It Began in Madras: The Eighteenth-Century Lutheran-Anglican Ecumenical Ventures in Mission and Benjamin Schultze*. Delhi: ISPCK, 2010.
Vicedom, George F. *The Mission of God: An Introduction to a Theology of Mission*. St. Louis: Concordia, 1965.
Villarreal, Sandra Ivelisse. "Puerto Rican Woman Invested as Bishop in Lutheran Church." *El Nuevo Día* (October 28, 2001): 4.
Vives, Papo. *La familia Heyliger*. QuebradillasPR.org, June 15, 2008, http://quebradillaspr.blogspot.com/2008/06/la-famila-heyliger-por-papo-vives.html.
Waddell, D. A. G. "The British West Indies." In *The Historiography of the British Empire-Commonwealth: Trends, Interpretations, and Resources*, ed. Robin W. Winks, 344–56. Durham, NC: Duke University Press, 1966.
Walsh, Ellen. "The Not-So-Docile Puerto Rican: Students Resist Americanization, 1930." *Centro Journal* XXVI, no. I (Spring 2014): 148–71.

Warneck, Gustav. *Outline of a History of Protestant Missions from the Reformation to the Present Time.* New York, Chicago, and Toronto: Fleming H. Revell Company, 1901.

———. *Outline of a History of Protestant Missions from the Reformation, to the Present Time: With an Appendix Concerning Roman Catholic Missions, Third English Edition Being Authorized Translation from the Eighth German Ed.* Edited by George Robson DD. Edinburgh and London: Oliphant Anderson & Ferrier, 1906.

Westhelle, Vítor. "Communication and the Transgression of Language in Luther." *Lutheran Quarterly* 17, no. 1 (Spring): 1–27.

———. *Voces de protesta en América Latina.* Mexico: Lutheran School of Theology at Chicago, 2000, 111.

Woolf, Daniel. *A Global History of History.* Edinburgh: Cambridge University Press, 2011.

Young, Robert J. C. *Postcolonialism: A Very Short Introduction.* Oxford: Oxford University Press, 2003.

Index

Abercromby, Ralph 36
Agostini, Rev. Francisco 105
Alfinger, Ambrosio 19, 26, 27
Alonso, Manuel 23, 33, 178
Anderson, Rev. Axel Peter Gabriel 97, 102
Anderson, Noemi 97
Anthony 81, 84
Arbaugh, Rev. Dr William G. 93, 96, 98, 100, 105, 114, 115, 119, 120, 121, 123, 125, 126, 127, 128, 129, 130, 131, 134, 135, 136, 137, 138, 139, 142, 147, 164, 165, 185
Asociación de Educación Teológica Hispana (AETH) 89

Bainton, Roland H. 159
Baker, Kathryn L. 6
Bastian, Jean-Pierre 19, 27, 28, 30
Bean, Joseph 51
Bíblicos, Los 38, 40, 57, 72
Brown, Antoinette 161
Badillo, Antonio 38, 40, 57, 138
Black legend 17
Black soldiers of Company L. 51
Blanca

Blank, Rodolfo 18, 19
Blenk, Bishop James E. 55, 58, 66, 67, 93, 94
Blomgren, C. A. 82
Breckling, Friedrich 21
British Guiana 135
Brook, General John A. 124
Browne, John Christopher Owen 80, 83, 173, 195
Burgos Fuentes, Rafael 140
Burk, Peter 3, 9, 10

Cabán, José N. 106
Cabán, Rev. Leopoldo 79, 80, 90, 94, 102, 103, 105, 106, 115, 128, 130
Campos, Pedro Albizu 131, 139, 140, 141, 142
Canales, Blanca 141
Caribbean Synod 5, 7, 12, 14, 44, 66, 110, 130, 135, 136, 137, 138, 139, 140, 141, 143, 144, 145, 146, 151, 152, 169, 172, 176, 177, 178, 179
Catarina Lutero: Monja Liberada 160
Charles V (emperor of the Holy Roman Empire) 18, 19
Charleston, Steven 195
Chesterton, G. K. 75, 77

INDEX

Chimpo Ocllo, Isabel 3
Christmas Inspirations 75
Church in Puerto Rico's Dilemma, The 131
Cobián, Rev. Sergio 80, 103, 106, 126, 139, 164, 192
Collazo, Oscar 14
Colom, José E. 56
Cook, David 13
Corbe, Zenan M. 104
Crespo Vargas, Pablo L. 23
Critchlow, Rev. G. W. 87
Cuchilla 175, 176
Cuervos, Gabriela 79, 80, 83, 92, 146, 163, 164, 165, 169, 186

Davis, J. Merle 120, 131
Decolonial 4, 10, 181
de Bastidas, Bishop Rodrigo 23
de Deza, Felícita Rosario 164
de Haro, Juan 36
de las Casas, Bartolomé 19
Casiodoro de Reina, Casiodoro 18
de Sardén, Juana 167, 168, 169, 186
Deiros, Pablo Alberto 18, 19, 29, 30
Díaz Alfaro, Abelardo 175, 177
Dios hoy nos llama a un momento nuevo 165
Dober, Leonhard 81
Documentos históricos de la iglesia Episcopal en Puerto Rico 50
Donoghue, Eddie 22, 32, 59
Drury, Rev. Philo W. 102

Ehinger, Enrique 19, 71
Ehinger, Georg 19
Enrico, Balduino 36

Espín, Orlando 74
Esteves, Rosario 104

faith of the people 74
Falcó, Ofelia 167, 168
Falcó Esteves, Evaristo 80, 106, 113, 162
Federman, Nicolás 19, 26, 27
Florida of the Inca, The 3
Francke, August Hermann 15
Francis, Sister Emma 22, 31, 188
Franke, Merle George 135, 143
Franqui-Rivera, Harry 43, 61
Freeze, Joseph W. 138
Friede, Juan 18, 19, 23
Fry, Rev. Franklin F. 105, 137

Gaceta de Puerto Rico, La 39
Gaenslen, Rev. Richard A. 132
García, Ismael 6
García-Rivera, Alejandro (Alex) 73, 85
Gerhard, Johann 15
Gichtel, Johan Georg 21
González, Rev. Balbino 105, 106
González, Justo L. 6, 67, 74, 85
Gotay, Samuel Silva 38, 58, 84, 85, 92, 93
Goveia, Elsa V. 3, 9
grand marronage 24
Granquist, Mark 7, 17, 84
Granskopp, E. H. 127
Grenville, Sir Richard 36
Grito de Lares, El 38, 40, 59, 139, 198
Gritsch, Eric W. 13, 18, 26, 162
Gutiérrez, Angel Luis 35, 39, 58, 59, 60, 84, 85

Hacienda del Moro, La   39
Hall, Neville A. T.   24, 34
Hankey, Rev. Benjamin F.   70, 73, 81, 91, 161, 181
Hanson, Rev. Mark   169
Harvey, Henry   36
Hazelgreen, Clara   95, 145, 163
Hemsath, Rev. Charles H.   94
Hernández Aponte, Gerardo Alberto   93
Heyliger, Eduardo   38, 39, 41, 57, 71, 197
Heyliger, Johannes   39
Heyliger Barnes, Eduardo   39
Hidalgo, Manuel   99
Higman, B. W.   3, 188, 192, 193
Hines, Florence   79, 101, 105, 167
Historia del Protestantismo en América Latina   19
historiography   9, 10, 23, 158, 172
Hoh, Frieda M.   101, 150, 167
Hohansen, Augusta C.   97
Hopkins, Barry   6
How to Be a Minister's Wife and Love It   160
Huebner, Roberto   19
Huerga, Alvaro   23, 33
Huf, Rev. Gustav K.   80, 97, 104
Hurtado, Lorenzo   99

Ideal Católico, El   92
Imparcial, El   10, 99, 135, 177, 189
Inquisición Española y las supersticiones en el Caribe hispano, siglo XVI, La   23
Interamerican University   5
Isles of the Sea, The   41

Journal of Augustana College and Theological Seminary   80

King, George Glen   44–47, 194
Knoll, Rev. C. F.   55
Knubel, Rev. Frederick H.   128

Libro de Puerto Rico, El   103
Lindke, Rev. Fred W.   79, 93, 96, 97, 102, 104, 105, 106, 111, 138, 144, 183
López, Pascual   99
Luther, Martin   11, 12, 13, 14, 17, 25, 64, 68, 74, 79, 82, 84, 93, 104, 114, 159, 183
Lutheran   5, 22, 23, 68, 75, 76, 81, 92, 97, 105, 106, 108, 129, 135, 138, 140, 143, 175
Lutheran World Federation (LWF)   17, 23
Luvis, Agustina   6

Malpica-Padilla, Rev. Dr. Rafael   5, 171, 193
Manual de Culto Cristiano   128
Marks, Charles H.   164
Maroon   31
Marrero, Guillermo E.   101, 104, 131
marronage   22
Martel-Otero, Loida I.   89
Martínez, Margarita   169
Martínez, Miguel   42
Martínez-Fernández, Luis   23, 38
Marx, Karl   11, 26
maestre Juan   23, 34, 157, 178
Mayer, Alicia   17, 28
McDavid, Lillian Ainslay   92

INDEX

McAllister, James A. 42, 99, 100
Meléndez, Andrés 107
Mellander, May 90, 91, 97, 149, 166
Mercé, Peyo 175–77
Mile, Major General Nelson 49, 51, 54, 59
Molina, Rev. Francisco 102, 104, 106, 114, 126, 139, 163, 164, 166, 184, 185
Morales-Rosa, Rafaela Hayde 169
Muhlenberg, Henry Melchior 16, 161, 181
Mundo, El 97, 105, 138, 178, 192
Muñoz Marín, Luis 56, 131, 133, 139, 140, 141
Müntzer, Thomas 21
Murga Sanz, Vicente 23, 33

Naether, Rev. Hans 97, 103
Naffier, Vernon H. 20, 28, 31, 32
Nationalist Party 139, 141
Negrón, Rev. Idalia x, 141, 146, 170, 197
Negrón, Jose 141
New York Herald Tribune 125
Nitschmann, David 81
Notes and Quotes from the Correspondence of William George Arbaugh 120, 183
Nuevo Día, El 10, 41, 152, 193

Obama, Barak 56
Okenve, Enrique 6
Olson, Betty 95
Operation Bootstrap 132, 133

Orlandi, Rev. Dr. Carlos F. Cardoza 1, 2, 8, 73, 85, 178, 179
Ortiz, Rev. Alfredo 106
Ostrom, Rev. Alfred 66, 73, 74, 75, 79, 80, 95, 96, 97, 99, 102, 103, 105, 106, 119, 125, 129, 130, 145, 160, 163
Outline of a History of Protestant Missions from the Reformation to the Present Time 178

Parker, Charles E. 49
Pedersen, Jans C. 144
Peñaranda, Nicolette 30, 31, 32
Pérez, Carmín 141
Pérez, Eliseo 6
Piñeiro, Jesús T. 56, 131, 139
Plitt, Gustav Leopold 14
postcolonial 4, 10, 66, 172, 181
Probst, Sofía 97, 105
Puerto Rico Evangélico 10, 79, 89, 94, 95, 96, 97, 100, 101, 105, 107, 123, 130, 138, 140, 153, 156, 191, 194

Qualben, Lars P. 19
quipus 2, 9

Rabell, Carmen 183
Reading the Bible in Spanish 74
Richards, Rev. Herbert F. 70, 71, 75, 81, 86, 91, 143, 145, 162, 181
Riquelme, Isabel 39
Rivera Martínez, Sarahí 40, 42, 45, 61

226

INDEX

Rivera-Pagán, Luis N. 6, 24, 29, 67
Robertson, James 6
Rodríguez, Rev. Dr. Raquel E. 5
Rodríguez, Víctor 139
Roig, Eduardo 10, 79, 80, 96, 99, 103, 106, 114, 118, 120, 129, 131, 137, 138, 139, 140, 143, 144, 145, 146, 184
Rosas, Johnny 175–77
Rothenberger, Orpha 102
Royal Commentaries of the Incas: And General History of Perú 3

Saenz, Michael 61, 83, 114, 116, 126, 128, 129
San Ciprián 124
San Ciriaco 124
Santa Claus 176, 177
Santiago-Vendrel, Ángel 41, 99
Sayler, Jerónimo 19, 71
Sanz, General Jose Laureano 39
Scherer, James A. 13, 14, 16, 21, 26, 27, 28
Schindel, James Carl 48, 49, 52, 63
Schmid, Emma R. 97, 104
Schmucker, Samuel Simon 161, 181
Schoen, Nanca 97, 104
Schreiter, Robert 73
Scott, James C. 4, 107, 156, 162, 177, 182
Seminario Evangélico de Puerto Rico (SEPR) 5, 6, 11, 177
Seminario Teológico de Mayagüez 99

Seminario Teológico Puertoricense 99
Seminary 80, 98
Shaw, Leonor 79, 80, 149
Sheen, Fulton 75
Sherman, Chaplain Thomas E. 52, 53, 54
Shoemaker, Helen Smith 160
Singmaster Lewars, Elsie 89
Slagelse, Kjeld Jensen 21, 30
Small Catechism 92, 104, 106, 114, 127
Smidt, Erik Nielsen 21
Snydermann, Rev. Gunder Thomas 22
Soler, Rev. Jaime 102, 105
Sosa, Rev. Francisco L. 41
Sousa, Adela 42
Spanish Cortes 36
Spener, Philip Jacob 15
St. Croix 31, 32, 39, 40, 41, 74, 80, 92, 105, 135, 178, 182
Steuernagel, Valdir R. 179
Stover, Chaplain Earl F. 47
Strong, Josiah 168
Suárez de Figueroa, Gómez (Garcilaso de la Vega El Inca) 3
Swensson, Gustaf Sigfried 23, 70, 72, 73, 76, 77, 78, 79, 80, 81, 82, 83, 86, 90, 91, 92, 100, 125, 136, 137, 161, 181, 185

Taylor, Alice 160
Teología en conjunto1: A Collaborative Hispanic Protestant Theology 89
Teología y Misión en América Latina 18
Terrazo 153, 156, 186

INDEX

Testigo, El 5, 55, 75, 79, 80, 81, 86, 88, 89, 90, 92, 93, 94, 96, 98, 99, 100, 102, 103, 104, 105, 108, 110, 114, 115, 116, 118, 119, 120, 121, 123, 126, 127, 128, 129, 131, 134, 136, 137, 138, 139, 140, 141, 142, 143, 144, 145, 146, 147, 149, 150, 165, 182, 183, 184, 186, 187, 191, 193, 196, 197, 198
Texidor, Demetrio 79
Thomson, James 72
Thorensen, Joel 6
Torres, Rev. Carlos A. 132
Torres, Father Jorge Juan Rivera 50, 65
Torresola, Doris 141
Torresola, Griselio 141

Underwood, Judson 42, 99
United Nations 139, 140
University Institute ISEDET in Buenos Aires 6, 171
University of Puerto Rico 5
University of Halle 15
University of the West Indies (UWI) 1, 6, 13, 26, 32, 188, 190, 192, 198
United Theological College of the West Indies (UTCW) 5, 12, 33

Ursinus, Johann Heinrich 20, 21
USS Maine 44
USS Yale 45, 51

Vattmann, Chaplain Edward J. 52, 54, 55, 65, 66
Vázquez, Germán 107
Vigo Verestín, Milka T. 6
Vilá, Rubén Arrieta 41, 61
von Bora, Katherine 159
von Welz, Justinian Erns 15, 20, 21, 27
Voz Luterana, La 138

Wahlstedt, Annette 88, 95, 143, 147, 161, 162
Walter, Alicia E. 160
Wariboco, Waibinte 6
Warneck, Gustav 3, 7, 8, 9, 13, 14, 26, 178, 179, 180
Welser, Antonio 18
Welser, Bartolomé 18
Westhelle, Vítor 68, 75, 85, 175, 196
Whitt, Jacqueline E. 47, 63
Winship, Blanton C. 56, 60
Woolf, Daniel 3, 8